THE MASTERS OF GOLF

Learning From Their Methods

THE MASTERS
OF GOLF
Learning From Their Methods

Dick Aultman and Ken Bowden

Illustrated by Anthony Ravielli

Galahad Books · New York

Published in 1994 by

Galahad Books
A division of Budget Book Service, Inc.
386 Park Avenue South
New York, NY 10016

Galahad Books is a registered trademark of Budget Book Service, Inc.

Published by arrangement with Macmillan Publishing Company.

Library of Congress Catalog Card Number: 88-8007
ISBN: 0-88365-846-1

Printed in the United States of America.

Contents

Foreword

This book is the product of more than fifty years of research. That is the combined period of time that its two authors have been professionally involved in studying and writing about golf technique.

One or other of us, and in many cases both, have frequently watched and regularly talked about golf technique with each of the golfers discussed herein, with the exceptions of Harry Vardon and Walter Hagen. One or other of us has collaborated with nine of them in one or more of their literary efforts. One or other of us has played golf with the same number.

In preparation for writing this work it was, of course, necessary to search out and study the very substantial amount of literature published by these great golfers over a ninety-year period. This turned out to be primarily a refresher course, because both of us previously had read the bulk of it at least once.

In choosing who should be included herein, our objective was to select the world's eighteen greatest male golfers of the twentieth century (we hope we shall one day write a book about the great women players!). It was a difficult task, involving much debate, because there are at least four other players who might have been included on the basis of record, let alone technical interest. Obviously, in the final analysis, our selection was personal and is thus subjective. But we do believe that most knowledgeable golfers who had fully evaluated the record book on a worldwide basis would have come to much the same choice.

The actual treatment of the golfers we did finally select is also subjective, and because we have not collaborated in our assessments and analyses of them (beyond technical editing of each other's work), we have personally signed each chapter. We would stress, however, that the broad perspective within which the book was conceived and written is the modern American approach to the art, craft, or science of swinging a golf club, as best exemplified in professional tournament play.

After fifty years of 'background' and two years of intensive research it was our intention when we sat down to write the book to evaluate and discuss the specific playing methods of the great champions in a hopefully interesting but primarily a technically instructive manner. We hope we have done that. But as soon as we began to write, it became apparent that we would have to do more. We quickly realized that, in golf as in any other area of life, you cannot separate the method from the man—the performance from the personality. Thus there is much in these pages about the people as well as their playing techniques. And because of the amazing diversity of character and attitude among the superstars, we believe this will add greatly to the reader's entertainment.

As we proceeded, one further unexpected element emerged from the writing, that being a narrative of how the golf swing has actually evolved from its original crude Scottish form into the almost machine-like action of the modern greats. As no attempt has yet been made to document that evolutionary process in full and in depth, we hope that this book will contribute something not only to the lore of golf, but to the continuing worldwide effort to improve and refine its ever-complex, ever-difficult playing techniques.

Golf is one of the most 'written about' sports in history, and in that respect we were fortunate in the abundance of material that was available to us for research. We are particularly grateful to the players covered herein for their generally extensive, occasionally prodigious, and almost always excellent literary output.

We are also grateful to many other players and to a handful of great golf teachers with whom we have worked over the years for their friendship, encouragement, and unstinted sharing of knowledge. Because there are too many of them to name individually, we felt that the least we could do would be to offer them collectively our thanks by dedicating our book thus:

To all those players who have shone the light
and those teachers who have shown the way

DICK AULTMAN AND KEN BOWDEN

Publisher's note

Almost a decade and a half has passed since this book was first published. In that time it has won high renown among aficionados of golf technique, from top-name teaching professionals seeking ways to advance their craft to everyday hackers desperate to narrow the chasm between themselves and its subjects. It has also, with that passage of time, become both incomplete and difficult to obtain in some parts of the world. Thus this newly expanded edition, being published just about everywhere in the English-speaking world where golf is played.

The two new golfers under analysis are Tom Watson and Seve Ballesteros. While the authors don't doubt that, as with the original edition, some people will feel that other players merit inclusion, they are even more certain that no addict or fan in his right mind will argue with these two additions.

There was discussion as to whether every reference to and comment about the originally included golfers who are still active should be brought bang up to date. The decision to revise only those that might seem jarringly antique was based on the fact that none of their playing fundamentals has changed significantly, and that any detailed updating of playing records would itself quickly become out of date.

Introduction

by Herbert Warren Wind

I am not a cardplayer, and so it astonishes me that devotees of bridge, regardless of how many years they have pored over the game, never lose their passion for it. At the same time I can understand their perpetual keenness because as one of the many thousands of men and women who have been happily enslaved by golf since childhood I have always been astonished by the way one never tires of discovering more and more about the golf swing—dissecting it, restudying its various phases, practising its movements, discussing the latest theories about its basic facets, examining the methods and manners of the game's champions, and so on and on, ad infinitum. It is one of the comforts of this life, in which one involuntarily loses his zest for so many things, that thinking about and learning about the golf swing are one of those rare enthusiasms that never pall, never get boring. Age cannot wither it nor custom stale its infinite variety—or something like that.

Because every golfer wishes to become a better shotmaker, or at least a lower scorer, ever since the good old mauve days of Horace Hutchinson and Willie Park, Jr., golf instruction books have been sound publishing ventures. In recent years, however, the heavy majority of these books have not been as good as they should have been, trafficking in clichés and banalities rather than in newly appreciated fact or freshly minted opinion. There have been, fortunately, some exceptions—to name two which come quickly to mind, Percy Boomer's fascinating *On Learning Golf* and Ben Hogan's brilliant and original *The Modern Fundamentals of Golf*. (I am also reminded of the tender, loving care that Bert Yancey has lavished on his articles in which he has investigated the classic swing and the modern swing.) The book that you are holding in your hands is also an exceptional piece of work. Never before to my knowledge have the individual techniques of the great champions from Vardon to Nicklaus and Trevino been scrutinized so carefully and diagnosed as thoughtfully as Dick Aultman and Ken Bowden, the two authors of this book, have done, and

they have set down their findings in clear, helpful, and enjoyable prose. *The Masters of Golf*, a study of how the great golfers of the century have in their separate ways contributed to the evolution of the modern game, is an important book, and the wonder is that it has never been attempted before.

Dick Aultman and Ken Bowden are the perfect team to have prepared this book. Both are accomplished, low-handicap golfers, both are experienced in the operation of instruction schools and teaching clinics, and both have been established for quite some time as among the most knowledgeable golf writers in the world. The fundamental reason they have produced such a fine book is that they took the time that was needed to do justice to their considerable subject. They read every pertinent work. They spent endless hours studying hard-to-obtain photographs and motion pictures of the great players. Then, further to embellish their book, they enlisted the services of Tony Ravielli, the Da Vinci of golf artists. The book has both substance and style.

My guess is that *The Masters of Golf* will become one of those uncommon sports books to which golfers will return time and time again—intellectual golfers, weekend golfers, and serious tournament-level golfers. After all, it never hurts to refresh one's understanding of, say, why Walter Hagen may have fared even better with metal-shafted clubs, how Gene Sarazen went about assembling the swing that would complement the dominant left hand in his interlocking grip, why it was that Bobby Jones placed so much value on the extension through the ball, how it was that Henry Cotton came to emphasize hand action primarily, why it was important for Byron Nelson to have his legs lead on the downswing, what facets of Sam Snead's style account for his amazing longevity, and how Lee Trevino was able to compound a remarkably dependable hitting action out of five unorthodox moves. It is all here in a book that both informs and entertains and that possesses the real flavour of the game.

KEN BOWDEN

Harry Vardon

THE MASTER MOLD

Prominently displayed in the foyer of the South Herts Golf Club, north of London, is a commanding bronze sculpture of a golfer's hands gripping a club. Because this was the course where Harry Vardon ended his days—he is buried a few paces away in the Totteridge parish churchyard—every visitor knows or quickly guesses whose hands they are. But take those hands of golf's first true superstar out of their commemorative setting, and not one golfer in ten thousand would be able to identify their owner.

The sheer size and muscular power of the hands would surely prompt a strong vote for Arnold Palmer. To the more intense student of technical nitty-gritty, the fairly "strong" placement of the left hand might suggest Billy Casper or Lee Trevino. Perhaps the purposeful "short-thumbed" snugness of the overall grip would even bring Jack Nicklaus to mind. But it would be a guessing game at best because the fact is that this grip, for all practical purposes, is the grip of just about 99 percent of today's top professional and amateur golfers the world over.

It won't, of course, be news to anyone who

can break 90 that Harry Vardon popularized the principle of "wedding" (to use his word) the hands together by wrapping the little finger of the bottom hand around the forefinger of the top hand. What may be news is that he didn't actually invent this overlapping technique: His fellow member of the "Great Triumvirate," J. H. Taylor, developed it simultaneously but independently, and a fine Scottish amateur, John E. Laidlay, had used it in winning the British Amateur championship in 1889, the year before Vardon played his first round of tournament golf. What may be even bigger news to the modern golfer is the exceptional degree of influence that Vardon had on the golf swing as a whole, far beyond his popularization of a grip style.

Harry Vardon's achievements were awesome—every bit as overwhelming in his own time as Nicklaus' are today. But, looking back now, what impresses most about him is not so much his inevitably mist-shrouded victories as the method through which he achieved them. The deeper one gets into his technique, the more dramatically apparent it becomes that he was the greatest technical in-

HARRY VARDON

Born: May 9, 1870; Grouville, Jersey, Channel Islands
Died: March 20, 1937; Totteridge, London, England

Major victories:

British Open: 1896, 1898, 1899, 1903, 1911, 1914
U.S. Open: 1900

A. Ravielli

novator in the history of golf. The swing style of his predecessors is so foreign to the form we know today as to be almost unrecognizable—indeed, if we didn't know better, its practitioners would often seem to have been playing an entirely different game. But when one watches Vardon on film, one sees, in essence, the swings of Gene Sarazen, Walter Hagen, and Bobby Jones—even the timeless Sam Snead. In basic principles at least, here is the swing with which countless good senior golfers—and others who cannot physically or temperamentally accommodate the stressful body-controlled actions of the game's young lions—still continue to win golfing prizes and pleasure. Here, in short, is the master mold; the mold from which Byron Nelson built in initiating the method now so successfully refined on the U.S. professional tour; but a mold which remains, almost in its original form, a wonderfully valid swing pattern for the purely recreational golfer.

Harry Vardon was born the son of an artisan in the spring of 1870 in Grouville, Jersey, one of the Channel Islands between England and France at the gateway to the Atlantic Ocean. Almost from the time he could walk he would occasionally swing a homemade club in rudimentary backyard golf games with his five brothers and two sisters, but he had slight interest in the sport. When he began work at twelve, in domestic service, cricket and soccer consumed most of his sparse leisure time, and the rest was spent supplementing family income by such means as collecting and selling sea shells. Between the ages of thirteen and seventeen, when he worked as a pageboy and waiter, he played virtually no golf at all. In 1887 he took a position as under gardener in the household of a member of the Royal Jersey Golf Club and would play on the four annual British national holidays and occasionally with his employer at other times. But the game was certainly no more than a casual pastime for him during adolescence. He never had a lesson, never formally studied technique, never consciously copied anyone's swing. His clubs were a ragbag of discards and homemades, and he ferreted his gutta-percha balls out of Royal Jersey's wiry sea grasses. In 1922 he

wrote: "Up until I was twenty years of age, I played so little golf that even now I can remember every round as a red-letter event of my youth. In later days people often said to me: 'I used to know you when you were playing golf as a boy at Jersey.' In point of fact, it was my brother Tom they knew, for he obtained a good deal of golf, whereas I was not far from being a stranger to the game."

By the time he was twenty, Vardon had, by his own estimate, played no more than twenty full rounds of golf, and the closest he had come to practicing shots had been hitting balls around a cultivated field to scare away crows in the course of his gardening duties. Then, while still in his twentieth year, he entered a tournament at the local workingmen's club and won the first and only prize—a vase—with ease. Simultaneously news arrived that his brother Tom had won a professional tournament in Scotland and with it a prize of $20. Said Vardon Later: "This seemed an enormous amount to me and I pondered long and intently over it. I knew that, little as I had played, I was as good as Tom. If he could win that vast fortune, why shouldn't I?"

So began a career that was not only to immortalize the name Vardon but was massively and permanently to alter the character of the golf swing.

Prior to Vardon's appearance on the professional tournament scene, such as it was in the mid-1890's, golf was played at every level with what had become known as the "St. Andrews Swing." As today, there were individual variations on its basic theme, but fundamentally the St. Andrews Swing consisted of a long, flat, slashing action deriving from an ultraloose grip, a huge swaying body turn away from and through the ball, and an uninhibited slinging of the clubhead through the ball with the hands, wrists, and shoulders. Unquestionably the equipment of the day—the long, whippy, wooden-shafted clubs and the stonelike, rise-resistant guttie balls—had helped father this free-style formula. The few action paintings and prints, and the limited amount of technical exposition in the golf literature of the era, indicate that one or two outstanding players—notably

Young Tom Morris—employed a somewhat more compact style. But basically the St. Andrews Swing predominated, both in achievement and esthetically.

Vardon changed all that. His first three British Open wins in 1896, 1898, and 1899 severely dented confidence in the old Scottish style, even though many leading Scots vigorously defended their invention, often to the point of bad-mouthing the "English" method that was beating them so soundly. By the time Vardon won his sixth and last British Open in 1914, the St. Andrews Swing—at least in its most extreme form—had disappeared. And its demise would probably have come even sooner had two bouts of tuberculosis not forced Vardon out of competition and into sanatoriums for long spells between 1904 and 1911.

At a time so far removed, and in a world where excellence of strike is commonplace at the highest levels of the game, it is difficult today to fully appreciate the brilliance of Vardon's shotmaking, especially during his halcyon years before the long battle with tuberculosis. His greatest victories were won with the guttie ball, which he always preferred to the rubber version because of the thoughtfulness and precision it demanded in conceiving and executing every shot. From tee to green he was in his day totally without peer. He flew the unresponsive guttie appreciably higher than his rivals, thus gaining the twin advantages of long carry and soft landing that have so aided Nicklaus. He drove straight and, when necessary, extremely far. No one before—and probably no one since—played more majestically with the brassie: Vardon himself said that, on form, he could expect to hit the ball consistently within fifteen feet of the pin with this equivalent of the modern two-wood. With the shorter clubs he grew, if anything, even more adept. "No one ever played irons more prettily," eulogized Bernard Darwin, Vardon's equivalent among writers of the game. "He merely shaved the turf and did not take cruel divots out of it." He was an expert manufacturer of special shots with every club in the bag, describing as his best-ever stroke a shot over a clubhouse that was situated just a few feet away from his ball. The ball, struck with an open-faced niblick (eight-iron), appeared to rise almost vertically and then arc forward over the building's roof to fall softly within a yard of the cup! "His play was enough to break the heart of an iron horse," said Andrew Kirkaldy, a demon performer in the big-money challenge matches that interspersed the few tournaments of the day, and a frequent Vardon victim. "In truth, in his great years, no one had any real hope against him," wrote Darwin.

It was only when Vardon reached the green that he sank to the level of his contemporaries. "A grand player up to the green, and a very bad one when he got there," was how Darwin—never a man to mince words—put it. "But then," he added, "Vardon gave himself less putting to do than any other man." Contemporary reports constantly refer to Vardon's ineptitude with the putter as the cause of his either winning by only a smallish margin or actually losing when clearly he should have won, especially during the second half of his career after his illness. Ultimately it was the missed "gimmee," caused by a distinct twitch or jerk in the right hand and forearm, that caused him to give up tournament play. But, although he lost power as he aged, the majesty—the "supreme grace," as Darwin called it—of his long game remained with him to the grave.

The overlapping grip, although Vardon's most famous legacy to golf, was actually one of his least drastic departures from the St. Andrews Swing, which featured a mechanically passable if somewhat loose and sloppy ten-fingered hold on the club. Vardon was an average-size man—5 feet 9½ inches and 165 pounds in middle life—but he had unusually large hands and long fingers. Almost certainly, wrapping the little finger of his right hand around the forefinger of his left was originally simply a way of compacting his hold on the club. It took him no time at all, however, to discover the real value of this type of grip, which is the "wedding" of the hands into a single unit, and he strongly advocated it for this purpose for all players very early in his career.

The modern golf teacher would find little

fault in Vardon's grip and a lot to praise. The club passed from the inner knuckle joint of the first finger of his left hand across the base of the second and little fingers, which placed it a little more in the fingers than is currently fashionable. But this was essential to the light grip pressure and fluid motion of Vardon's swing, as it is to many good modern "hands" players. In most other respects Vardon's grip could have come right out of the 1970's. His left thumb sat just to the right of the center of the shaft and was snugly covered by the right palm when this hand was added. The club lay at the roots of the fingers of the right hand, and the right thumb rode just to the left of top-center on the shaft. The V's formed by the thumb and forefinger of both hands matched exactly, both pointing somewhere between his right ear and shoulder.

About grip pressure he expressed himself with a bit more flourish than might your twentieth-century teaching pro, but the mes-

An American writer commented in 1924: "The outstanding impression of watching Vardon play is that of utter ease and lack of physical effort. His hands, arms, body, and legs appear to work as a well-oiled machine, and there is always present that element denoting complete coordination, ordinarily referred to in golf matters as rhythm." This gracefulness derived from a lack of muscular stress or tension at any point in the swing, the polar opposite of modern professional technique. But, apart from his famous bent left elbow, the overall character of Vardon's action set the pattern for many of today's mechanical features.

sage was the same: "In the ordinary way of things, the tight grip creates a tautening of the muscles in the body and when the player is in this condition the chances of executing a perfect stroke are remote. The golfer's muscles should be at once healthy and supple—like a boxer's. When they are encouraged to develop hardness and size—like a weightlifter's—they retard the ease and quickness of hitting, which count so much at the instant of impact." Vardon did vary from modern theory, however, when he added that "it is quite sufficient to grip a little tighter with the thumbs and forefingers. They will prove sufficient to keep the clubhead in position. The other fingers may be left to look after themselves in the matter of the strength they apply."

Modern grip principles call for maximum pressure in the last two fingers of the top hand and the middle two fingers of the bottom hand. But this is much more a matter of feel than mechanics. From photographs of grips only, few average golfers today would be able to distinguish Vardon from 70 percent of present-day tour players.

It is a forgiveable human failing to bestow originality on current practice, and nothing more piquantly exemplifies this tendency in golf than three of Vardon's basic grip principles.

The modern golfer is frequently advised to face the back of the left hand and the palm of the right to the target at address. This point was also stressed by Vardon: "The left-hand knuckles should face [down] the line of play and the right-hand knuckles the other way," he instructed many times in his books and magazine articles. Then there is the question of which hand should grasp the club most firmly. Modern teaching favors either equal grip pressure or a slightly softer hold with the bottom hand. Said Vardon: "I grip equally firmly with both hands at the start, but the pressure of the right hand decreases during the backswing." And finally the matter of which is the master hand and arm. Although the very latest theories lean strongly toward "left-sidedness," a consensus of international teaching opinion would probably favor a balanced effort. Wrote Vardon: "I don't be-

lieve in a master hand or arm. All should work as a unit, and I believe the overlapping grip best achieves this."

Harry Vardon played all his competitive golf in knickers, fancy-topped stockings, a hard collar and tie, and a tightly buttoned jacket ("A cardigan or jumper permits too great a freedom in the shoulders," he said). Re-dress him in a sport shirt and double knits and he would still look incongruous on today's pro tours because, champion innovator that he was, certain elements of his swing definitely conflict with modern theory.

His manner of starting the club back, for example (although also employed by Jones and Hagen), would create horror at any present-day PGA teaching seminar. Vardon's first move was a pronounced drag backward and inward of the hands, with the clubhead trailing the hands almost until they reached hip height, at which point a free wrist-cock from a cupped left wrist position set the hands very much "under" the shaft and established a wide-open clubface. That is certainly about as far as you can get from the "one-piece" policy of the 1960's and light years away from the "square-to-square" and "set-the-angle-early" edicts of the 1970's!

Conceivably, Vardon's famous bent left arm would be less sinful in principle today than his takeaway, in that a number of top golfers currently play with discernible "give" at the elbow (including Europe's top teacher and former tournament star, John Jacobs). But Vardon's elbow didn't just "give"; it categorically *bent*—during his early years almost at right angles! When teaching, he did not insist on so great a kink, but he strongly advocated relaxation in the elbows to prevent tension and to produce smoothness and rhythm, arguing that centrifugal force would automatically straighten the leading arm at the appropriate moment in the downswing. "I am constantly having to cure patients ruined by the stiff left arm," he wrote in an American golf magazine, and he stressed the bent arm frequently and persuasively in his books.

Vardon's swing contained other departures from what is presently regarded as good form; for example, he allowed his hips to turn very freely in the backswing; his right elbow to rise high and away from his body (into almost the same position as Nicklaus!); his left heel to swing high at the completion of a full backswing (again like Nicklaus!); and he "crossed the line" at the top—pointed the club right of target. But these were minor aberrations compared to his thoughts about the correct way to start the downswing.

Golf instruction over the years has been liberally sprinkled with tips from leading players who inadvertently advocated something they genuinely felt they did, but actually did not do. Vardon was not to escape this trap. To return the clubhead back to the ball, the golfer using the long, flat, floppy St. Andrews Swing was forced to make a throwing action with the hands, wrists, and arms as the first move of the downswing. This was the one element of the old Scottish method that Vardon *thought* he retained. In many of his writings he talks of "leading the downswing with the clubhead," of "throwing the club to the right and a little behind the body" starting down, of "only the arms moving until halfway down," of "early uncocking of the wrists"; in short, of what we know today as "hitting from the top."

There is no doubt that Vardon "released" his wrists in plenty of time to deliver the clubhead solidly into the back of the ball, traveling low enough to the ground to catch the ball cleanly with a divotless sweep rather than an abrupt downward hit. Indeed, the smoothness and comparative slowness of his swing, as captured on film, are such that one can actually *see* his wrists beginning to uncock as his hands pass hip height on the downswing—a movement far less visible in films of modern tournament players. There is also no doubt that the pattern of wrist-hand action Vardon employed to release the clubhead would not be regarded as ideal today, in that his left wrist arched inward—became concave—through the impact zone (modern methods call for the left wrist to maintain a firm straight-line relationship to the forearm while turning anticlockwise through impact).

But whatever his stylistic differences and whatever he thought he did, Vardon categorically *did not* "hit from the top." In every one of the scores of pictures of him studied by the authors, it is blindingly apparent that the set, or cock, of Vardon's wrists is at least maintained—and sometimes on a full drive increased—early in his downswing. In fact, in hitting what in his day was a famous specialty of both himself and J. H. Taylor, a low-flying mashie (five-iron) "push shot," Vardon hit the ball as "late" as any golfer on the tour today. For proof, see the photograph on page 19.

Whatever Vardon's variations from modern standards, they are vastly outweighed by his similarities. In fact, discovering from Vardon's literature how little is truly new in golf was an educational experience for this writer, despite his long-held suspicion that so-called modern methods draw more from the recycling of old ideas than from solid invention.

See, for example, how many of the following principles, paraphrased from Vardon's writings, you can fault as conflicting with modern practice:

- The body should be easy and comfortable at address.
- The stance should be open, with the rear foot square to the line of play and the leading foot angled toward the target.
- The ball should be addressed opposite the left heel or, if not there, nearer to the left heel than the right—unless you wish to play a low shot.
- I like my ankles to be free, which is why I play in shoes, not boots.
- When the clubface is against the ball, the end of the shaft should reach to the flexed left knee.
- The arms do not touch the body at address, but neither do they reach.
- The weight should be divided equally between both feet.
- It is necessary only to find the correct stance and the shot is certain to be a success.
- The head should be steady throughout the swing because if it moves, the body goes with it, disrupting the club's path.
- The eyes should focus on the back of the ball or on the ground just to the right of the ball.
- An upright backswing offers the shortest

and therefore the most efficient route from and to the ball.

- Avoid straining for too wide a backswing, for if you do, you will likely sway your body.
- The backswing is wound up by the swinging of the arms, the hips turning, and the left knee bending as the body pivots from the waist.
- As the backswing proceeds, the right knee holds firm, but does not quite become stiff.
- Don't lift your left heel too much, but let it come comfortably up as you pivot onto the inside of the foot in response to your body pivot.
- The grip relaxes a little as the backswing proceeds, especially the right hand.
- The right shoulder rises gradually as the body pivots. The body turns on its axis in the backswing and the downswing.
- There is no pause between the backswing and the downswing; they flow into each other.
- Don't jerk or snatch at the top or coming down or let the right wrist get on top of the club.

Dressed in a modern shirt, double knits, and a golf hat, Vardon at address would be almost indistinguishable from a dozen present-day tour players. The bent left elbow causes the club to set low at the top, but the full, free upper-body turn has been common to most great golfers and remains classic form today. The poised and balanced follow-through indicates superb timing and a freewheeling release of the clubhead into the ball.

- The downswing is faster than the backswing, but there should be no conscious effort to make it so.
- At its simplest, the swing is a matter of winding yourself up with your arms and unwinding yourself with your arms.
- The grip automatically becomes firmer as the downswing proceeds.
- Let the shoulder movement be steady and rhythmic, especially in the downswing.
- The club accelerates gradually to impact.
- The wrists should be held fairly firmly as the ball is hit. Do not bend the right wrist toward the target until after the ball has been struck.
- At impact the feet should be flat on the ground.
- As the club goes through, the weight moves to the left, the left leg resists the blow, the right leg bends, the body fronts the line of flight, and the right foot raises almost vertically. At the finish the arms are up, the hands level with the head, the club beyond horizontal, and the body and shoulders face the target.
- I have always preferred an open stance because then I am not in the way of the clubhead as it swings through the ball. Also, an open stance encourages the upright swing that I favor.
- Don't scoop with the iron; thump down on the ball.
- The straight shot is difficult to repeat. Intentional pulls (hooks) and slices are golf's master shots.
- Good driving is the foundation of a good game. Learn to drive first with the brassie, for it is easier than the driver.
- I believe I use lighter clubs than many of my contemporaries. My driver is 42 inches long and weighs 12¾ ounces; my brassie is the same length but 12 ounces.
- Never throw the clubhead or make a hit with it; swing it all the way.
- There is no such thing as a pure wrist shot in golf, except for putting.
- The shorter the swing or the shot, the narrower the stance, the less the foot and body action, and the more the emphasis on the knees. The length of the backswing deter-

mines the distance of the less-than-full shot.
- The most successful way to play golf is the easiest way.
- To play well, you must feel tranquil and at peace. I have never been troubled by nerves in golf because I felt I had nothing to lose and all to gain.

Good action photography of Vardon is scarce today, but what is available of his mature swing depicts a number of strikingly modern features—all of them seminal departures from the St. Andrews Swing.

Vardon's "centeredness" throughout the swing is one such. A 1927 commentator graphically described it thus: "Imagine that, as he addresses the ball, a pole is passed downward through the center of his head and body, and into the ground: then his swing is a rotating movement performed by the shoulders and hips, around the pole, while the arms are being lifted up and the left knee is bending inwards." The writer goes on to quote Vardon as saying that his ability to maintain a fixed axis was perhaps the major factor in his accuracy and control—why he "would not be off the fairway six times in six rounds."

Another remarkably modern feature of Vardon was his address posture: knees slightly flexed; upper body angled forward from the waist; back straight; arms hanging easily and freely; head high; hands slightly below a straight line from the clubhead to the left shoulder. Compare the picture of him on page 17 to any modern tour player if you still need proof that it really wasn't Arnold Palmer who invented golf.

Leg action, the core of the modern golf swing, was little discussed as such by Vardon in his writings, but he did recognize it obliquely, and he certainly employed it, albeit unconsciously, as an effect rather than a cause. As photographs prove (see page 19), his open stance and speedy return of the left heel to earth immediately on starting his downswing definitely brought his legs and hips into play, even though he felt that he started down by moving the clubhead with his hands and arms. The reason he never thought or wrote much about the legs is, in this writer's view, very simple: His lower-body movement was a natural, unconscious, *reflex* reaction to the winding of his upper body in the backswing (as it is with every golfer who makes a full body turn and free arm swing). Thus, because his legs operated so instinctively and automatically once he'd got to the top of the swing, Vardon never had occasion to think about them consciously—or, if he did, he could quickly put the matter out of mind as being a natural reflex movement not needing or warranting conscious direction.

It would seem that Vardon was definitely way ahead of most of the moderns in at least one respect, that being his swing's appearance of grace, ease, and economy of effort. Today only a handful of tour players, such as Sam Snead and Gene Littler, would seem to come close to matching what Bernard Darwin called the "beautiful free movement of one having a natural gift for opening his shoulders and hitting clean." "Time after time," Darwin extolled, "he [Vardon] would come right through, drawn to his full height, the club round over his left shoulder, the hands well up, the left elbow tolerably high. It was the ideal copybook follow-through, and he did it every time with an almost mo-

Left: Modern theory has eliminated the hands-before-clubhead takeaway, but it was employed to a greater or lesser degree by most fine golfers until the Second World War, including, notably, Bobby Jones. The effect was a fluid start to the swing. Center: The impression has long been given that all olden-day golfers hit "early"—"threw" the club from the top with the hands and wrists. Vardon's writings imply that he personally felt—and thus favored—such a motion, but this picture seems to prove that he actually hit just as "late" with his hands and wrists as any of the moderns. Right: The momentum of the freely released clubhead wheels Vardon into a classical follow-through. Compare it to the modern stars for a measurement of his massive influence on the evolution of the swing.

notonous perfection." An even better word picture of Vardon's overall motion comes from Walter Cavanaugh, writing in *The American Golfer* in 1924: "The outstanding impression of watching Vardon play is that of utter ease and lack of physical effort. His hands, arms, body and legs appear to work as a well-oiled machine, and there is always present that element denoting complete coordination, ordinarily referred to in golf matters as rhythm."

How many of today's stars, one wonders, will evoke such prose?

A recurring theme in this book is the influence the master golfers' personalities have had on their playing methods. Unquestionably Vardon's swing style and general approach to the game were born of his remarkably placid, easygoing nature. "He had a calm and cheerful temperament," wrote Bernard Darwin. "The game seemed to take little out of him, and he could fight, if need be, without appearing to be fighting at all." This quiet, considerate, and unfailingly courteous nature threaded every facet of Vardon's life. At no time did he make any effort to impose his grip or swing on the world or even to suggest that they were superior to any others. Particularly in his early days he simply let his achievements speak for his technique, which, in the small, clubby golf world of that

time, they did with nuclear force. Later, when he came to write about the game, he did so with great modesty and lucidity and only the gentlest chiding of what he regarded as erroneous or befuddled theories. Perhaps his open-minded, nondogmatic approach stemmed as much from his almost happenstance entry into the game as from his easygoing personality. Threading all his writings is the impression that initially he really had little idea about what he did when he swung a golf club and that he found out only when, as a superstar, he was forced to think about technique in order to communicate about it.

In fact, in 1922, reflecting on the "shock" his swing initially created, he wrote revealingly: "My own brother and Edward [Ted] Ray [and other Jersey golfers] all drifted involuntarily into the habit of taking the club to the top of the swing by the shortest route, whereas the popular way before was to swing flat at the start and make a very full flourish. . . . Why we hit upon the other way we do not know. Personally, I never thought about the matter until I obtained my first professional post at Ripon, Yorkshire. And it was only when I was twenty-one and in my second appointment, at Bury, Lancashire, that I began to study and learn golf in real earnest. So you can see that there is every chance for you."

A fine illustration of what Bernard Darwin meant when he described Vardon's swing as the "beautiful free movement of one having a natural gift for opening his shoulders and hitting clean."

DICK AULTMAN

Walter Hagen

"THREE OF 'THOSE' AND ONE OF 'THEM' COUNT FOUR"

There is a theory that golfers play the game, even swing the club, in much the same way they live life off the course. The same Julius Boros who idles gently through the years, occasionally casting line and sinker into a placid pond, also strolls lazily down the fairway, stopping now and then quietly to swish his clubhead through a ball that, ho-hum, happens to be in the way. Jack Nicklaus swings deliberately, methodically, much in keeping with his purposeful Teutonic temperament. Quick-swinging Lee Trevino hops from shot to shot like a Mexican jumping bean, chattering at the fans whenever his hyperactive Latin temperament needs venting.

If ever a golfer played as he lived, it was Walter Hagen. Hagen swung the driver and the swizzle stick with equal flair and flamboyance. Frequently both led him astray. Yet no golfer in history could recover so successfully so quickly as Hagen, whether it be from an errant tee shot or a whiskey hangover.

A typical Hagen showing occurred in 1926 when he played his only head-to-head match with Bobby Jones. Their meeting, a two-day,

72-hole affair in Florida, was billed as the "Battle of the Champions." On the first hole Hagen pulled his drive deep into trees on the left, where the ball finished on bare sand. He rifled his second shot through a narrow opening to just short of the green, pitched on, and dropped a ten-foot putt for a win. That hole set the pattern for the match: a wild drive by Hagen, a crash from the trees with the ball spewing forth into position for par or birdie.

"By the time Bobby got the idea," Jones' "Boswell," O. B. Keeler, later recalled, "Walter had a miraculous spin of 32 on the second nine of the second round. With half of the match played he was eight up."

After Hagen finally settled the matter the next day, winning 11 and 10, Jones summarized his feelings about playing Hagen head to head: "I would far rather play a man who is straight down the fairway with his drive, on the green with his second, and down in two putts for his par. I can play a man like that at his own game, which is par golf. If one of us can get close to the pin with his approach, or hole a good putt—all right. He has earned something that I can understand. But

22

WALTER HAGEN

Born: December 21, 1892; Rochester, New York

Died: October 5, 1969; Traverse City, Michigan

Major victories:

U.S. Open: 1914, 1919

British Open: 1922, 1924, 1928, 1929

PGA championship: 1921, 1924, 1925, 1926, 1927

For maximum length and accuracy, Walter Hagen advocated and employed a tension-free swing, as one would use to clip tops from daisies. He stressed light grip pressure ("no more than you'd need to write smoothly with a fountain pen"), plenty of preswing waggling of the club and pumping of the knees ("to get your muscles unstrung"), and a free-swinging acceleration of the arms forward through impact and beyond. Indication of Hagen's arm-swing freedom is shown in the downswing photos (turn page) by the rapidly expanding gap between his hands and his right shoulder. Note also his excellent footwork, despite his wide stance, as his left knee shifts rapidly to his left at the start of his downswing. Also observe the steady head position, with absolutely no indication of the famed "Hagen sway" until the ball is well away.

when a man misses his drive, and then misses his second shot, and then wins the hole with a birdie—it gets my goat!"

Hagen's amazing ability to save shots in the face of disaster contributed heavily to his winning two U.S. Opens and four British Opens at stroke-play, but even more so it made him golf's all-time match-play champion. As Keeler observed of Hagen's miraculous escapes: "These shocking upsets do not affect the card and the pencil in a medal competition, but they do work havoc with the equilibrium of a single human opponent at match-play."

In the PGA championship, then determined by 36-hole matches, Hagen won 32 out of 34 times between 1916 and 1927. He beat the best—MacDonald, Barnes, Farrell, Watrous, Cooper, Mehlhorn, Diegel, Joe Turnesa, McLeod, Armour—and he beat them resoundingly; his average victory margin exceeded five holes. He lost only to Jock Hutchinson on the final hole and to Gene Sarazen on the 38th. He won the championship five of the seven times he entered it.

In short, Hagen was a scrambler without peer. Perhaps British writer Arthur Croome said it best when he wrote: "He makes more bad shots in a single season than Harry Vardon did during the whole period 1890–1914, during which he won six [British] Open championships. But he beats more immaculate golfers because three of 'those' and one of 'them' count four, and he knows it."

To understand why Hagen made so many of "them," we must study his attitudes toward golf. Conceivably his commonsense approach could help many of us on those frequent days when all our shots seem to be one of "those."

First of all, Hagen learned to accept with equanimity the fact that there will always be such days. "One thing a tournament golfer has to learn," he said, "is that it is not the game he played last year, or last week, or probably will play the week after next, that he commands in any one event. He has only his game at the time; and it may be far from his best—but it's all he has, and he'd just as well harden his heart and make the most of it."

Realizing that bad days are inevitable helped to free Hagen's mind of any qualms about the overall quality of his method. When playing atrociously, as he sometimes did, he did not begin to search for a new technique, but merely accepted the setback with a smile, went to a party, and waited for a better day. Thus he eliminated the paralysis from self-analysis that has stifled so many potentially fine golfers.

Hagen's first try at the British Open, at Deal in 1920, typified his attitude. Twice U.S. Open champion, he was a highly favored entrant. He shot the front nine of the first round in 37, then required 48 blows to get home. He failed to break 80 in any round and finished 26 shots behind the winner, George Duncan. "I'll be back," Hagen told the gallery around the scoreboard as his final-round 84 was posted. Two weeks later he handsomely beat much the same field in the French Open.

Such massive swings of fortune characterize Hagen's entire career. Invariably he was

at his best shortly after playing his worst. Perhaps the most spectacular example of his ability to bounce back occurred in a highly promoted challenge match he played in 1928 against the outstanding (and equally colorful) British professional, Archie Compston, over 72 holes for the then-record purse in England of $3,750. Hagen entered the match, at the tricky Moor Park Golf Club northwest of London, after having spent two months in Hollywood making a movie, riding a train cross-country to New York, and sailing on the *Aquitania* to Southampton, where he arrived a day before the big event. His only practice during that period consisted of driving a few balls off the boat while crossing the Atlantic.

Compston, a giant of a man physically and in personality, was ready. He played the first nine in 32, the second in 35 for a 67 total. In the afternoon he shot 36-30–66. Hagen was 14 down after the first day! Compston shot 70 the morning of the second day and ended the duel on the first hole of the fourth round.

Hagen's 18 and 17 defeat was one of the worst in the history of the game, but photos taken after the match show him happily congratulating Compston. A cigarette juts jauntily from Hagen's smiling face. He looks for all the world as if he'd just breezed to victory. The next week he did just that, beating Compston and everyone else in the British Open at Sandwich!

In 1929 Hagen again reversed an embarrassing defeat with a major victory. Duncan whomped him 10 and 8 in their Ryder Cup singles match in Britain. Hagen's caddie was crestfallen, but not Hagen himself. He immediately bought his disappointed bag toter a new suit of clothes, took him to Muirfield for the British Open, and won the championship for the fourth and final time with a 292 total. No Briton broke 300 in the harsh Scottish winds and rain.

Hagen not only recognized that good rounds would eventually follow bad; he also learned early in his golfing life the invaluable lesson that bad shots are part of the game. He observed that they are best forgotten, that the only shot that really matters is the one coming up.

"I've never played a perfect eighteen holes," Hagen once said. "There is no such thing. I expect to make at least seven mistakes a round. Therefore, when I make a bad shot, I don't worry about it. It's just one of the seven."

The 1913 U.S. Open at Brookline, Massachusetts, is remembered primarily as the one in which the American amateur Francis Ouimet, then a twenty-year-old ex-caddie, beat golfing giants Harry Vardon and Ted Ray in a play-off, thus establishing the "rich man's sport" as a game for the masses. A lesser-known fact about that tournament is that Hagen, also twenty, also an ex-caddie, also playing in his first U.S. Open, finished the 72 holes just three shots behind Vardon, Ray, and Ouimet.

The final day of that tournament was cold and dismal, and so was Hagen's play. He three-putted the first green for a bogey, caught a bunker at the second for another, and double-bogeyed the third, three-putting for a seven—four over par after three holes.

The fourth hole at the Country Club required a blind second shot over a hill to the green. Despite his horrendous start, Hagen, ever the optimist, walked ahead of his drive to the top of the hill. As he surveyed his upcoming approach, he noticed a boy running out of the woods behind the green. Hagen returned to his ball, selected a five-iron, and played what seemed to be a good shot.

"When I walked to where I could see the green," he recalled, "my ball was not in sight. I had a hunch that boy I'd seen running out of the woods had picked it up. I yelled at him, far down the fairway, and sent my caddie after him with orders to search him. Meantime, I went hunting through the rough. Then my playing partner thought to look in the hole . . . and there was my ball nestled real snuglike. I had scored a deuce. I figured right then the two would take care of the seven on the previous hole."

On the fifth hole Hagen smashed a two-wood shot to within one inch of the hole for another birdie. On the sixth his approach hit the top of the flagstick, caught in the flat itself, and dropped next to the cup. That birdie

brought him back to even par for the round. He just missed another birdie on the par-three seventh hole when his twelve-foot putt for a two lipped out.

For the first seven holes of that round, Hagen's score read 6-5-7-2-3-3-3. Though he bogeyed the eighth and ninth holes, he finished the front side tied for the lead. A double-bogey seven on the 14th hole, where Vardon and Ray made fours, ended his chances for victory, but Hagen had learned a valuable lesson about forgetting a bad shot—even a putt—and positively approaching the one ahead.

This lesson was to be particularly valuable to him on the greens—that area of maximum frustration—throughout his career.

"I believe the great majority of golfers expect too much in holing out," Hagen later advised. "There is no tragedy in missing a putt, no matter how short. We have all erred in this respect. Short putts are missed because it is not physically possible to make the little ball travel over uncertain ground for three or four feet with any degree of regularity.

"The mental side will overcome the physical side if we begin to worry about a missed putt. It is far better that we count missed putts as part of the game and leave our minds free and open to make one, without the suggestion entering the head that our putting stroke is all wrong."

Hagen's ability to accept—and forget—bad shots made him one of the game's greatest come-from-behind competitors. "I can tell when Hagen is losing," Walter Travis, three times U.S. Amateur champion, said in 1924. "He's fighting harder than ever. He gets a big thrill in going after a three- or four-stroke lead. No golfer in history has come from behind oftener to win."

Another aspect of Hagen's makeup that made him a winner was his ability to accept luck—both good and bad—as an inherent aspect of the game. Unlike so many tournament players of that day and this, he did not blame the course when it failed to reward all his good shots because he knew it would also fail to penalize all his bad ones. Thus he seldom let bad luck divert his concentration from the

job ahead. Bobby Jones summed it up well when he said: "I love to play with Walter. He goes along, chin up, smiling away; never grousing about his luck, playing the ball as he finds it. He can come nearer beating luck itself than anybody I know."

All in all, the attitudes that made Hagen a super stroke-saving, come-from-behind, escape artist on the golf course sprung from a bottomless pit of self-confidence. His was not the kind of self-confidence that reflects itself in vanity or conceit, not the kind that needs constant reinforcement from the putting down of others. Nor was it the kind that requires periodic reminding that "I can win because I'm Walter Hagen." Hagen's self-confidence was of the kind many Americans of his period developed during a fend-for-yourself childhood; reinforced through successes over the years; tempered by an ebullient, carefree personality that allowed him to view life with a "So what if I lose today, life is still fun and I'll win sooner or later" attitude; and, finally, firmly reinforced by a basically sound golfing technique that worked very well indeed most of the time.

Compared to others of the 1920's, Hagen's swing was considered "slashing." Today, with smash more fashionable than smoothness, it would be categorized as "well paced," perhaps even rhythmical. From the standpoint of overall tempo, Hagen may have seemed to be the Arnold Palmer of his era, but actually his swing pace was almost identical to that of Billy Casper today.

The whippy wood-shafted clubs of Hagen's era bent and twisted more readily than do the more rigid, torque-resistant metal shafts of today. They required a more precise timing of the delivery of the clubface to the ball, demanding that the player give himself a moment more between backswing and downswing. Perhaps Hagen's chief fault was that he did not always allow himself sufficient time to change direction. Slow-motion movies show him starting forward to the ball with his legs and lower body a shade before his hands and clubshaft had finished swinging back and up. This sequence is fairly common to the swings of modern professionals, but it was sometimes a little too stress-producing for the shafts of Hagen's day. Unquestionably it was one reason for his wildness off the tee with the long-shafted driver. In fact, it could be argued that Hagen's amazingly modern-looking early lower-body action during the downswing was, ironically, better suited for play on the professional tour of 1975 than 1925.

Hagen himself remarked in 1925 that "for accurate driving a whippy shaft is a hopeless proposition." To offset the twisting effect of the softer wooden shafts and to help him square the clubface by impact, Hagen employed a trick that would actually be illegal under today's rules. He put a slight kink or bend in the shafts of his wood clubs at the bottom of the grip, so that the handle, if extended, would point to the *center* of the clubhead rather than to its heel. A few years ago this writer had the opportunity to hit shots with metal-shafted clubs that had been bent in this fashion. It was truly remarkable how readily the clubface returned squarely to the target line no matter how much effort was made to swing badly.

Another feature of Hagen's style that led to occasional wildness with the long clubs was his unusually wide stance. He spread his feet much father apart than did most of his contemporaries and certainly wider than any modern star except, perhaps, Doug Sanders.

Maybe Hagen's unusually wide stance stemmed from his baseball-playing days. He was proficient enough as a baseball pitcher to be invited to try out with the Philadelphia Phillies when he was twenty. His fine showing in the aforementioned U.S. Open of 1913, along with his preference for golf's challenge to the individual rather than baseball's to the team, eventually caused him to turn down the invitation. The wide stance that baseball players step into to meet the oncoming pitch remained, however, a distinctive feature of his golfing address position until late in his career.

Much has been said about Hagen's tendency to sway sideways as he swung. This impression has been furthered, no doubt, by the many photos that show him with his head and upper body well forward toward the target at the finish of his swing. In truth, however, Hagen did almost all his forward swaying *after* impact. Movie and sequence photography show that during actual impact, his head was either in its original address position or even slightly behind it.

Hagen's head position, both before and during his swing, was almost identical to that of Jack Nicklaus and Bob Jones. He set it well back of the ball as he stepped into his stance; he looked at the ball with both eyes as he waggled; then, like Nicklaus and Jones, he gradually turned his chin to his right just before starting the club back, to allow a full shoulder turn on his backswing. By the time his clubhead had moved back a foot or two from the ball, he was looking at the ball only with his left eye. He then held this head position until after impact, when he allowed the weight of the moving clubhead to pull his arms, shoulders, and head forward and upward.

Above all, Hagen advocated a free swinging of the arms through the impact area and well beyond. "The golfer who gets into this habit," he advised, "will soon forget that he's ever topped a ball. He will also be surprised at the distance obtainable, which will be in marked contrast to the ball hit with the club checked before it has done its work."

Hagen understood fully that we are all intimidated to varying extents by the ball itself. He knew that the unconscious urge is to scoop or lift the ball, especially from a tight lie. He realized how difficult it is to avoid trying to guide the clubhead squarely to the ball on a critical tee shot, a practice that inevitably causes a checking of the club "before it has done its work."

In keeping with his role as a great recovery artist, the strongest areas of Hagen's game were his chipping and putting. He handled varying situations by making more or less the same swing with different clubs, rather than a variety of strokes with one club. His chipping stroke was crisp, with most of his weight remaining on the left foot throughout the swing.

Hagen's putting stance was also very wide and considerably "open," with his left foot pulled three to four inches farther back than his right from the target line. He set most of

his weight on his left foot as a guard against swaying, positioning the ball opposite his left foot and setting his hands slightly in advance of the putterhead.

Hagen's putting stroke was a little wristier than most of those on the pro tour today. As a result, his putterhead swung back relatively high on lengthy putts. However, he seldom lifted it upward, and he tried, consciously at times, to continue accelerating his forearms freely forward on his through-stroke. Thus his putterhead kept moving forward relatively low to the ground well beyond the ball.

Hagen stressed being as relaxed as possible when putting, but his main thought was simply to make the ball go into the hole. "Probably the most important single thing," he said, "is to feel that you are going to hole the putt, then stroke the ball the right way. This has to be mostly instinctive, for you certainly can't be thinking of two or three things when you are trying to putt." And he added: "Gripping the putter too tightly is one of the surest ways to miss."

As Hagen neared the end of his career in the 1930's, his wood and iron shots became more accurate—quite probably because he gradually narrowed his stance. His putting, however, began to deteriorate along with his confidence in this part of his game. As always, Hagen had no excuses:

"My putting touch was definitely off," he recalled. "I tried standing with my feet close together. . . . I tried standing with my feet wide apart. I tried bending over a bit more, and I tried standing straight.

"Actually, my main trouble was just a whiskey jerk."

Hagen's stance was one of the widest of his or of any other era.

31

Gene Sarazen

HITTING IT HARD FOR FIFTY YEARS

Gene Sarazen entered golf with the force of a thunderclap in 1922 by winning the U.S. Open as an unknown twenty-year-old, prevailing by one stroke over Bobby Jones and a forty-three-year-old grandfather called John Black by birdieing the last hole and shooting 68, equaling the then-lowest final round in the history of the championship.

In 1973, at age seventy-one, Sarazen retired from tournament golf with equal élan by hitting a five-iron straight into the famous 126-yard "Postage Stamp" eighth hole at Troon, Scotland, while on television during the British Open.

In the fifty-one tumultuous years between these stirring events this pint-sized issue of poor Italian immigrants became not only one of the greatest-ever players of golf but one of the most colorful and charismatic personalities in the game's history.

Among professional golfers, only his archrival and lifelong sparring partner, Walter Hagen—and possibly, of modern times, Arnold Palmer—ever won more newsprint than Gene Sarazen. And every inch of it was thoroughly well earned, if not by sheer golfing achievement, then by a bold, bouncy, and often provocative attitude toward life.

It was impossible in his day not to admire Sarazen as a golfer and not to be entertained and intrigued by him as a man. He was the first golfer to win all four major championships—the U.S. and British Opens, Masters, and PGA championship. He was—and is—the youngest-ever winner of a major championship (the 1922 U.S. Open). He was almost certainly the first superstar to practice as much as he played, frequently hitting balls for six or seven hours a day throughout his career and swinging a 22-ounce practice club daily into his seventies. He was one of the fastest golfers in history—once shooting 70 in the final round of the Masters in 1 hour, 57 minutes—and a vociferous critic of tardy play. He habitually wore what the British call plus fours and Americans knickers on and off the golf course (and, suggested some of his rivals, also in bed). He used some of the heaviest clubs wielded in this century, including a 15-ounce driver. He claimed to have—and is generally credited with having—invented the modern sand wedge, as the

GENE SARAZEN

Born: February 27, 1902; Harrison, New York

Major victories:

U.S. Open: 1922, 1932
British Open: 1932
PGA championship: 1922, 1923, 1933
Masters: 1935

result of a one-time ineptitude in bunkers, and credited his 1932 British Open victory to this club. He hit perhaps the most famous single golf shot in history, a four-wood into the 15th hole at Augusta National for a double eagle in the 1935 Masters, to tie Craig Wood and go on to win the play-off. He was the smallest great golfer pre-Gary Player—5 feet 5 inches and 145 pounds in his spikes. On the course he emitted an aura of urgent, combative confidence and a Palmer-like sense of going for broke while wondering who was going to be second. He fought a sometimes bitter, sometimes good-natured, but ever-relentless battle with Walter Hagen for titles, money, recognition, and the *bon mot*—a battle often enlivened by the fact that in many personal tastes and habits he was Hagen's opposite: openly ambitious, industrious, intense, mercurial, health-conscious, temperate, and usually early to bed. And he was a self-admitted loner; a man who never tried to hide the fact that he was out for himself; who said many times in his career: "Your game counts for you and mine for me. In other words, look out for number one, because in doing that you'll find you have plenty to care for."

As a swinger of the golf club, Sarazen commanded less attention in his heyday than he did either as a competitor or a personality, with one striking exception—his grip. Nothing like it had been seen before at the highest levels of the game, and certainly nothing like it has since won fame and fortune on the professional tour.

The first unique factor about Sarazen's hold on the club was that for much of his career he actually used two grips, an interlocking arrangement for full shots and an overlapping configuration for chips, pitches, and other around-the-green finesse strokes. Both were unorthodox in mechanical form, but by far the stranger animal was the interlocking version.

This grip evolved in large part because hitting the ball hard suited Sarazen temperamentally and was also mandatory for a man of his short if strong and stocky physique. Particularly during his formative years, however (he began to play golf at age eight as a

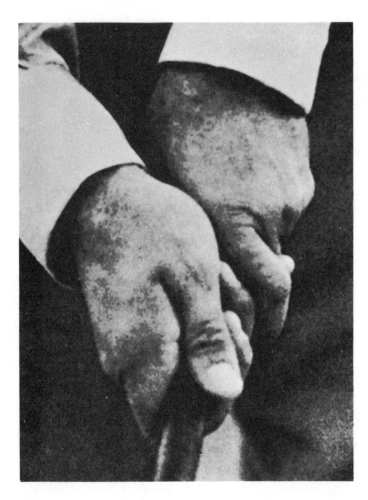

Sarazen's grip featured a "strong" left-hand placement; interlocking of the little finger of the right hand with the forefinger of the left; and—unique among champions since the nineteenth century—the thumb of the left hand hanging free from the clubshaft. The "strong" placement of the hands particularly influenced his entire swing.

Because of his grip, as well as his approach to golf, hard-hitting Sarazen had to deliver the clubface "late" with his hands and wrists to prevent closing it disastrously through the ball. This in turn demanded sprightly use of the legs and lower body during the downswing to clear a path for the arms to swing freely past the body without the wrists being forced to roll counterclockwise. As a result of building a swing around his grip/hand action, Sarazen's overall style came to incorporate many elements that would be considered excellent form today—compactness and economy of movement being two of them.

caddie), the smallness and comparative weakness of his hands inhibited his instinctively vigorous approach. For a while he attempted to increase his power by allowing the club to slip down into the slot between the thumb and forefinger of the right hand at the top of the backswing (as the British star, Dai Rees, similarly did), but this device cost him too dearly in control. He discovered exercise to be a better solution; throughout his playing career he worked assiduously to build up his hands, wrists, and forearms. But there were limits to what could be achieved through muscular condition, and these he overcame by developing a grip whereby the strongest part of the leading hand could sustain the stress and shock of impact.

In assembling his basic full-shot grip, Sarazen placed his left hand almost entirely on top of the shaft, enabling him easily to see all four knuckles at address. He then added the right hand in a slightly less "strong" position, but with the thumb positioned off the left side of the shaft so that it touched the tip of his "triggered" right forefinger. To marry the hands better, he interlocked the little

finger of the right hand with the forefinger of the left—in itself an unusual if not unacceptable device at a time when Vardon's overlapping technique had come to be regarded almost as the eleventh commandment. But all of this was rampant orthodoxy by comparison with Sarazen's ultimate idiosyncrasy. His left thumb, instead of lying down the shaft and snuggling nicely into the palm of the right hand, went the way of the St. Andrews Swingers: It hung out in space off the shaft under the outer edge of the right hand! And just to put the finishing touch to what one critic of the day called "the most contorted bunch of bananas I've ever seen," Sarazen had his club grips built up to about one and a half times the standard diameter where his left hand held on.

Sarazen did not promote this configuration in his teaching, favoring the overlapping grip for golfers with large- or normal-size hands and the interlocking formula primarily for small-handed men and most women. But he never departed from it personally, and he has never ceased to advise a very "strong" placement of the left hand on the club for all play-

ers. In 1933 he said in an interview with Grantland Rice: "The left hand should be placed far enough over toward the right so that the player can see all four knuckles out of the corner of his eye. The right hand should be placed so that the V formed between the thumb and forefinger points approximately to the upper edge of the clubface as you look down upon it in the position at address. It is very important to get the left hand well over as indicated, and to hang onto it firmly with the club throughout the swing. . . . I have seen far too much loose, flabby gripping."

As a contemporary of Sarazen's, player/writer P. A. Vaile, perceived in 1922, the principles behind this grip were actually exactly those of the lumberjack and the practitioner of karate. Wrote Vaile: "He has his left hand so much above the shaft of his club that at the moment of impact, and during the adhesion of the ball and the club, the shock of the blow falls *across the flat of the wrist,* in the way of which that joint cannot possibly yield to the sudden strain. [His] grip on the club *at the moment of impact* is mechanically

almost the same as that of a man wielding an axe or sledgehammer, and they are not exactly theorists when it comes to getting the most they can out of their stroke.

"I know very little of [the Oriental martial arts] but I do know that one of the most effective blows is dealt with the side of the hand. It is a backhanded blow, and the shock falls across the wrist joint in a way in which it cannot bend. This is also the root-principle of the finest backhand in tennis. Without it a swordsman could only use his weapon one way. A woodsman would be lost if it were barred to him. A few facts such as these may serve to show the great underlying merit of Sarazen's grip, for it must be remembered that . . . in Vardon's grip . . . the left, at the moment of impact, is in a comparatively impotent position, presenting the back of the hand, instead of the side, to the hole."

Irrespective of the merits Vaile saw in this grip—and the fact that children, women, and weaker men players tend instinctively to place the left hand well on top of the shaft—the Sarazen format would be unacceptable to the majority of modern teaching profession-als. There are some good reasons why, the chief one perhaps being the amount of training necessary to ensure that the left hand always swings through the ball side-on to the target, instead of instinctively turning to a square (back of hand facing target) alignment at impact. The untrained golfer using as strong a grip as Sarazen's would be certain to smother-hook or block out to the far right as many balls as he hit straight—smothering when his left wrist collapsed or was overpowered by his right hand through impact and blocking when, as a countermeasure, he failed to release his wrists at all.

Yet the fact is that Sarazen won seven major championships and a score of other tournaments between 1922 and 1938 and was still sprinting around Augusta National in the high 70's in the Masters in his eighth decade. All that with a faulty grip?

The answer, of course, is that Sarazen's grip wasn't faulty—*for him.* He is, like so many of the golfers analyzed in this book, a dramatic example of the fact that there is more than one way to skin a cat. What Sarazen did was simple and logical—and work-

able if you can devote your life to golf and you have the drive and determination to become great at it. First he found a way of holding the club that he believed would best allow him to generate maximum power. Then he built a golf swing around that grip—and stuck to it.

A few years ago Deane Beman, one of the more prescient technicians among professional tourists, wrote a series in *Golf Digest* magazine about "mutually exclusive" (compatability) factors in the golf swing. It did not win wild hosannas from readers because it demanded thought, work, and the prospect of uncomfortable change, rather than instant par-busting. But it was actually some of the best material ever presented on golf technique in that it told the thoughtful player exactly which swing factors will blend together and which will not. Discovering a swing that complemented his grip, then sticking to it through thick and thin, was the key to Sarazen's success as a shotmaker, as it has been the key to all great golf (although often not consciously rationalized by the players themselves).

Sarazen's overall action offers an instructive study of how compatibility is more important than orthodoxy in golf.

The heavy emphasis on delayed release of the wrists in modern swing theory tends to create the impression that all olden-day golfers must have "hit from the top." If Sarazen, with his grip, had hit from the top, the only sport in which he might have made a living would have been baseball, because every golf shot he hit would have trundled worm-high somewhere near third base. Sarazen *had* to hit "late" with the clubhead and probably did, in fact, unhinge his wrists as late as any golfer in history with the possible exception of the late Tony Lema. Sarazen talks constantly in his books and magazine articles of "hitting the ball with the hands, not the wrists"; of "firm wrists through impact"; of "hanging on with the left hand"; of "not letting the right hand turn over too quickly"—even writing, in 1928, "I have stood on the first tee and watched one golfer after another drive off, and one thing that struck me was that most of them hit too soon. Roughly speaking, the clubhead should be two-thirds

of the way from its position at the top of the backswing down to the ball before any hitting force is exerted; in other words, the hands should be down about waist level." Photographs from that time show his own hands to be almost as far ahead of the clubhead approaching impact as are the hands of one of today's strongest grippers (at least with the right hand), Lee Trevino.

Technical analysts of Sarazen's era paid scant attention to leg action, although the need to clear the left side out of the way to make room for the arms to swing past the body and out toward the target has been recognized since Vardon's day (and there is no way that can be done without some leg movement toward the target). Except for the fact that he braced his left leg immediately after impact to keep his body behind the ball—a fundamental of 1930's golf teaching—Sarazen's leg action was identical to that of the modern tour player. And the fact is that with his grip and swing plane, it *had to be that way.*

Immobility in Sarazen's legs at the start of the downswing would have caused him to pull-hook every shot, by forcing his right shoulder over and around instead of under and through, thus obliging him to deliver the clubface to the ball in an acutely closed position from outside the target line. He emphasizes the need for flexibility in the leading knee through impact in an article written in 1927 about getting distance: "The left knee should bend very slightly out towards the hole . . . before impact. The knee is pushed out as the clubhead comes down and . . . practically the whole weight of the player is thrown onto the left foot by the bend of the left knee, but the action is done so smoothly as to be practically unnoticed by the onlooker. However, if the golfer omits to bend the left knee, and the left leg tightens up too soon, the chances are that the shot will be a bad one."

Sarazen's swing as a caddie was long and upright, but as his grip strengthened in his search for power, it became shorter and flatter and more dependent on the winding and unwinding of the body than on simply a swing of the arms. Here again he was influenced by the compatibility factor: As the practice-tee lineup at any present-day tour event conclusively proves, a strong grip and an upright plane simply do not go together.

Other mutual exclusivity, or incompatibility, factors are to be found in Sarazen's early problems with, and eventual cure of, a troublesome hook. The stronger the grip, the flatter the natural swing plane; and the flatter the plane, the more "inside out" the club swings at impact. Also, the stronger the grip and the flatter the plane, the greater the danger of closing the clubface prematurely. During his early years Sarazen tended to compound his built-in hook-makers by addressing the ball fairly well back in his stance, which in turn had the effect of closing his shoulders to the target line. Periods of truly prodigious roundhouse hooking resulted. By 1932, however, the year he won both the U.S. and the British Opens, Sarazen was the consummate golfer—able to flight the ball from right to left or left to right at will. And the reason was plain to see in his setup, the ball now being positioned opposite his left heel and his shoulder and foot alignment now being square to slightly open. A modern golfer who began to win big only after going through a similar process is Lee Trevino. And, inevitably, there is much that is reminiscent of Sarazen in Trevino's present setup and shoulder and hand action through the ball, not to mention his basic stature and physique.

Although Sarazen thought of himself primarily as a "hands player" (although not a "wrists player"), his writings strongly emphasize body action, both directly and indirectly. He exhorts the golfer to make a wide stance; to strive for the fullest possible turn of the shoulders in the backswing; to pivot around a fixed axis and create maximum body torque by taking the weight on the inside of the right foot during the backswing ("It is always better to overdo than underdo the pivoting"); to start the club back low and wide in what today would be called a one-piece takeaway; to extend the left arm going back without pronating or supinating the wrist, so that the swing may be given "a wider sweep, providing a means of employing the muscles of the shoulders, body and legs as well as those of the arms"; to allow the body to turn freely during the down-and-through swing.

In sum, Sarazen's swing at his peak in the early thirties was as modern as anything you'll see on tour today, with the minor exceptions of the very wristy waggle from which he went fluidly into the takeaway; an unusually wide stance ("To provide a strong base for a hard hit," he said); and the bracing of the left leg immediately after impact.

His "soft" right arm at address is a feature of Lee Trevino's setup. His cocking of the head to the right as the club went back in one piece is integral to Jack Nicklaus' swing and to Sam Snead's. His slight sway of the upper body away from the target in making a full shoulder turn is clearly evident in Tom Weiskopf's action. His fractional cupping of the left wrist at the top of the swing is the position Frank Beard attains. His full hip turn going back, raised left heel, and quick knee shift and hip clearance starting down are all features of Nicklaus' driver swing. His immobile head through impact is Arnold Palmer to the inch. His pronounced "down, under, and through" right-shoulder movement is Trevino all over. And his occasional loss of balance on the follow-through after a big hit is Gary Player to a T.

Technically proficient as he may have been, however, it was not Sarazen's swing that made him one of golf's greatest champions. Tracing back through his career, four characteristics that have nothing to do with playing method jump vividly from the pages. They are hard work, confidence, concentration, and competitive spirit.

Sarazen really did labor at golf and enjoyed doing so because he knew that for him it was the only route to the success he hungered for. And out of this endless work came his boundless confidence. Six months after his dramatic first U.S. Open win he wrote: "Golf requires a lot of practice—a whole lot, in fact. I really like to practice. I recently heard a fellow say that when one spent three or four or five hours practicing with one club, then the game ceased to be pleasure and became work. Maybe that's true, if you don't like to practice. To me it's interesting to see how

close to the pin I can come with a hundred balls at a hundred yards, and then from 75 yards, and so on. It is this kind of practice that enables me to play my shots accurately. I have practiced . . . six and seven hours at a stretch, and all with one club. That is why, when I am about to make a shot, I know exactly what I can do with the club I am about to use. I know whether I can stop the ball two feet from the pin at a certain distance, because practice has taught me just how much effort I must use to accomplish the end I seek. I am sure always of every shot I make. Of course, the best of them will go wrong at times, and when this happens I realize that I have neglected my practice. Then I go out and remedy the defect, and I practice until I am absolutely confident that I can do what I want to do."

Sarazen's ability to concentrate on one shot at a time and on a positive result rather than a multiplicity of technical maneuvers was hard earned. Thinking two holes ahead of the one he was playing, and playing his opponent instead of the course, cost him dearly until he learned to temper his ebullience and impatience and to blank out of his mind all but the task immediately confronting him.

In 1923 he said: "[I have learned] never to pay any attention to my opponent's play—[not] mind what he does at all—for it does not count anything for me. You cannot concentrate on your game if you are worrying about your opponent. I am always playing my card—I am trying to equal par on the scorecard. If I can equal par, I am satisfied. If my opponent gets a birdie or an eagle, well and good. But, in the long run, it is the player who shoots par, or as close to it as possible, who eventually triumphs."

And a little later that same year: "When the player steps up . . . to hit the ball, he should be thinking of nothing else in the world than hitting the ball. By that time he must have put out of his mind any thought of whether he is taking the club back right, whether he is hurrying the backswing, whether his grip is correct . . . or any of the other things that may enter into the correct making of the stroke. The time to work over

Apart from a stiffening of the left side through impact—hitting against a firm left side was considered good form in his day—Sarazen at impact met all modern criteria.

the grip is some time when you can turn your attention to this and nothing else. The time . . . to think about whether or not you are hurrying the backswing is beforehand, when you have time to put your mind strictly on that and train on that point alone. In other words, all of these details, important as they are, must be attended to beforehand, so that when you step up to hit the ball you have your mind on that and that alone. It's pretty much the same as driving a nail in with a hammer. There would be a lot of sore fingers if carpenters divided their attention between whether or not they were gripping the hammer too tightly, and how far back they were taking it, and so on. Keep your attention on hitting the ball, on bringing the clubhead [solidly] against it."

And in 1928, with even greater maturity showing: "Imagination is the death of a low golf score; it puts the player's nerves on edge, makes him visualize hazards that do not exist. . . . It is better to have a dull, nonchalant outlook, impervious to external influences."

In the realm of competitive spirit, Sarazen was always richly endowed—by nature, by his hard-scratching youth in a tough New York suburb, and perhaps by his small stature. O. B. Keeler, America's outstanding golf writer of the day, may have best captured this quality the year Sarazen burst into big-league golf:

"When Gene takes the field against any golfer, or any array of golfers, the only question in his mind is, in the first instance, how many holes it will take him to beat his man, and, in the second, by what margin he is going to finish in front. [He] fairly bristles with assurance. His confidence is aggressive—more aggressive than Hagen's, if not so philosophical. . . . Sarazen gives the impression of straining at the leash. When confronted by a tough and testing shot, he appears tremendously eager to get at it; not to 'get it over with,' as are so many nerve-ridden players; but rather with a fierce inspiration to conquer; with a certain joy of battle and a grim delight at the chance to extend his powers."

Bobby Jones

NEVER TINKER WITH TALENT

Bobby Jones had just finished third-round play in the 1927 Southern Open in Atlanta. It was a round in which he shot 66, a round that Jones himself later described as being "as nearly perfect as any I ever played."

Kerr Petrie, sportswriter for the New York *Herald Tribune*, began his report of that round as follows: "They wound up the Mechanical Man of Golf yesterday and sent him clicking around the East Lake course."

While Jones' precise shotmaking may have seemed machinelike to writers of his day—not to mention his disconsolate opponents—there was nothing "mechanical" about the way he actually swung a golf club. Jones was a student of the golf swing. As a trained engineer he understood its mechanics, its physics, its ballistics far better than most of his peers or even the vast majority of the great players who came later. But he consciously avoided letting this understanding inhibit the innate flow, rhythm, naturalness, and grace of his own stroke. He never lost sight of the fact that the purpose of the swing is simply to strike the ball forward with the clubhead, not to manipulate the club itself in a certain prescribed manner.

Sam Snead's swing has been described countless times as "natural." If natural means uncontrived, then Jones' swing must be similarly categorized. In researching this book the authors came across a photograph of Jones taken in 1909 when he was seven years old and just starting to play the game. It shows a wisp of a lad in short pants at the top of his backswing (Jones was a frail youth who couldn't take solid foods until he was five). The striking thing about this picture is the similarity of swing form between Jones as a rank beginner and as the man who later dominated major tournament golf as no one ever has or likely will. We see the same narrow stance, both feet toed out slightly. We see the same full hip turn that became a Jones trademark. Even the head position, with the chin turned noticeably toward the right shoulder, is identical. Bobby Jones was indeed a natural golfer, blessed with a fine swing from the start—certainly a magnificent sense of rhythm—who had the good sense to cultivate what he was born with and never to tinker too much with what nature had wrought.

Fortunately for Jones, Stewart Maiden, the

BOBBY JONES

Born: March 17, 1902; Atlanta, Georgia

Died: December 18, 1971; Atlanta, Georgia

Major victories:

U.S. Open: 1923, 1926, 1929, 1930

British Open: 1926, 1927, 1930

U.S. Amateur: 1924, 1925, 1927, 1928, 1930

British Amateur: 1930

That Bobby Jones' swing was natural and uncontrived is proved by the similarities between his championship form of 1930 and his original technique as a frail seven-year-old. Note the preservation over the years of the original—and natural—narrow stance, full hip turn, and cocking of the chin to the right.

professional at East Lake where the Jones family rented a cottage, also knew when to leave well enough alone. "I taught Bobby as little as possible," the stocky Scot later recalled. "I knew it was a mistake to confuse him with too many things."

Thus, unencumbered by theory, young Jones was allowed the run of the fairways at East Lake. Frequently he'd follow Maiden for a few holes, unconsciously absorbing the flowing grace of his swing. Youngsters seem to have a knack for mimicry that generally wanes with the years, and Jones certainly was no exception. Later, when he filled out physically into proportions similar to Maiden's, it became difficult to tell their swings apart when viewed from a distance. (Another East Lake youngster who successfully absorbed Maiden's graceful swing style was Alexa Stirling, winner of the U.S. Women's Amateur championship in 1916, 1919, and 1920.)

It has often been said that Jones had the perfect build for golf—tall enough at 5 feet 8 inches to develop a full arc, but short enough to swing compactly; solid enough at 165 pounds to possess ample strength without being cumbersome or muscle-bound. He was also blessed with what today's more professorial instructors of golf call "excellent hand-eye coordination." This gift or knack is a valuable asset in a game where the challenge is to make the club in hand strike what is seen on the ground with as little steering and maneuvering as possible. Perhaps this talent in Jones stemmed from the genes of his father, an accomplished college baseball player and much sought after by major-league teams.

Additional evidence of Jones' superb hand-eye coordination was given by W. H. Letton, of Atlanta, a crack shot who accompanied the golfer on his first attempt at trap-shooting:

"He [Jones] took hold of the gun as awkwardly as a woman would at first. Obviously he'd had no sort of training with a gun. Yet he broke the clay targets with a consistency that many a shooter of years' experience could not match. He broke the targets through sheer instinct. His judgment of distance was practically perfect." (Not coincidentally, Harry Vardon once described Jones as "the finest judge of distance I have ever seen.")

First as a golfer and later as a marksman, Jones realized that success depends largely on simply letting one's instinctive sense of coordination have free rein. In his writings he talks frequently of letting the clubhead freewheel through the ball and warns against last-second attempts to help it swing faster or strike too precisely.

"Many shots are spoiled at the last instant by efforts to add a few more yards," he warned in 1938. "This impedes, rather than aids, the stroke. Muscles tensed in making this sudden effort must hold the clubhead back. . . . I like very much the concept of a free-traveling clubhead at impact. This implies that the golfer will consider his job done once he has made a full wind-up of trunk, arms, and hands, and used these sources of power in proper order during his downswing. The clubhead is then released to strike the ball. . . . The difficulty in applying this conception is in acquiring sufficient confidence in the swing to resist making a last-instant correction or addition on the ball itself. . . . I believe most sincerely that the impulse to steer, born of anxiety, is accountable for almost every really bad shot. The sad fact is that no amount of steering can possibly do any good. And it may serve to magnify errors."

Jones relied on left-arm acceleration through impact to provide a freewheeling clubhead, with no conscious effort on his part either to guide or to accelerate it with his hands.

Readers might more fully appreciate the validity of Jones' comments by simply recalling the success they've had, in terms of both length and accuracy, when swinging in a more or less carefree fashion—when purposely laying up short of a water hazard, for instance.

No doubt the hallmark of Jones' swing was its overall rhythmical smoothness. "You must swing smoothly to play golf well," he said. Then came the all-important corollary: "You must be relaxed to swing smoothly."

In much of the description that follows about how Jones actually swung the golf club and played the game, we shall see that he did things in ways designed largely to control mental and physical tension, particularly in how he produced a state of relaxed alertness—not tension—that allowed him to swing smoothly.

It should also be noted that while Jones did benefit from an early start in the game and a healthy backlog of natural talent, his temperament certainly was not conducive to tension-free swinging. At the peak of his career he became so nervous that he could hardly eat prior to an important round and would need a drink and a hot tub to relax afterward. As a youth this tension, combined with his impatience with himself, was externally released in the form of club throwing. The low point came during a charity match with Alexa Stirling, then the national champion, when Jones was fifteen.

"Although I should have known that Alexa, not I, was the main attraction," Jones later admitted, "I behaved very badly when my game went apart. I heaved numerous clubs, and once threw the ball away. I read the pity in Alexa's soft brown eyes and finally settled down, but not before I had made a complete fool of myself."

That incident ended Jones' club throwing, but only during tournaments or exhibitions. He later admitted that "to the finish of my golfing days I encountered golfing emotions which could not be endured with the club still in my hands." And even after he had mastered this problem in public, he still tore up his scorecard in the British Open during his first encounter with the Old Course at St. Andrews (which he later came to love).

One thing Jones did to reduce such tensions was to grip the club lightly, especially with his right hand. He believed minimal grip pressure at address helped to relax his arms and shoulders for a slow, smooth start to his backswing. The light grip pressure also allowed him to make the long, free backswing that he valued so highly.

Jones also realized that standing too long in one position can cause undue tension. Therefore he tried to avoid becoming static while addressing the ball: "Although we are in the habit of thinking of addressing the ball as one thing, and of swinging the club as quite another, it is a great aid to relaxation if the two performances can be blended as intimately as possible. By all means one should make the placing of the feet, the grounding of the club, and the waggle, parts of the swing, but after they are completed, get the backward movement started before everything tightens up again."

To blend the two, address and swing, Jones waggled only once before his takeaway. "Whenever I hesitated or took a second waggle, I could look for trouble," he said.

Jones was not by nature a critical person, but in his excellent autobiography, *Golf Is My Game*, published in 1959, he did question the habit many modern players have of standing over the ball so long before swinging:

Jones' long, smooth, rhythmical swing (continued on following pages) set the standard for his generation and those that followed. As he pointed out at the time, long, smooth swings cannot be fast swings. Fast swings demand tight grip pressure to maintain club control, and this pressure creates arm and shoulder tension that stifles backswing length. Instead Jones advocated a light right-hand grip with club control resting largely in the last three fingers of the left hand throughout the swing but especially at address, during the takeaway, at the start of the downswing, and through impact.

"If there is a new method in golf," he wrote, "it seems to involve a more careful, even meticulous, 'sighting' of the shot. While we still have many graceful, comfortable-looking players, there are a number who have the appearance of being excruciatingly stiff. In some cases the traditional waggle of the club, designed to promote smoothness of movement, has been replaced by a waggle of the player's behind as he strives to place himself in precise alignment for the delivery of the blow.

"Some of these players are very effective," he added. "Once they have settled into a satisfactory position, the quick convulsive stroke seems to send the ball very straight indeed toward the objective. But the method involves a complete disregard to the amount of time consumed, and so is most trying upon the nerves and patience of any who may be watching."

Jones' observation is especially pertinent in the light of the fact that the modern professional's long-drawn-out setup procedures seem to be infiltrating the styles of thousands of handicap players. While the tournament pro playing for a $25,000–$50,000 prize each week might be pardoned for taking his time to seek positional exactitude or a feeling of divine inspiration while addressing a shot, the club golfer vying for a $2 Nassau hardly has the same excuse. In most cases, Jones would certainly aver, he's merely building tension—physical from standing and mental from thinking about a lot of things that have very little to do with actually hitting the ball.

Like his grip—standard overlap—Jones' address position was relatively orthodox. The only major departures from standard were the aforementioned very narrow stance, with even the right foot toed out, and the chin cocked toward the right shoulder. A slightly less apparent departure was the fact that he stood closer to the clubhead than is consid-ered standard nowadays.

Jones' narrow, close-in stance was another effort to relax at address. By standing close in, he avoided the arm and shoulder tension that comes with reaching outward for the ball. He sought to position himself close enough to the clubhead so that he need bend only slightly from the waist in order to let his arms hang down naturally. He avoided crowding the ball itself simply by addressing it off the toe of the clubface.

"Addressing off the toe is just as good, or perhaps better," said Jones, "to allow for some stretching in the actual moment of hitting. You [can] learn to hit the ball from its new position, but you can never learn to swing until you relax."

The narrowness of his stance helped Jones minimize tension in his legs. It also allowed him to make a full, free hip turn during his backswing and to use his legs fully during his forward stroke. Regarding the latter, Jones often quoted the old English champion

Abe Mitchell's expression that a golfer must "move freely beneath himself." He felt that these words graphically described the mobility which he himself liked to feel in his legs and which he could not feel when they were spread far apart.

Jones felt that the biggest problem golfers faced in swinging was the tendency to rush, especially at the start of the backswing and the beginning of the downswing. "A short swing is always fast, and a long one is always relatively slow," he noted. "But the speed controls the length rather than the length the speed. A fast backswing must be short because the grip is tight and the muscles tense. Invariably it is followed by a hurried start down and a messed-up shot."

To avoid starting back too fast, Jones personally favored a takeaway in which the club, held lightly, started moving slowly as a result of his left hip turning toward the ball. "I get the hip under way before my hands have made any effort to swing the head of the club," he said. "If the hands start the swing first, there will be a tendency to leave the hip behind—not to make a full body turn—which is one of the most common faults in golf."

Jones called a backswing made largely with the hands and arms the "gardener's stroke" because it excused the body from turning and left the golfer with nothing more than a chopping action.

It is in Jones' backswing that we see the greatest difference between his style and the so-called modern methods. Of today's champions, only Jack Nicklaus comes close to making as full a hip turn and as long a swing arc as did Jones, whose clubshaft swung well past horizontal even on iron shots. (Nicklaus' doesn't, but he achieves a comparable size of arc by carrying the club higher with his arms.)

No doubt it was the advent of steel-shafted clubs that made possible the shorter—and thus simpler—swing of today. As Jones said,

short swings are usually fast swings, and the whippy wood-shafted clubs of his day could not fully unbend and untwist by impact if they were swung short and fast. The metal shafts of today can.

In short, the club golfer of today who has a relatively fast, short swing can be thankful he doesn't have to play with the wood-shafted clubs of Jones' era. By the same token, however, the too-short, too-fast lasher of today would probably do well to adopt more of Jones' long, slow backswing with a fuller turning of the hips.

One danger in starting back with a turning of the hips, however, is that the clubhead stays at the ball too long. By the time it finally starts back, the hands have already moved a few inches and thus must "drag" the clubhead back and up. This causes a very late cocking of the wrists going back and frequently a too-early uncocking starting down. Given this type of backswing, it takes a Jones-like unhurried downswing to avoid "hitting from the top."

Jones himself was indeed continually aware of the need to start his downswing leisurely. He wrote in 1930 that the surest way to ruin a shot was to swing the clubhead outside or beyond the target line during the downswing. He realized that the proper clubhead path on the forward swing was from inside, to along, to inside the target line. He knew that the clubhead could never move along this line through impact if it had moved beyond it beforehand.

"There are at least two things that can be done to throw the clubhead beyond the line," he observed. "To start down with a pure turn of the body without first sliding hips forward is fatal, because such a motion pulls the hands forward [outward]. To swing outward and across the ball is then not only easy but inevitable. The same thing happens if the wrists are employed here to whip the club downward as is so often advised."

In short, said Jones, don't start down with

either a spinning of the hips or a whipping of the wrists. Instead, he offered a three-part plan to keep the clubhead inside the target line during the downswing: "First," he said, "the hips must be shifted quickly toward the front along the line of play, ever so slightly yet definitely. Second, the right elbow must return to the side of the body. Third, the hands must be moved backward and downward without straightening or trying to straighten the wrists. If this sort of start is made, the rest is easy."

The "rest," as noted earlier, was merely to let the clubhead freewheel *through,* not just *to,* the ball. Again, Jones felt that last-ditch efforts to add clubhead speed or to improve clubface alignment merely produced unneeded tension that actually reduced distance and accuracy.

"To the casual observer," he said, "it appears that at this point the club must be lashed forward by crossing the right hand over the left as we would do if we were trying to throw the clubhead off the end of the shaft.

"This is a grave mistake. It has been demonstrated beyond question that in the most effective methods this cross-over does not occur until perceptibly *after* the ball has been struck, until the clubhead has traveled over a foot beyond the ball, and then is never a conscious action, but only the natural effect of the club with its momentum carrying on over a relaxed physical mechanism.

"Throughout the downstroke, the player ought to have in his mind that he is going to drive the club through with his left hand and arm."

In analyzing Jones' game as a whole, it is difficult to find much to criticize. Its strongest parts were driving and putting, but no area was weak. Basically he favored a right-to-left draw shot, but could "work" the ball either way at will. Off the tee he was exceptionally straight and, when necessary, unusually long.

Much has been said about Jones' tendency occasionally to lift both heels off the ground prior to impact—an idiosyncrasy that he himself disapproved of but found no reason to change. Actually, he "swung from his toes" only on tee shots and then only on those where he sought extra distance.

Conceivably his preference for teeing the ball rather high, along with his close-in stance, was at least a partial cause for his rising onto his toes, as a way to give his outstretched arms room to swing forward freely. It is this writer's opinion, however, that Jones purposely teed the ball high to encourage himself to sweep it forward off the peg instead of chopping downward to it. Forward sweeping demands the inside-to-along-the-line clubhead path that Jones sought. Chopping downward results from throwing the clubhead outside the line into an ultra-steep angle of attack. Thus Jones programmed himself for swinging the clubhead on a proper path by teeing the ball high. The price he had to pay was going up on his toes at impact, but even then only on those occasions when he strove for extra distance.

Jones himself felt that he was at his worst on the early and late holes of a round, when not warmed up or when being overprotective of a lead. To offset early-round problems, he consciously played well "within himself" on the first few holes, never striving for full distance off the tee until he felt physically ready to do so.

He countered the problem of losing leads, both in match- and stroke-play, by simply concentrating on beating par instead of an opponent or the leaders in the field. By playing against par, Jones won four U.S. Opens, three British Opens, and a reputation as a peerless stroke-play competitor. Somewhat overlooked was his skill at match-play, during which he wore down his opponents with long and straight driving, putting consistency, and an aura of infallibility. Jones did not care for 18-hole matches, where the underdog might grab him with a hot round, but he always felt the master over 36 holes, the standard examination in championships of his day. In fact, his defeat by George Von Elm in the finals of the 1926 U.S. Amateur, four years before he retired, was the last time he ever lost a 36-hole match to an amateur.

Jones set his clubhead relatively close to his feet at address to avoid arm tension from reaching. He played the ball off the toe of the club to allow for the outward pulling of centrifugal force during the forward swing. He started his backswing by turning his left hip toward the ball. This produced a full hip turn and caused an early movement of the clubhead away from the target line and around his body. This relatively flat backswing plane allowed him to loop the club into a steeper

downswing plane yet still return the clubhead to impact from inside to along the target line. Starting down slowly with a free arm swing, instead of a shoulder shove, was vital to Jones in order to avoid an ultrasteep approach to the ball from outside the target line.

No discussion of Jones' game would be complete without mention of his excellent putting. His method on the greens was simple and to the point, that being to get the ball in the hole, which he did about as well as anyone ever has. As on full shots, he advocated and applied a long backstroke, especially early in the round, as an aid to attaining "that feeling of a smoothly floating club so necessary for a delicate touch." He also stressed a steady head and relaxed address position, which to him required a narrow stance.

In this writer's opinion, however, the real secret of Jones' success at putting—in fact, of all aspects of his marvelous game—rested, again, in the simplicity of his approach, a simplicity that gave full rein to his inborn natural talent, his excellent sense of rhythm, and his innate hand-eye coordination. He didn't like to think about how far to swing his putterhead back or even about aiming his putterface. He knew that these things would take care of themselves if he simply visualized the ball rolling along the line he'd selected and then dropping into the cup.

Though Jones retired from major competition at age twenty-eight, after winning the Grand Slam in 1930, he did play for several years thereafter in the Masters tournament he helped to found in 1934. Ironically it was putting jitters that finally caused him to decide, in the late thirties, that his days of playing in public had truly come to an end. Later, in his autobiography, he opined that these nervous twinges had nothing to do with the spinal affliction that by then had confined him to a wheelchair. Nor did he blame them on infrequency of playing under pressure after 1930.

"It is my own conviction," he stated, "that my putting troubles began when I started to struggle for a precision in my putting stroke which I would never have considered possible in any other department of the game."

In short, Jones' tremendous putting skills survived only so long as he relied on his natural resources. Once he allowed his mind to dictate to his body, his body lost much of its inherent ability spontaneously to respond correctly.

HENRY COTTON

Born: January 26, 1907; Holmes Chapel, Cheshire, England

Major victories:

    British Open: 1934, 1937, 1948

Died: December 22, 1987; London, England

Henry Cotton

THE SUPREME "HANDS" PLAYER

An elderly lady of this writer's acquaintance, although she has never so much as hefted a putter, enjoys golf on television because "it is always such a pretty place." But she has two criticisms of the game. First, it is "slow," at least by comparison with her great love, basketball. And second, "They [the players] all seem the same." When she is questioned on the second point, it becomes obvious that she isn't talking about swing form but about personality. Viewed from her long-distance, noncommitted perspective, professional golfers all look and act so similarly as to appear stereotyped. Not surprisingly, her favorite is Lee Trevino.

In terms of its appeal as a mass entertainment, there is no doubt that the measured, somber, almost clinically formularized behavioral pattern demanded at the highest levels of tournament golf has always been a drawback. But the real pity of it is that the casual fan gets to see only the performer, rarely glimpsing the person beneath that necessarily ultracontrolled and thus frequently bland exterior. In actual fact, the highly individualistic nature of golf has always drawn strong personalities to the game. Certainly at the su-

perstar level it is difficult to identify a sport that down the years has offered a richer mix of human foibles and character. In fact, by comparison with their differences in personality, the variations between the playing methods of the great golfers often seem almost inconsequential.

Henry Cotton was one of the most unusual of the great champions, both in his personality and in his technique. In 1934, shortly after he won his first British Open, a leading American golf writer of the day, George Trevor, caught his unique flavor:

"Henry Cotton might have walked right out of a Leonard Merrick novel. Dapper, suave, polished, Cotton is a far cry from the seamy-faced, leather-skinned, shabbily-dressed, old-line British professional. He buys his clothes on Savile Row, his boots from Peel, and selects his golfing ensembles with fastidious attention to detail. He prefers grays, fawns and beiges but has the nerve to flaunt a dash of color when he feels in the mood for gaiety. His slacks are creased to a razor edge.

"Physically, there is a suggestion of the Latin about this tall, svelte, limber chap with the swarthy complexion, dark lustrous eyes, and aquiline nose. He could double for Valentino in profile and is quite the best-looking and snappiest dressed golfer ever to hold the British Open title. A Belgian masseur kept Cotton's muscles supple and pliable during the Sandwich week. It is typical of Henry's methodical preparation that he should have brought this waxed-mustached roly-poly muscle-kneader along with him from Brussels; that he should have gone to bed at nine o'clock each evening despite the lingering English twilight; and that he should have taken the trouble to engage Ernie Butler as a caddie—the mascot who carried [Arthur] Havers' clubs at Troon in 1923, when a Briton last won the title. This was Henry's one concession to superstition.

"Cotton speaks French fluently—a prerequisite at a Belgian teaching post—drives a flashy red Mercedes roadster . . . and carries in his caddie bag a giddy umbrella which he uses as a sunshade when it isn't raining. Socially speaking, this independent, self-assertive young man has acted the role of

Iconoclastic as he was to seem to many in his theories and teaching techniques, Cotton's swing at his peak was one of the most powerfully efficient and economical in the history of golf, as well as one of the most esthetically appealing. Everything depended on his superbly trained hands. The effectiveness with which he used them to "hit past himself" is clearly seen in the two pictures on the opposite page. Few golfers have been able to use their hands and wrists well enough to stand as "still" through impact as Cotton does here.

emancipator for his fellow professionals. Alone, Henry tilted against the windmills of the British caste system, seeking to lift golf teachers from the servant class. If he hasn't quite succeeded in his crusade it is because most of the old-timers prefer 'to stay in their place' and not 'ape the Yankee upstarts.' Many of these reactionaries resented Cotton's swagger taste in dress, his cultivated accomplishments, his Bond Street look, and his personal initiative."

Three years later, after Cotton's second British Open victory, another American commentator, Brownlow Wilson, wrote thus about his polished but equally distinctive playing method:

"[Cotton] is almost mechanically perfect from tee to green. His swing is a model of style. He has developed a three-quarter swing under perfect control, absolutely grooved, tremendously powerful, and amazingly rhythmic. [He has] learned the art of hitting late better than any other golfers have ever done before. It is very hard to 'wait for it' . . . from a three-quarter swing. How-

ever, [he has] mastered the art to an amazing extent and seems to hit harder from the curtailed swing than most American players do with a fuller, longer arc."

Through his seventies and into his eighties Cotton has remained one of golf's most colorful and controversial characters: an elder statesman, perhaps, but still a sophisticate; still an innovator; still a loner; still an enthusiast; still hyper-health-conscious; still a perfectionist; still a wonderful stylist; still a few light years ahead of the bulk of his profession—at least in Europe—in worldliness, taste, articulateness, and the artifacts of success; and still utterly convinced that his individualistic approach to striking a golf ball is the best for the majority of players over the long haul and that it will one day prevail.

Because Cotton never won big in the United States (less from lack of desire or talent than because the Second World War caught him at his peak), younger American readers might well question his credentials as an arbiter of technique. The plain facts of his record should help mollify any skepticism.

From the mid-1930's to the early 1950's Cotton dominated European golf as no one had since Vardon and no one has since, including Tony Jacklin. He prevailed over American stars in all three of his British Open wins—among them, in 1937, Byron Nelson, Horton Smith, Sam Snead, Ralph Guldahl, Denny Shute, and Gene Sarazen. The only American to beat him head to head in Ryder Cup play was Sam Snead. He regularly whipped the best European and British Commonwealth players in tournaments and in the big-money challenge matches that added spice to the English golf scene. He was the king of the Continent, winning seven national championships in as many sorties. And his dozens of course record scores—many still standing—ran from 59 to 65. In short, Cotton could play, as all the American commentators of the day who saw him verified. In the article already quoted from, Brownlow Wilson went on to write:

"Cotton stands with his feet parallel and at right angles to the line of shot. This is natural to him, because a player should stand as he walks, in the most comfortable position, and Cotton walks slightly toed-in, Indian style. He places the ball, for a drive, about two or three inches in from his left heel. He swings back slowly, with a very straight left arm. His head turns back slightly . . . until he seems to be looking at the ball over his left shoulder with his left eye at the top of his backswing. His right elbow is kept well into his side; the hallmark of a compact swing under absolute control. At the top of the backswing his wrists are cocked and his clubface is open. His hips have turned through 45 degrees, while his shoulders have rotated the full ninety. His left heel is barely off the ground, and the whole position is so perfectly poised that it gives the impression he could never hit a crooked shot.

"Cotton starts down lazily, until you think he will never generate enough acceleration to hit a hard blow. However, once his hands are pressed down almost to the bottom of their arc, with the club in the horizontal position, his wrists begin to do their work and apply their whip. They sling the clubhead into the ball with an amazing flicking motion, much faster than the eye can follow. He hits later than any other player I have ever watched, and hitting late is the real secret of the crack professional's supremacy over the ordinary amateur.

"Cotton hits past his chin in the approved Bobby Jones manner, and at impact his hips have unlocked to permit the uninterrupted flow of power. His shoulders have opened slightly beyond the address position; his left arm is still straight, while his right arm is partially bent. His forearm applies the power. He hits against a braced left leg and side, which makes for firmness and leverage. His heels are both firmly on the ground at impact, which is rare indeed but makes for unusual control. . . . When a player hits in this way, you may be sure he is hitting primarily with his wrists. Some years ago I compared an action shot of Cotton hitting the ball with Bobby Jones. The similarity was truly extraordinary.

"Cotton's finish is as controlled as his backswing. His grip never relaxes throughout the whole operation. His right wrist rolls over by the time the club reaches the horizontal again, and his right foot rolls over onto its inside edge after impact, to rise slightly at the finish. . . . His long shots through the green are thrilling to watch, and easily the longest and straightest of anyone playing today."

From this description the modern golfer might fairly be puzzled as to why Cotton's theories on technique and his actual teaching practices could have become as controversial as they now are. He combined great power with almost monotonous accuracy in a compact and extremely elegant swing that would seem to have incorporated a great many of today's most favored technical elements. Why, then, so much debate?

Part of the answer lies in the amount of exposure Cotton's ideas have enjoyed, especially in Europe. A vigorous and prolific writer, he has authored nine books and has almost never been without a newspaper or magazine column in Britain since he first came to prominence. Inevitably there has been reaction against the sheer power of his pen, especially in a country where golf professionals are even less in agreement about swing tech-

How the hands work in taking the club away and in applying it to the ball. The bottom right-hand picture leaves no doubt at all that Cotton hit as hard with his right hand as he claims he did—and as he claims everyone should, given properly trained hands.

nique than they are in the United States.

But the real answer, of course, lies in the message itself. Cotton is golf's ultimate "hands" man, an unrepentant iconoclast who relentlessly insists: (a) that the ever-growing accent on body action is at best wrongheaded and at worst physically injurious and (b) that there is no way mechanically to program and fundamentalize the golf swing, at least insofar as the average mortal is concerned. Exacerbating his unremitting sounding of these trumpets is the fact that the alternatives he proffers offer no instant success or "secrets," but only hard work, much of it of a sweat-producing nature.

We shall look into Cotton's specific "hands" theories in a moment, but before doing so a word or two about his evolution as a golfer might help the reader further to assess his credibility. Historically the best teachers of golf have been those players not blessed with an overabundance of natural talent, those who themselves had to struggle the hardest to master the game. If ever a golf swing was "manufactured" out of thin air, it was Henry Cotton's. The son of well-to-do parents, he took up golf at eight years of age and spent the next twenty grinding himself a game with a fanaticism and stoicism perhaps equaled in history only by Ben Hogan. Singularly unathletic as a youth, Cotton had sparse talent for golf, but an almost maniacal passion to master it. It is a certainty that no one, except Hogan, has hit more practice balls for longer periods of time and that no one, not even Gary Player, has experimented with more "methods." The stories told in British clubs of the youthful Cotton having to be carried off practice putting greens because of muscular seizures resulting from bending over the ball so long are not apocryphal. Since early middle age he has had to do calisthenics to counter bone and muscle distortions resulting from endless hitting of golf balls.

The theories he now so emphatically promulgates about hitting a ball would therefore seem to be drawn from an extremely valid source—a vast and wide-ranging amount of personal trial and error resulting in one of the most effective swings in history.

In proclaiming that the key to sound and long-lasting golf lies in the condition and action of the hands, Cotton does not deny that other methods work—simply that the hands method, once mastered, is the easiest, most effective, and longest lasting. The only really adamant stance he takes is against the concept that the golf swing can be mechanically standardized—a position born of his own failure to do just that after one of the greatest single efforts in history to accomplish such a goal. He had clearly recognized this personal failure as long ago as 1938, when he wrote in an American magazine:

"I have always admired the attitude of American golfers in general towards the game of golf, and have gained much encouragement from their enthusiasm, although I must say that I never quite understood the idea of those seeking to standardize golf instruction throughout the world. It was perhaps in theory a worthwhile idea, but one destined to fail.

"At one time I felt it would be possible to perfect a standard system, but now, whilst I am prepared to concede there are certain fundamentals in the golf swing, I believe the whole art of teaching golf lies in helping the pupil to translate the fundamental principles via his own physique. I have wasted . . . much time trying to copy assiduously different leading players. This was especially true when I began to study the game. But it was not until I decided I could not play their way that I made much improvement.

"Golf is an individual game and will ever be so, whilst human beings vary in physique. The thoroughness with which American golfers have analysed golf in an attempt to find 'the secret' has further convinced me there is no secret. To watch a first-class field drive off must surely convince everyone that a golf ball can be hit in many ways."

Later he also conceded that his original highly mechanistic approach to developing a putting stroke was one of the chief reasons he was so poor a performer on the greens, compared with his prowess at reaching them.

Cotton's preferred way of swinging a golf club, the "hands" way, starts with three basic premises: first, that the key (actually he often uses the word "secret," but in quotes) to excellence of strike lies in finger tension, which determines how the hands control and motivate the club; second, that proper finger tension and thus correct club control can only be achieved through assiduous and sustained exercising and training of the hands; and third, that the right hand (left for the southpaw), properly trained, plays the imperative role in delivering the clubface squarely and powerfully to the ball.

Although he enjoys teaching, Cotton has never underpriced his services, a fact which has caused him to give fewer lessons than most golf professionals. But a session with him has usually been regarded by the pupil as well worth the cost, not only in terms of what is learned about one's own limitations in the above areas but for sheer novelty and entertainment value. Here, in rough outline, is how Cotton would typically set about teaching an average golfer the facts of hand action:

Comfortably seated in a chair or on a shooting stick, à la Tommy Armour, the maestro would invite the pupil to open fire. As soon as the cobwebs had been shaken free, he

More examples of Cotton-type hand action—of using the clubhead to hit "past" rather than "with" the body. Note also the firm left side and the beautifully centered and "quiet" head.

would ask the pupil to hit teed balls one-handed, first with the right hand, then with the left. The results were usually disastrous, but Cotton's comments at this point were always encouraging: "Good try." "Not quite so fast." "Now you're getting the hang of it."

Next, five or so balls would be teed and the pupil would be asked to strike each of them without regripping the club: "Just swing through and then readdress the ball with your hands remaining wherever they may have become positioned on the shaft." Invariably, after a couple of shots thus, the two feelings fighting for dominance in the pupil would be great digital discomfort and—especially if he were a good player—profound embarrassment. But Cotton's enthusiasm and encouragement would continue unabashed—nothing gave him more pleasure than showing a sinner the light. So onward, with ten or so balls now being teed in a line and the pupil being asked to stroke them without stopping between each shot: "Just inch yourself forward as you swing the club from the end of the follow-through up again into the backswing. Just hit the balls as you swing to and fro in continuous motion." Very few pupils got to the last ball, and by now most probably didn't care—the mechanics of respiration having become far more important than those of golf.

"Okay, have a breather," Cotton would say, rising from his seat. Taking up a four-wood, he would then hit maybe a dozen teed balls first with his right hand alone, then with his left hand alone. Each shot would travel somewhere between 160 and 180 yards, usually with a slight draw. "Watch my hands," he would say, teeing more balls. Again with a wood, he would hit a half-dozen immaculate shots without regripping the club. Finally, he would line up and dispatch ten or so teed balls in one continuous fluid, flowing and apparently effortless swinging motion, each of them landing within a circle twenty yards wide.

Shortly after this writer first underwent this eye-opening and muscle-wrenching experience, he watched Cotton give a clinic at the British equivalent of a state amateur championship. The five top finishers were in-vited to attempt the above drills. Their performances were uniformly pathetic. None could make even a passable shot one-handed with more than a short-iron; none could hit more than two shots without having to regrip the club; none could make much better than glancing contact with ten balls while swinging continuously.

Critics of Cotton have claimed that this sort of approach to teaching golf simply emphasizes his biggest failing: overkill. They maintain that it simply is not necessary to be able to perform such feats with the hands to play great golf, especially when the swing is built around body action. Cotton's answer comes in three parts: first, that the endless playing and practicing of all outstanding golfers has automatically finely trained and conditioned their hands, even though they may not be conscious of the fact and thus are prone to focus maximum attention on their body actions; second, that unless a golfer's hands are involuntarily or deliberately well trained and conditioned, his career will be foreshortened by the back troubles that inevitably accompany the stressful body actions inherent in all "nonhands" methods; and three, that it is simply impossible for a golfer to overstrengthen and overtrain those parts of the body which, at the moment of truth, whatever the method, must control the delivery of the club to the ball—in short, the hands, wrists, and arms.

Here, paraphrased from his writings, are some of the specifics Cotton has used to flesh out these beliefs:

- Golf is a game of fingers and hands working in coordination with other parts of the body. Good hands plus balance and a swing of the clubhead in a free arc will take care of all the so-called positional basics.

- The best swing in the world is only as effective as the strength of the fingers to hang onto the club at impact. If your hands are weak, the shock of impact will move them on the club. Exercise your hands, overtrain them—they can't be too strong.

- The secret of golf lies in finger-tension control. The ideal tension is loose at first, firm as the ball is struck, and loose again immediately after impact. The stronger the hands, the greater your control over this tension—and the bigger the range of shots you can hit by varying the finger tension. Start the education of your hands by holding the club tightly enough only to prevent it from turning in the hands during the stroke.

- The hands must hit *past* the body, not *with* the body. To achieve that, I teach hitting with the right hand *past* the left, making the clubhead do the work. I have personally played my best when I have had a pronounced feeling of hitting *past* my left wrist with the clubhead.
- Through impact the left hand *gradually* turns down and over as the right hand hits past it. The action is a rolling or turning of the hands, *not* an inward collapsing of the left wrist or a forward bending of the right wrist.
- A grip in which the back of the left hand faces the target at address allows that hand to turn more freely through the ball at impact while allowing the right hand to supply the power.
- The right hand is the "finder" hand. Think of it as being an extension of the clubface. It will naturally come from any backswing position to hit the ball squarely if it is properly trained and you will allow it to do so.
- Most people's hands instinctively return to the same alignment at impact that they were in at address. If the back of the left hand and the palm of the right hand parallel the clubface at address, then they'll do so at impact if they are properly trained and if you swing freely without manipulating the club.
- I like to feel that I hit the ball hard, but that I disguise the hit in a swing as much as possible. That comes from trained hands, allowing me to get my maximum clubhead speed just before impact by whipping the clubhead through the ball at the last split second. This is certainly a "late hit"—but it is a very definite hit with the hands and the clubhead.
- Consciously "hitting late" is the worst mistake in golf for the average player. Most

of the slices you see come from not using the right hand to sling the clubhead through the ball, which forces the golfer to hit with his shoulders. You can't hit too early with a trained right hand if your right arm stays bent until impact.

- A closed clubface, caused by a strong grip and/or a shutting (counterclockwise) movement of the clubface in the backswing, makes my kind of hand action impossible. The shut-faced golfer is forced to use a lot of hip and body action getting down to and through the ball in order not to arrive at it with the clubface disastrously closed. In effect, he's hitting what golfers of old called a "push" shot, with the clubhead restrained by the hands instead of being whipped by them through the ball. It's a clumsy and physically stressful way to play and one that only physically strong players can usually master—and then not often for very long.

Since Cotton's retirement from tournament golf in the early 1960's (as a result primarily of his by then embarrassing incapacity with the putter), a substantial number of young European professionals have sought his help. Like the American club golfers who have sought him out for lessons over the years, most have benefited but few have been able to complete the full course. A gracious and gentle coach with the admittedly play-for-fun golfer, Cotton is a hard taskmaster with anyone who goes to him in search of real excellence. He will not compromise his belief in the need for total dedication, involving as that does a disciplined and abstemious life-style. He will not teach "positional" golf (meaning body action) until the would-be world-beater can properly motivate and control the club with his hands. And he does not believe he can teach that proper hand motivation and control without a pupil's total commitment to a heavy and an arduous physical-training program.

In short, if you want to play like Cotton, then you will have to work like Cotton did. And that is an assignment which few who have crossed his path have been able to sustain.

BYRON NELSON

Born: February 4, 1912; Fort Worth, Texas

Major victories:

    U.S. Open: 1939

    Masters: 1937, 1942

    PGA championship: 1940, 1945

DICK AULTMAN

Byron Nelson

THE BIRTH OF THE MODERN METHOD

There is a fascinating similarity between how the golf swing has developed over the years and the evolutionary process in nature itself.

In nature the plant or animal that is best suited to its environment is the one that dominates and survives. In golf, to a large extent, the player who has dominated his peers—survived the best—has been the one whose swing has best suited his environment, that being largely the clubs and balls of his day and the course and weather conditions under which he played.

In nature the unusual strengths that allow the fittest to survive are passed on to their progeny. In golf the strongest swing characteristics of the dominant players are assimilated by those who watch them play.

During their respective heydays Vardon, Hagen, Jones, Snead, Hogan, Palmer, Nicklaus, and others have all influenced the swings of their contemporaries, especially young people, who seem most capable of successful mimicry. This influence has naturally become stronger with the growth of golf books, magazines, movies, and, finally, tele-vision. Palmer, for instance, has caused millions of viewers to realize that a slashing "hit-it-hard" approach *can* be a successful alternative to the leisurely, flowing action that Vardon, Jones, and Snead helped to make the vogue. Nicklaus no doubt has been influential in modifying, if not burying, the concept of a "tight" right elbow and, in so doing, has probably raised the average swing plane of today's junior stars at least a few degrees.

It is fitting to air these thoughts about golf-swing evolution here because the subject of this chapter is Byron Nelson, a man who, for a short time, dominated his peers as no one ever has or ever will and who did it with a swing that departed dramatically from the norm. Nelson set a new standard of shotmaking excellence, and quite naturally some ingredients of his unusual technique became the model for those that followed. In fact, it can be safely said that if there is a watershed between the classical stroke spawned eighty some years ago by Harry Vardon and the swing method employed in large part by the top players of the world today, it was the one-piece, upright, left-side dominant, flex-kneed swing of John Byron Nelson.

Nelson's role as a pioneer of the golf stroke is most apparent when one studies movies of tournament professionals in the 1940's. Seemingly anyone who was anyone on the United States pro tour at that time paraded before the camera to make at least one swing for posterity. None of these 1940's swings was identical, of course, but one striking similarity soon becomes apparent. The finest players of that generation were all "hitting against a firm left side," a phrase that was to remain a part of the golf-instruction lexicon for at least another quarter of a century. Just prior to impact these players' left legs would straighten and remain all but immobile while their arms continued swinging forward. Of the dozens of players filmed only Nelson retained some left-knee flex throughout his entire swing as he drove forward with both legs. Instead of hitting "against" his left side, Nelson hit *with* his left side.

Nelson, like most of his peers, had started playing golf with wooden-shafted clubs. The few golfers of his era who hadn't were still highly influenced in their swing development by teachers and players who had. As a result, the vast majority of the swing techniques of the late 1930's and early 1940's had grown out of the need to accommodate very flexible shafts, which demanded a high degree of control, if not manipulation, with the hands and wrists to throw the twisting clubhead back to a square position by impact.

The metal shafts that began to appear around 1930 did not twist and bend as much, required less hand-wrist manipulation, and thus allowed players greater use of their legs as a source of power. While all great players, even as far back as Vardon, had used their legs to some extent, none had done so to the degree that Nelson did. In short, the metal shafts created a new golfing "environment." Byron Nelson adjusted to it first and best.

Another environmental change that Nelson

Byron Nelson was the first of golf's superstars to retain left-knee flex through impact and well beyond, a technique that keeps the moving clubhead more or less at ball height for a longer duration in the hitting area and thus improves one's chances for consistent solid contact. Earlier players stiffened the left leg prior to or during impact—hit "against" a firm left side—a result of

right-side domination as opposed to left-side control and hitting WITH the left side instead of AGAINST it.

adjusted to supremely well was a larger golf ball. The United States Golf Association, concerned that extra distance resulting largely from the new shafts would render existing courses obsolete, had ruled that as of January 1, 1931, no ball less than 1.68 inches in diameter would be legal for tournament play in America. The difference in size between the 1.62-inch ball that had been allowed in this country prior to 1931 (still the size played in most parts of the world) and the new 1.68-inch ball required thereafter may seem infinitesimal, but it dramatically affected the evolution of the golf swing in the United States.

The larger ball, for instance, would backspin more readily. Thus it rose into the air more easily than did the the small ball. Whereas the smaller ball had required throwing the clubhead under it with a wristy swing to flick it upward, the new ball would backspin to adequate height even when hit with a definite *downward* clubhead motion. Good players found that they could contact ball first, turf second, thus minimizing the chance of "fat" shots. The best downswing stroke for producing this ball-turf contact was one in which the legs led the way. Nelson, flex-kneed throughout, quickly proved that he had the fittest swing to survive in a world of stiffer shafts and larger balls.

In addition to using his legs dramatically, Nelson did several other things in his swing that departed from the styles of most of his contemporaries. These departures were really simplifications of the swing, and they led to superior shotmaking consistency. As we shall see, these departures also set the format for the swing pattern utilized by the vast majority of today's top professionals and amateurs, especially in the United States. Let's examine these departures as they occurred in Nelson's action.

The first alteration involved the way he swung the clubhead away from the ball. Ear-

Byron Nelson, influenced by the then-new larger ball and metal-shaft clubs, developed a swing style far different from that set by Bobby Jones. These departures—revolutionary at the time, but now accepted swing technique—include a one-piece takeaway in which the hands do not lead and drag the clubhead back; far less hip turn than Jones employed; a full, deep shoulder turn coupled with a relatively short backswing—indicating little or no wristiness at the top; strong left-hand, left-arm pulling in the downswing; and a firm, straight-line back-of-the-left-wrist position—with no inward cupping—through impact and beyond. (Other aspects of Nelson's technique are defined in the subsequent swing series later in this chapter.)

ly in his career Nelson's takeaway was similar to that of most of his fellow professionals and those who had excelled before him. His hands led everything else, moving a couple of inches or so to his right before the clubhead started to be dragged away. It was the "drag and whip" technique, used by the hands-and-wrists players who for decades had flicked the smaller ball off the soft, short-bladed grasses of the great Scottish and English links courses, the technique that had been brought to the United States by the British professionals who first showed Americans how to play the game.

During the 1930's, however, Nelson worked on developing what has become known as a "one-piece" takeaway. His hands, arms, and club moved back together, with his left hand and straight left arm initiating the movement. He gradually eliminated the initial "reverse cocking" during the takeaway that had led to so much wristiness among the old players and thus demanded such ultraprecise timing.

Nelson also avoided the habit of quickly fanning the clubface open during the takeaway, a technique employed by most of the early British professionals to help them flick the ball into the air. Nelson kept his clubface more or less square to its path of movement throughout his swing. He did so by establishing a straight-line relationship at the back of his left hand, wrist, and forearm during his backswing and by maintaining it well into his follow-through.

Nelson's hip turn on his backswing was considerably less than that of most of his peers, including Bobby Jones, whose game and instructional writings and movies were still highly influential when Nelson first began to make an impact on the professional golf tour in 1935. Nelson's hip turn on full shots was less than 45 degrees, yet his shoulder turn was at least 90 degrees. When coupled with his one-piece takeaway and one of the straightest left arms in the history of the game, Nelson's minimal hip turn and full shoulder turn resulted in a highly compact

backswing. His club never moved past horizontal at the top, even on his fullest swings.

His was also an upright backswing—perhaps the most upright of any great player except Nicklaus. By reducing his hip turn, Nelson was able to swing his arms and club more directly back and up than can the golfer who turns his torso on a shallow plane. As a consequence, Nelson's clubhead remained on the target line longer during his takeaway than anyone he competed against. He also swung his hands higher.

Most average golfers would find it difficult to copy successfully Nelson's high, upright swing plane and minimal hip turn. Less skilled golfers who swing on such an upright plane run the risk that any slight casting with the hands or shoving with the right shoulder from the top of the swing will move the clubhead outside the target line prior to impact, thereby forcing an outside-to-inside path during contact. The golfer with the upright swing plane must give himself plenty of time to change directions between backswing and downswing, time for his legs to lead his shoulders into the forward stroke to ensure that the clubhead will swing from inside to along the target line during impact.

"If the club does not come to a reasonably slow motion, almost a pause, at the top of the swing," Nelson once told this writer, "then it is hard to keep the downswing coordinated well enough to make any sort of solid contact." Nelson, however, had the swing pace that gave his legs time to lead, just as does Jack Nicklaus, the current exemplar of the style that Nelson initiated.

Taken in sum, all the ingredients of Nelson's swing described thus far added up to an attractively simple method. He minimized moving parts and thus built a swing less likely to break down under pressure. His action was firm and positive, both starting back and at the top—the two most critical areas. His backswing was relatively short, his hip turn minimal, his leg action excellent even by modern standards. So was his ability to control the club with his left hand, arm, and side.

All in all, Nelson incorporated practically all of the swing factors that are part of what came to be called, more than a quarter century later, the "square-to-square method."

Perhaps the most graphic way to explain Nelson's amazing shotmaking consistency is to look at his swing purely from a ballistic or geometrical point of view. Because his plane was relatively upright, his clubhead moved along the target line slightly longer, both going back and coming through, than does the clubhead of the player who swings more around his body. Thus, by his uprightness, Nelson increased his chances of contacting the ball while the clubhead was moving along his target line.

Because he did not fan his clubface open to its arc going back, Nelson also avoided the necessity of fanning it precisely back to square during his downswing in order to hit a straight shot. Thus he increased the odds that his clubface would be looking at his target during impact.

His pattern of swing also decreased the chance that his right hand, in an effort to throw the clubhead back to square, would break down the straight-line relationship at the back of his left wrist, a breakdown that could either close the clubface to the left of target or throw the clubhead too much upward instead of forward.

Finally, by retaining his knee flex well past impact, Nelson more or less "flattened" the bottom of his swing arc, thereby lengthening the period that his clubhead moved through impact at ball level.

While these geometric or ballistic advantages may have been slight, they were sufficient to give him a considerable edge over the rest of the field. "Even when Nelson is only halfway putting," Tommy Armour once said, "he can't be beaten. He plays golf shots like a virtuoso. There is no problem he can't handle—high shots, low shots, with the wind or across it, hooks or fades, he has absolute control of the ball. He is the finest golfer I have ever seen."

Several factors led to Nelson developing a "virtuoso" swing. Certainly the conditions under which he played as a youngster had a lasting influence. Nelson grew up amid the winds and hardpan fairways of Ellis County, Texas, just south of Dallas–Fort Worth. The conditions demanded a wide variety of shots and precise striking. Wind is especially unforgiving of high shots, and Nelson sensed early on that lots of leg drive on the forward swing helped to produce shots that bore well into the breezes. He also found that a firm left arm and wrist through impact helped to drive the ball forward instead of upward.

Most good golfers suffer through a period of hooking. Nelson, with his exceptionally large, strong hands, was no exception. Leading with the legs—more or less dragging the clubhead toward the ball—helped him avoid prematurely closing the clubface and thus to avoid the duck hooks that ran seemingly forever in disastrous directions off those bonny Texas fairways. It was a lesson that years later another Texan, Lee Trevino, was to learn so well.

People as well as course conditions also influence a player's swing development. In 1927 the great Walter Hagen came to Dallas seeking his fourth straight PGA championship. Throughout his final match against Joe Turnesa, a fifteen-year-old youngster trailed at Hagen's heels every step of the way. At one point Hagen squinted into the sun and remarked that he wished he had a hat to wear for the next shot. The youth gladly proffered his tiny baseball cap, which Hagen, to the delight of the gallery, donned above one eye and somehow managed to keep in place during his swing. Twelve years later, in the same tournament, Bryon Nelson's mother introduced herself to Walter Hagen as the mother of the boy whose cap he'd once borrowed. By that time the son himself had already won the Masters and the U.S. Open.

It may seem ironic that a quiet and abstemious fellow like Byron Nelson would choose an outgoing, round-the-clock swinger like Hagen for an idol. What influenced Nelson, however, was Hagen's swinging on the course. Many players of Hagen's era—most notably Bobby Jones—swung the club well around their bodies early in the backswing, then up and slightly over, and finally down to the ball. As a result, the club moved on a slightly steeper plane during the downswing

Looking at Nelson's swing from this angle, we see additional departures from the Bobby Jones style. Nelson, using far less hip turn than Jones, thus kept his clubhead swinging more along his target line during his takeaway. He moved into a straight-line relationship between the back of his left hand, wrist, and forearm early in his backswing and maintained it through impact, thus ensuring maximum left-hand control for pulling, rather than throwing, during his forward swing. He maintained some right-knee flex throughout his backswing for maximum leg drive to the left early in his forward swing. This leg drive helped Nelson pull the club back to the ball on a shallower plane, from farther inside the target line, than did Jones, who looped outward into a somewhat steeper downswing plane.

than it had early in the backswing.

Hagen was one of the first stars to reverse this process. By starting down with his hips sliding to the left, he pulled his club down to the ball on a slightly flatter plane than it had followed going back and up. This increased his chance of returning the clubhead from inside to along (rather than from outside to across) the target line at impact. Nelson, with his upright backswing and strong forward leg drive, produced an even greater lowering or flattening of plane on the downswing, much in keeping with the action of modern players like Nicklaus, Player, Miller, Weiskopf, and Trevino.

An even stronger influence than Hagen on Nelson's game was George Jacobus, head professional at the Ridgewood Country Club in New Jersey, where Nelson assisted in the mid-'30's. Jacobus encouraged Nelson to work on developing the ultrastraight left arm that became a hallmark of his technique and

74

to eliminate exaggerated fanning open of the clubface during his takeaway.

"I had an idea to get the club higher and to keep the clubface square to the swing," Nelson says. "George was very helpful in developing my style of play."

The fact that Nelson was not a great putter—he was more in a league with Vardon, Cotton, and Hogan than with Hagen, Jones, and Locke—does even more credit to his driving and iron play. Nelson's first round in the 1937 Masters more or less symbolizes his tee-to-green excellence. During that 18 holes at Augusta National, he hit every par-3 green in one shot and all others, including the four par-5s, in two. He one-putted only two greens, yet shot 66. The two one-putts were from two and three feet.

Nelson, of course, is best remembered for his amazing feats in 1945, when he won 19 of 30 tournaments he entered, 11 of them in a row, and averaged only 68.33 strokes per round. Even taking into account the 1974–1975 exploits of Johnny Miller, it is difficult to conceive that any of these records will ever be broken.

There are those who tend to diminish Nelson's achievements because some of the better touring pros were still in the armed services for at least part of his supreme year. Perhaps these additional facts will put Byron Nelson's career in better perspective:

—He was a full-time touring pro only in 1945. He won 26 additional PGA tournaments while doubling more or less as a club professional.

—He won money in 111 straight events.

—He finished second in seven of the 11 tournaments he entered in 1945 that he failed to win.

—His stroke average in 1945 was almost a shot per round, or four per tournament, lower than anyone has ever recorded in a given year.

—In the nine stroke-play tournaments he won in 1945, his average margin of victory was 6.3 strokes.

—Most of the best players *did* compete in 1945: Hogan, Snead, McSpaden, Demaret, Harmon, Revolta, Shute, Mike Turnesa, Laffoon, Byrd, etc.

Nelson's fantastic success throughout his career, but especially in 1945, stemmed in large part from a basic character trait found in most great athletes. Nelson was and still is a perfectionist. Throughout his ten-year career he had tried to "play each shot for what it was worth," but in 1944 he actually charted every shot he made, hoping through this analysis to find some means of reducing his scoring average.

In reviewing his little black book, Nelson realized that despite his efforts to concentrate fully on all shots, he was still blowing an occasional stroke because of carelessness. "I recall once I had the ball an inch from the cup," he later revealed. "I just pushed at it. The putter hit the grass behind the ball—never reached it." Thus Nelson went into 1945 vowing to reduce his stroke average by one shot per round. Actually, he chopped off almost 1.5 strokes, having averaged 69.67 in 1944.

Perhaps none of Nelson's fellow competitors felt the sting of his precise shotmaking more than Mike Turnesa, his second-round foe in the 1945 PGA championship. Nelson went into that major event with eight straight tournament victories, but it appeared that the string would end when Turnesa led 2-up

with four holes remaining at the Moraine Country Club in Dayton, Ohio. Turnesa played those last four holes well, scoring three pars and a birdie. Nelson, however, shot birdie, birdie, eagle, par, to win 1-up. "Nelson chews you up and spits you out," said Turnesa, seven under par for the round. "How can anyone beat him?"

Nelson himself solved that puzzle early the next year when, after winning the first two tournaments, he announced his retirement from the pro tour. He had decided to settle down with his wife, Louise, on the Texas ranch he'd always wanted, away from all the off-course demands that were increasingly sapping his time and energy. He was only thirty-three at the time. Contrary to popular belief, his nerves were not shot. Much ado has been made about Nelson's inability to retain food before an important round when, in fact, he'd played with a nervous stomach all his life and welcomed it as a sign of being "up" for the competition. Recently, of course, he has been well known as a television golf commentator, whose main characteristic is modesty, exemplified by the unstinting praise and admiration he offers his successors.

It is difficult to imagine the heights that Nelson could have achieved with his 1975-model golf swing had he not retired in 1946. Perhaps our best appraisal of his prowess should come from another who also retired at the peak of his career:

"At my best I never came close to the golf Nelson shoots," said Bobby Jones.

Sam Snead

A SWING FOR ALL AGES

It is the year 2000. The 100th United States Open championship has just been completed. The winner accepts the first-place check for $200,000. He studies it a moment to make sure it's certified, and then he looks up at the gallery, his bright eyes twinkling under the brim of his straw hat.

"Ah figured ah was about due," says eighty-eight-year-old Sam Snead.

As this chapter is being written, in August, 1974, Sam Snead is sixty-two. It's an age when pro golfers sit back in the soft chairs on the clubhouse verandas at major tournaments, recalling the days of Hagen, Jones, and Sarazen and accepting warm handshakes from members of the Hospitality Committee.

Not Snead. Last weekend he finished third in the PGA championship behind Trevino and Nicklaus and in front of Player, all whom were just out of diapers when he first won the event thirty-two years ago. A few months previously he placed second in the Los Angeles Open, six shots under par on the demanding Riviera Country Club course. All told, he has averaged over $4,000 per tournament entered in 1974.

In short, Sam Snead is playing golf just about as well today as he did thirty-seven years ago when he made the United States Ryder Cup team as a rookie touring professional.

There are many reasons for Snead's amazing longevity. Largely they fall within one or more of the following broad categories:

—The way he learned to play
—The way he swings the club
—His unusual suppleness
—His enthusiasm for the game

Within each of these categories the reader will find not only explanations of why Snead has played so well so long but also some clues to how he or she can also minimize the toll of advancing years.

Legend would have us believe that Sam Snead climbed down from the trees just shortly after Neanderthal man, ripped off a limb, and with it started winning golf tournaments—barefooted.

Actually, Snead did grow up in the Back Creek Mountains of Virginia. He did carve clubs out of swamp maple limbs, leaving some bark on for better gripping. And he's al-

SAM SNEAD

Born: May 27, 1912; Ashwood, Virginia

Major victories (through 1974):

British Open: 1946
PGA championship:
    1942, 1949, 1951

Masters: 1949, 1952, 1954

Sam Snead's swing remains a classic example of simplicity and smoothness. Its simplicity stems in large part from his coordination of movement. Notice how his arms seem to swing in perfect coordination with the turning of his body and the movement of his legs. Meanwhile his hands and wrists and club operate merely as a result of this coordinated movement. There is no independent manipulation of the club with the hands and wrists. Snead's smoothness of swing is another result of his coordinated movement when coupled with his immaculate sense of tempo and rhythm. Many golfers can quickly improve their own swing tempo and rhythm simply by hitting iron shots with their feet touching together. Once square striking occurs, continue the drill but sense the pace of rhythm of your swing as you do. As this sensation becomes stronger, gradually spread your feet to normal width.

ways found it easier to make a balanced swing when bereft of shoes.

While fact and legend often become inseparable in Snead's case, there are two things that are certainly true about his formative years in golf. First, he learned to play more or less by trial and error. Second, he learned to play largely by feel.

There were far more amateur whiskey distillers than professional golf instructors around Ashwood, Virginia, during the 1920's. Snead learned golf by watching his oldest brother, Homer, wallop 300-yard drives across the back pasture of their small cow-and-chicken farm. With his swamp maple, Snead imitated Homer's roundhouse swing by the hour. If he sliced the ball, it fell off into some mucky bottomland. Therefore he experimented with different grips and stances until he found one that would keep his limited ball supply intact. (Perhaps the fact that Harry Snead's pasture lacked sufficient drainage on the right side is a major rea-

son why his fifth son, Sam, has always preferred to draw his shots from right to left.)

As Snead experimented with his swing, he gradually learned what would work for him and what would not. He found, for instance, that he could overcome his tendency to smother-hook his drives by positioning both hands a bit more to his left on the shaft (counterclockwise). He also discovered that he could hit the ball much farther and straighter if he held the club more lightly, especially in his right hand, than he did when swinging a baseball bat.

To this day Sam Snead has seldom looked elsewhere than into himself for counsel about his golf game. Learning by trial and error has given him the wherewithal to find a cure somehow for any problem that might occur, whether it be smothered drives or putting "yips," the bugaboo that has stifled so many fine players in middle age, including Vardon, Cotton, and Hogan. Snead knows exactly what works for Snead, and that is a big

reason why he has played so well so long.

Another reason is that what works for Snead is usually what feels right for Snead, apart from what some textbook on golf advocates as being proper. This is not to say that Sam doesn't understand textbook fundamentals. He can talk technique about as perceptively as any man I have met. The point is that he has always made a conscious effort to avoid too much conscious thought while swinging.

"Thinking instead of acting is the No. 1 golf disease," he says in his excellent autobiography, *The Education of a Golfer.* "If I'd become tangled up in the mechanics of the swing when I first hit shots, chances are I'd have been only an average player."

Snead certainly doesn't knock golf instruction, either written or oral, but he does feel strongly that information about the swing is in itself of little value to a pupil until he or she can learn to apply it in a way that *feels* comfortable. He also points out that some things simply don't feel comfortable until you've done them over and over again, per-

haps thousands of times, on the practice tee.

Once the editors of *Golf Digest* magazine asked some playing and teaching professionals what each did or advocated to achieve proper swing tempo. Various pros described various swing mechanics to produce a smooth swing pace. Snead closed down the subject when he said simply: "I try to feel oily."

As golfers advance in years, they generally find it more difficult successfully to direct themselves *mentally* to make a given move *physically.* A common complaint is: "I keep telling myself to slow down my backswing but nothing happens." Wouldn't it be so much simpler to play good golf longer if, like Snead, we'd simply learned to "feel oily"?

Playing by feel makes it simpler to think simply. The student of the game who continually absorbs swing theories may find six or seven different ideas running through his head between the time he steps up to the ball and actually starts his takeaway. Three or four other thoughts may creep in while he swings. Too often the result is an inhibited

swing that breeds inconsistency from shot to shot.

Snead has reduced his thinking to a few simple "keys," as he calls them. The result is a free-flowing stroke that has remained amazingly consistent over the years. It is a simple swing. It has no unnecessary moving parts that might cause variances from shot to shot.

One of Snead's keys is merely to set the club in "the slot" during his backswing. No one knows better than Sam that the main purpose of the backswing is simply to put the club into such a position that a freewheeling forward swing will deliver its head along the target line at great speed through impact. His slot at the top of the backswing is the space between his right shoulder and his head. He merely swings the club around and up so that at the top it lays in this slot and points more or less in the direction he wants to strike the ball.

To set the club in this same slot time after time, Snead has said that he imagines his swing as being a wheel, with his head as the hub and his straight left arm as a spoke. By swinging this spoke around and up so that his hands finish in the slot, his clubshaft automatically becomes properly positioned.

Most golfers do not swing back and up on the same plane that they swing down and forward. Some, in changing directions from backswing to forward swing, loop the club more inside, behind themselves, and thus swing back to the ball on a flatter plane. More commonly, others loop the club in the opposite direction, forward or outside, so that the downswing plane becomes steeper than that of the backswing. The inside loop is preferable because it is more likely to return the clubhead from inside to along the target line during impact instead of from outside to across the line. The flatter downswing plane also keeps the clubhead moving at ball level longer through impact, on a shallower arc than does the steeper plane that results from the outside loop. The force of the blow thus becomes directed more forward, toward the target, rather than downward into the ground.

Snead's swing, however, has remained consistent over the years largely because he,

more so than any other great player, swings back and up and down and forward on practically the same plane. He sets the club into a position at the top—in the slot—from which it becomes unnecessary to swing into either a flatter or steeper downswing plane. Thus he eliminates the inconsistencies that can result from looping.

Most golfers, even the best, need a slightly flatter downswing plane to assure swinging the clubhead back to the ball from inside to along the target line. They need this flatter downswing plane for insurance against the deadly outside loop that must inevitably swing the clubhead across the line—outside to inside—during impact. Snead, however, does not need this insurance for several reasons.

The first deals with the alignment of his body at address, especially his shoulders. Snead has always aligned himself in a slightly "closed" position, one in which a line across his shoulders would point at the target or even a bit to the right of it rather than parallel to the target line in the so-called square alignment. By setting up slightly closed, he can be sure that he will always swing the clubhead into the ball from inside to along the target line—even on those few occasions when he happens to loop a bit outside onto a slightly steeper plane than he adopted going back.

Snead seldom loops to the outside, however, because of his excellent rhythm and tempo. He has always stressed starting both his backswing and his downswing slowly. This gives him sufficient time in changing directions from backswing to downswing to allow his feet and legs to initiate his forward stroke. With legs leading, his shoulders and hands are relegated to being followers. They do not have an opportunity to shove or throw the club into the outside loop.

Snead's unhurried swing pace results largely from his second key, that being always to swing at less than full power. He has estimated that on a normal stroke he uses only 80–90 percent of the power that is actually available to him. On those occasions when he needs extra distance, he relies on what he calls his "supercharger," which is

Seen from this angle, Sam Snead's swing photos indicate further evidence of the simplicity of his technique. Whereas most golfers swing the club back and up on one plane, they return it to the ball on another. Snead, however, swings up and down on a seemingly identical plane. Note again the complete coordination between the swinging of his arms and the turning of his body. Snead's simplicity of movement also stems from his conscious effort to keep his thinking simple whenever his swing should happen to falter. Then his key checkpoints are merely to set the club in the slot between his right shoulder and head at the top of his backswing, or to return to his original address-position, arm-club relationship at impact, or to finish with his hands high, or simply to swing with less than full-out effort.

nothing more than a somewhat more aggressive forward driving of his feet and legs at the start of the downswing. Most golfers, in attempting to add extra yardage, unconsciously use their hands and/or shoulders too soon too aggressively, from the top of their backswings, which invariably forces the club onto an outside loop and thus into a too-steep downswing plane. Leading with the feet and legs in Snead-like fashion increases leverage while maintaining a proper downswing plane.

A third Snead key is simply to think of returning his arms and the clubshaft back to the same position at impact that they were in at address. Purists will find that actually there is a slight variance between Snead's overall body position at address and impact. By contact his legs have shifted farther toward the target and his head and shoulders a bit farther away from it. There is a close, if not identical, similarity, however, between his arms-club relationship at the two stages.

This writer believes that it is Snead's thought of returning his arms to their address relationship that helps him swing his arms so freely on his forward stroke. The outstanding British instructor, John Jacobs, has noted a feature of all great golf swings, especially true in the case of Snead's. That feature is a rapid and dramatic increase in the space between the hands and the right shoulder during the downswing. Golfers who shove with the shoulders and thus do not swing their arms freely forward will not get nearly the separation that we see in those, such as Snead, who swish their arms freely down and through as they drive their knees smoothly forward and their hips around. The golfer who fails to achieve this separation will tend to top his or her shots and would be much helped by Snead's key.

Another Snead key thought is to finish with his hands high. This is the thought he uses when he finds his shots are pulling to the left. Thinking "hands high" helps him avoid the too-steep downswing plane that causes the relatively low finish position. It helps him to return the clubhead from inside to along the target line.

Snead's swing is probably best known for its unhurried, flowing grace. It gives this appearance largely because it is so unified. When he came on the scene in the 1930's, the emphasis was still on "hand action." While Sam certainly does nothing to stifle normal use of his hands, his swing exemplifies the "one-piece" unification of body, legs, and arms. His arms swing back and up in direct conjunction with the turning of his body. There is absolutely no independent lifting or turning of the club with his hands and wrists, no flippiness at the top, no casting with the hands at the start of the downswing. In short, his hands are "quiet" throughout his swing. It is this lack of wristy jerking above all else that makes Snead's swing look so smooth. It is also a major reason for his remarkable consistency over the years.

No discussion of Snead's longevity as a winner would be complete without mention of his remarkable physical assets, most notably his unusual suppleness. On request he will demonstrate his flexibility by high kicking, cancan style, a normal eight-foot-high ceiling. He will also bend forward, with legs stiff, and pluck golf balls out of the cup. Even today, although his equator has broadened considerably, he still makes a fuller shoulder turn on his backswing than do most of the youngsters he competes against.

Beyond inheriting some exceptional genes, however, Snead also employs certain techniques in swinging a golf club that enhance suppleness. These are techniques that less well-endowed golfers could also adopt to help themselves play better longer:

—He holds the club lightly, thus avoiding arm and shoulder tension. He controls the club largely in the last two fingers of his left hand, but with a pressure he has likened to holding a fork or a billiard cue.

—He waggles the club freely at address, all the while shifting his feet and legs, trying to feel "oily."

—He cocks his chin toward his right shoulder just before swinging, thus moving it out of the way for a free turning of his shoulder.

—He starts his swing with a definite for-

ward press, easing his right knee and his hands slightly toward the target before swinging immediately thereafter into his backswing.

—He addresses the ball with a slightly closed shoulder alignment. For average golfers this minimizes the degree of shoulder turn required to place the club in proper position at the top.

—He starts the club back low and slow, thus encouraging a full left-arm extension and a full shoulder coiling. Starting back slowly minimizes any involuntary grabbing with the right hand in order to control the club—grabbing that will tense the right arm and shoulder and abbreviate the backswing.

—He keeps his swing thoughts to a minimum. As he's said, too much analysis causes paralysis.

No golfer can play golf so well so long as Snead unless he has a tremendous love for the game and a great pride in his ability to excel. Once, at a *Golf Digest* seminar, Bob Toski, the outstanding American golf teacher, asked Sam why he has been able to strike the ball better and score better for longer than any player who ever lived. For answer, Snead revealed that during the forty-odd years he had played golf for a living, he had never gone more than two weeks without somehow playing a few holes or hitting balls.

"The only time I came close was when I went to Africa on safari," Sam said. "We were right out there in the bush, shooting elephant and buffalo and all that stuff. But somehow a couple of golf clubs came along and the next thing you know a guy called Gordon Fawcett and me have got a little game going.

"We've got a hole from here over to the wall and we're using elephant droppings for balls. Only trouble was you couldn't hit 'em too hard, 'cause they'd explode. Seem to remember I beat this guy. I'd hit my ball on its hard side and it'd stay in one piece and I'd make five. His kept falling apart.

"The point is I couldn't keep away from golf. I'd been gone two weeks and here I was playing again. I reckon if I'd ever taken a year off, I wouldn't have been able to play at all when I started again."

It is the year 2001. The 101st United States Open championship has just been completed. The winner accepts the first-place check for $210,000. He studies it a moment to make sure it's certified, and then he looks up at the gallery, his bright eyes twinkling under the brim of his straw hat.

"Ah figured it was so much fun ah'd try it again," says eighty-nine-year-old Sam Snead.

KEN BOWDEN

Ben Hogan

"THERE IS ALWAYS SOMETHING LEFT TO IMPROVE"

In the course of researching this chapter, the writer spent the best part of a day repeatedly watching two films of Ben Hogan practicing full shots. The first of these movies was made around 1939, when he was in his late twenties and had yet to win a tournament. The other was shot in the late 1950's, by which time Hogan had come to be regarded by many people as the greatest shotmaker who ever lived. Here, in précis, are the tape-recorded observations made that day:

The Early Hogan

- Very purposeful-looking in setting up—Palmer-like.
- Sights down line over left shoulder with feet still together after placing clubhead squarely behind ball.
- Stays in motion from moment of stepping up to ball to takeaway.
- Feet relatively wide apart for his height (5 feet 9 inches)—wider than the width of his shoulders. Toes of both feet pointed slightly outward. Weight seemingly toward the heels.
- Shoulders square to target line at address, with feet slightly open, hips a bit more so.

- Very erect stance. Only the slightest flex at the knees, slightest bend at the waist. Head high, butt out, back very straight, arms hanging easily.
- A line upward through spine at address would tilt five to 10 degrees away from target. Head in line with spine and only very slight chin rotation away from target starting backswing.
- Hands opposite center of body at address, with clubshaft angled slightly *away* from target.
- Sets clubface very square to target at address. Seems to set club very lightly behind ball—doesn't press it on ground.
- Much waggling of club with the wrists and forearms. Moves directly into backswing from final waggle.
- Hands lead clubhead very slightly into takeaway—slight dragging, but nowhere near as much as most of contemporaries.
- Definite pronation (clockwise rotation) of left hand and arm early in backswing.
- Apart from this dragging and pronation, a one-piece takeaway—everything in line from the left shoulder to the clubhead as hands reach hip height.

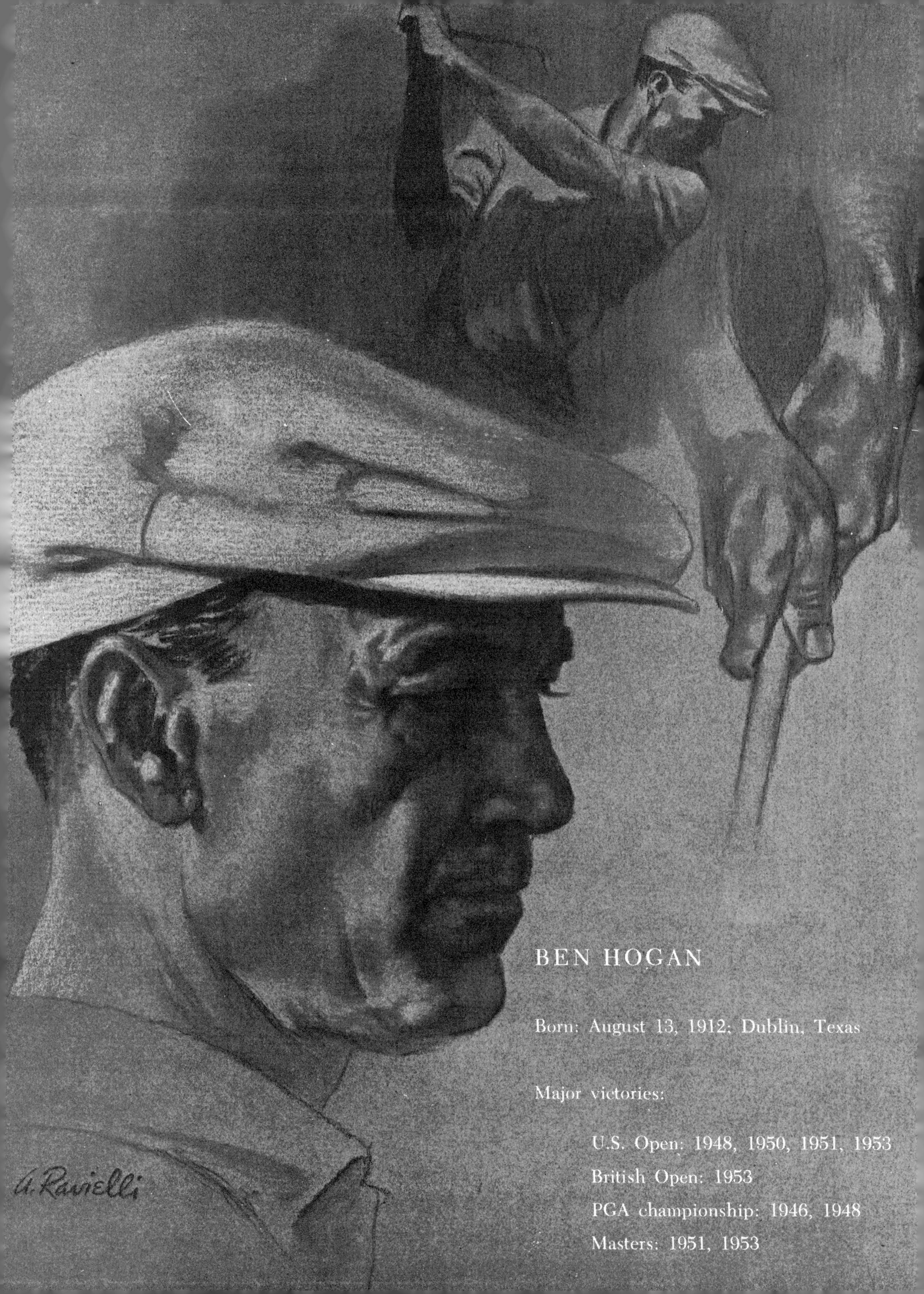

BEN HOGAN

Born: August 13, 1912; Dublin, Texas

Major victories:

U.S. Open: 1948, 1950, 1951, 1953
British Open: 1953
PGA championship: 1946, 1948
Masters: 1951, 1953

A. Ravielli

- Very full and pronouncedly flat shoulder turn.
- Power of the shoulder turn pulls the hips around, eventually through about 45 degrees. Also pulls left knee back behind the ball and left heel slightly off ground—although action is more a roll onto inside edge of foot than a heel lifting.
- Right leg straightens as body winds up, but leg doesn't move an inch laterally.
- Wrists are cocked very fully, but late in the backswing—seemingly by the weight and momentum of the clubhead rather than deliberately.
- Left arm is firm and extended at top, the hands high above the head.
- Clubhead drops way below horizontal at top, shaft almost to a 45-degree angle. Also, club slightly "crosses line" (points right of target).
- Knees drive toward target as first move of downswing.
- As legs continue to drive laterally toward target, left shoulder seems to drive slightly forward with them.

Here is the swing that, at its prime, many experts believe to have produced the cleanest-struck and most accurate shots in the history of golf. Note particularly the incredibly late release of the wrists deriving from superb leg and lower-body action; the "inside" attack on the ball; and the way in which the entire upper body stays behind the ball as the left arm and hand lead the clubhead through it.

- Hips begin to turn and clear almost simultaneously with leg drive.
- Wrist-cocking actually increased by initial leg drive. Hands and arms are pulled, or dropped, backward onto even flatter, "more inside" plane. This appears to be increased by or associated with slight arching, bowing, or backward bending of the left wrist as the downswing starts.
- Swings very much "underneath" body with head centered at all times.
- Extremely late release of wrists in downswing. Hands are inches ahead of ball before wrists fully uncock. Ultra-late release undoubtedly owing to immense thrust generated by leg/hip action. Also causes massive "extension" through ball—amazing for so small a man.
- Left leg straightens through impact, hits against "braced left side."
- Huge follow-through—sheer velocity or momentum of clubhead pulls arms high and way back behind head, violently twists shoulders around, almost spins player off feet.

The Late Hogan

The basic characteristics and "mood" of swing were the same, but there were some definite differences:

- Even greater impression of power and purposefulness at address, especially in the firmness and security of set of hands and forearms on club.
- Stance slightly narrower. Right foot now square (at right angle to target line).
- Knees now pronouncedly set, or "cocked," more toward target at address.
- Hands a little higher at address, giving more "arched-wrist" appearance.
- Fewer waggles, and what there are are more to the "inside."
- Clubhead moves back momentarily *before* hands start back—all "drag" eliminated.
- Plane of shoulder turn discernibly flatter.
- Swing much shorter, with shoulder turn cut from about 110 to 90 degrees and less wrist-cocking.
- Hands at top much lower, now level with tip of right shoulder (goes with flatter plane and lesser shoulder turn).

- At top of swing back of left wrist, previously slightly "cupped," now in line with back of hand and forearm.
- Club now "laid off" (pointed a little left of target) at top of backswing, rather than "crossing line."
- More right-arm folding. Elbow even closer to body at top. Points more downward during backswing and until hands reach hip height on downswing, when right arm begins to straighten. More compact.
- Greater impression that "triangle" formed by shoulders and arms stays constant throughout swing. More compact.
- Right knee no longer straight at top of backswing—entire right leg remains slightly flexed but immobile (where it was at address) throughout backswing.
- Left knee remains flexed longer after impact, although sheer extension and momentum of follow-through still force it to straighten eventually.
- Because of flatter plane, swing is more "rotary" and less "up and under." Right shoulder higher through impact.
- Shoulders appear to unwind earlier, more in unison with fast hip clearance.
- Extension through ball seems even greater. Right arm stays straighter longer after impact than that of any player except Nicklaus.

What inspired Ben Hogan to change his swing so radically over the years, and how much were the changes responsible for his phenomenal achievements? Only the man himself knows for sure. One would have to believe that some of the changes were forced on him by the appalling injuries he sustained in the 1949 car smash that nearly took his life and that unquestionably would have ended the athletic career of almost any other person. Undoubtedly his change in preferred "shape" of shot—from a draw to a fade—provoked certain modifications. Conceivably some of the changes were simply the result of aging—Hogan was forty-one in 1953, when he became the only man ever to win the

92

Masters and U.S. and British Opens in the same year. And, if only because of the nature of some of the changes, it seems at least a possibility that the innovative methods of a fellow Texan (and, in the early 1940's, chief adversary), Byron Nelson, might have had some influence.

Irrespective of the part these or any other factors may have played in the evolution of his game, one needs only the slightest awareness of Hogan the man to know that, in the final analysis, whatever he did and whatever he achieved sprang from only one source: inside himself. It is inevitable that a book like this will contain superlatives and that some will be better cast than others. But if there is one thing for sure in the history of human endeavor, it is that no one ever applied himself to mastering a sport more ferociously and single-mindedly than did Benjamin William Hogan. To many people (including this writer) he remains certainly the greatest shotmaker who ever lived, if not the greatest golfer of all time, and to most others the latter choice

would be finely drawn among him, Jones, and Nicklaus. But when it comes to effort, there is no contest. Sarazen, Cotton, Player, and Trevino are certainly strong runners, but at the tape in the practice stakes it is Ben Hogan all alone and looking back.

There is no question that Hogan temperamentally was a loner, but there is also no question that throughout his playing days he was too busy with golf to be otherwise. Like Cotton a few years previously, he had realized while still in his twenties that he would never achieve the utopia he might originally have aspired to: mechanical shotmaking perfection. But he also recognized the need never to stop striving toward that impossible goal because "there is always some fellow in there against you shooting just as good golf or better than you." And he never did stop searching and striving. If contemporary accounts may be believed, throughout his competitive years when he wasn't sleeping, eating, or traveling, he was either playing or practicing. And for long afterward—in fact,

right up until the aftereffects of his car smash recently began to incapacitate him seriously—he continued the search, hitting balls almost daily in solitude at his club in Fort Worth, partly to test new technology for the golf equipment company he directs, but also because there were still things to learn about the making of golf shots.

Hogan has never been much of a communicator about the game he so distinguished, but he did publish two books, *Power Golf* in 1948 and *The Modern Fundamentals of Golf* in 1953, both best sellers and the latter a classic. Some of the changes in his swing previously noted are mentioned therein, if not always rationalized in detail. What is certainly true is that he became a great (rather than a very good) player only once the majority of those changes had been effected; thus the later swing inevitably is the more interesting. Let us now look at what today might be regarded as some of its most productive elements.

Although he does not particularly stress the point himself, Hogan had what may have been one unusual and important natural

Comparison of these pictures taken early in Hogan's career with those on previous pages of vintage Hogan illustrates some of the changes he effected in his swing over the years. The basic character and mood of the actions are the same, but there are some interesting and educational differences in both the overall scale of the swing and in its details.

advantage as a golfer: He is left-handed but played right-handed. The fact that he came to make his dominant hand (probably in terms of both strength and deftness) the leading hand was a pure fluke—there just weren't many left-handed clubs around when as a boy he started caddieing as a means of enlarging a limited family exchequer. But in terms of current swing theories at least, it was a fortuitous move. It gave him a head start in controlling the club with the leading side of the body or, to put it another way, reduced the natural tendency of what modern teachers say should be the subservient side to take over.

A pronounced feature of Hogan's game has always been the purposeful, super-secure-looking set of his hands upon the club at every point in the swing, with the shaft locked by the last three fingers of his left hand against that palm and the right hand riding high on and welded to its brother. Undoubtedly the comparatively greater strength of his left hand contributed much to this marvelous security and unity. Another contributor, perhaps, was the way he came to hook—

rather than wrap—the little finger of the right hand around the index finger of the left when he changed early in life from an interlocking to an overlapping grip.

Whatever the contribution of these particular grip factors or others, Hogan's hand action through the ball was exemplary. Never at his best, when hitting a normal shot, did Hogan's clubhead catch up to his left hand until after the ball had been struck. His impact position—superfirm, back of left hand to target, slightly arched and high-wristed—is today the epitome of fine form and the ideal to which most tournament professionals enviously aspire.

Hogan was not alone in eliminating the hands-before-clubhead, dragging-back takeaway movement that was such a feature of professional golf swings prior to Nelson's best years. But his adoption of the one-piece takeaway certainly helped speed what Nelson had started and to establish unified movement from the left shoulder to the clubhead starting back as a fundamental of good form (and one that will, in this writer's view, survive the latest fashion of dramatically

"setting the angle"—cocking the wrists—as the first movement of the backswing).

But in another facet of form that has been endlessly debated since the days of the St. Andrews Swingers, Hogan was close to being unique. This was in the area of swing plane. Hogan actually came to maturity at a time when Nelson's example was just beginning to move the golf swing onto a more upright path, but here Ben did not follow the new fashion. In fact, he went, if anything, in the opposite direction: He got flatter (and better!)

Even in the days of his fuller backswing, Hogan exhibited massive control over his entire action and a tremendous power and authority—all the product of the most intensive study and practice regimen ever known in golf.

as he got older.

An advantage of an upright plane, as exemplified so well today by Nicklaus and Johnny Miller, is that it allows the clubhead to travel along the target line slightly longer through impact than does a flatter angle of attack. Unfortunately an upright plane also has disadvantages, primarily two. The first is that, unless it is accompanied by strong leg action, the club stays at ball level for less time than it does when delivered on a shallower arc. The second is that it is very easy, in attempting to swing on an upright path, simply to lift the club with the hands and arms and thus fail to coil the body fully. Nicklaus, Miller, and other pronouncedly upright swingers obviate both dangers through the width of arc emanating from their tremendous arm extension and prodigious coiling of the upper body. The average golfer who lacks their physical capabilities but tries to ape their style regrettably often ends up with a powerless chopping action, in which the clubhead is delivered so steeply downward to impact that it

cannot possibly drive the ball solidly forward. Thus are born many of the fat shots, bloops, and slices that so plague club golfers.

As a comparatively small man, power—distance—was of utmost importance to Hogan. As a youth and in his adult years prior to his accident he achieved it largely through a very long and comparatively wristy arm swing, combined with what might be called a "neu-

tral" swing plane—neither flat nor upright but halfway between. As time went on, the probability is that swinging long became either unappealing to Hogan because it did not offer sufficient control or impractical for him physically or both. He thus sought or was obliged to shorten his swing, but in a way that did not cost him power. A flatter plane was certainly a sound solution me-

chanically, in two respects. First, the shallower the plane, the more the shoulders going back must turn rather than tilt, and the more the shoulders turn, the greater the torque, and thus leverage, and thus clubhead speed that is created coming down. Second, the shallower the plane, the longer the clubhead will be at ball level through impact and thus the greater the amount of force driving directly forward instead of downward.

For whatever reasons, by the time he reached his peak, Hogan had definitely come to swing the club on a shallower plane than any of the other champions discussed in this book. And he had a great deal to say about this previously highly neglected matter in *The Modern Fundamentals of Golf.* There artist Tony Ravielli illustrated Hogan's plane with Ben swinging beneath a tilted sheet of glass that extended from across his shoulders down to the ball, a drawing that has become perhaps the most famous single golf-instruction illustration in history.

Basically Hogan's message was that the golfer's ideal plane is represented by an imaginary straight line running at address from his left shoulder to his clubhead, the angle of this plane being automatically established by the player's build, distance from the ball, and address posture. But he does come down heavily in favor of shallowness should there be any deviation from the ideal, writing: "As golf faults go, it is not too injurious if your club and arms travel on a plane a little flatter than the ideal one. *However, you are heading for disaster if you thrust your arms up above the plane so that they would shatter the pane of glass.* Poor golfers make this error at any and all stages of the backswing, but it occurs most commonly when they are nearing the top of the backswing. Then, when their hands are about shoulder high, they suddenly lift their arms almost vertically toward the sky—crash goes the glass . . . and their shot."

This writer, for one, knows exactly what he means!

Hogan also wrote extensively in *The Modern Fundamentals* about the rotation of the arms, hands, and club going back from and through the ball that is necessary with a shallow plane and that he believed to be integral to good form irrespective of the angle of swing. Indeed, these passages first introduced the words "pronation" and "supination" into the lexicon of golf; and although as usual he has refrained from commenting publicly, Hogan privately might be scathing about today's so-called square methods, especially the technique of "curling under" (turning the hands slightly counter-clockwise starting back). A few years ago this writer and a colleague had the pleasure (and honor) of watching Hogan hit balls for a couple of hours at his Fort Worth club. Lunchtime conversation had touched on the then recently launched "square-to-square" method. As his two-man audience watched the endless stream of flawless shots, Ben would occasionally turn to them and say: "See that? See how I curled under on that one?" The pronation—clockwise rotation—of his arms and hands on each swing was, of course, just as pronounced as in the films discussed earlier.

One movement of Hogan's that became increasingly pronounced as his game evolved, and one that this writer believes contributed mightily to his superb striking, was a slight arching or bowing of the back of his left wrist and/or backward dropping of the hands as he flowed from backswing into downswing. It is difficult for the untrained observer to spot this very slight and therefore seemingly insignificant movement, but it is present in the actions of many fine strikers, from Hogan to, most notably, Gary Player. (Player, of course, learned much from Hogan when he first visited the United States in search of swing improvement.)

With Hogan, this movement was certainly deliberate—his swing contained nothing that wasn't. Among other players it is perhaps unconscious or simply the product of other actions—most probably the controlled thrusting of the legs toward the target with which all great modern players have initiated the downswing. Whatever its origin, however, it would seem to have at least two great benefits. First, it firms up and forces the left wrist into the straight-line relationship with the forearm that makes for powerful hands-ahead-of-clubface impact (the relationship that square-to-square advocates seek to establish by "curling under" during the take-away). Second, it ensures that the clubhead is delivered to the ball traveling from inside the target line by reversing any instinctive tendency to throw the hands forward as they begin to swing down. (Hogan had a definite "inside-to-out" swing-path picture.) Little has been written by any of the top golfers about such movements, but despite their subtlety, this writer believes that they could actually be important keys to solid, powerful striking.

To the golf fans of his day Hogan was an awe-inspiring figure, not least because of his remoteness. On the course his depth of concentration on managing his play as much as actual shotmaking (he was probably the greatest strategical analyzer and placer of shots in history) left him nothing for howdy-doodying. Off the course his extreme sense of personal privacy, plus his preoccupation with becoming ever a better golfer, kept him far removed from both the public and the majority of his contemporaries. As he often said, he was content to let his golf speak for him.

It did so with unrivaled eloquence, particularly in terms of the amount of power a person of slight build—135 to 150 pounds during his prime—can develop given a superhuman effort. Hogan in his day was not only terrifyingly accurate but extremely long. Often his full power was not unleashed—he was essentially a positional player (Nicklaus' little-recognized strongest weapon, incidentally). But it was there when he needed it, with the driver and particularly with the long irons.

Where did this power come from? Obviously, in sum, from strength, suppleness, and a magnificently tempered golf swing—certainly not from any one single technical idiosyncrasy or action. But if there was one movement that did contribute more than others to the size of Hogan's shots, it was, in this writer's opinion, his hip action. Therein also may lie the clue to his remarkable "extension through the ball," the most pronounced of any champion and a matter of constant debate by technically inclined golfers ever since Hogan first showed his mettle.

One of the chief reasons that even fairly good golfers do not send the clubhead whistling widely out toward the target in hot pursuit of the ball as Hogan did (and Nicklaus does) is that they are "in their own way" at this most critical point in the swing. The reason they are in their own way is that their hips have not turned sufficiently in the early and middle parts of the downswing to allow their arms to swing freely past their bodies as the club traverses the ball. In short, they are "blocked" by their bodies, as a pure anatomical result of which the wrists must hinge toward the target prematurely, the left elbow must bend, and the club must abruptly rise and quickly move left of target. If the reader will suffer yet another of this writer's personal beliefs, a prime reason for the lack of post-impact extension today is the heavy emphasis on lateral (targetward) leg action in initiating the downswing, leading to an exaggerated sideways lurch of the entire lower body, leading in turn to insufficient, or insufficiently early, unwinding or clearance of the hips before impact.

In his writings Hogan talks of starting the downswing by turning the hips toward the target as soon as the left foot has been firmly replanted. Such a movement is dramatically visible in his swing, as it is in Nicklaus' (stand behind Jack driving if you want to see really energetic hip clearance). And therein, in this writer's view, lies the main applicator of both golfers' phenomenal distance-producing leverage, the cause of their prodigious "extension" of the arms and club toward the target, and the supplier of the momentum that sends their drivers flying way up and around and down behind their backs at the finish of the swing.

Taken as a whole, Hogan's swing, like his record, was breathtaking—a thing of beauty and majesty in its machinelike repetitiveness and in almost every respect a model for all ages, especially for the slightly built golfer. The only element that the present-day teacher might not want to hand on was Hogan's idiosyncrasy of addressing the ball with his hands in line with (sometimes, it even appears, behind) the ball. But that was common to many of the best players of old and is not a rare sight on the present tour (witness Arnold Palmer). Indeed, with possibly that exception, Hogan's setup particularly—shoulders squarely aligned to squarely aimed clubface; ball positioned just inside the left heel for all normal shots; erect, unstrained, resiliently ready posture—is the master model.

Will anyone ever surpass Hogan's ability as a shotmaker? It is difficult to imagine, but the last person to be surprised if anyone does would probably be Hogan himself, if he still believes these words he wrote in 1940: "It is my conviction that in the years ahead there will be many changes in style and form, just as there have been in the past. We never come anywhere near reaching perfection—there is always something left to improve."

BOBBY LOCKE

Born: November 20, 1917, Germiston,
        Transvaal, South Africa
Died: March 9, 1987, Johannesburg, South Africa

Major victories:

British Open: 1949, 1950, 1952, 1957

KEN BOWDEN

Bobby Locke

BENIGN IMPERTURBABILITY—AND THE HOTTEST PUTTER IN HISTORY

A portly golfer walks slowly onto a green surrounded by expectant, craning spectators, pauses contentedly to allow a caddie to present him with a long, wooden-shafted, thin-bladed putter, then ambles across the green to a ball lying some fifty feet from the cup.

The golfer is dressed in white buck shoes, white stockings, baggy black knickers, a long-sleeved white dress shirt, a black tie tucked into the shirt between the third and fourth buttons, and a white linen cap. Slowly he squats behind the ball and peacefully contemplates the rolling real estate betwixt ball and cup. One hand lightly rests the putterhead on the grass; the other gently settles the white cap.

Now, with the stateliness of an emperor rising from his throne, the golfer rises and proceeds slowly across the greensward, inspecting it minutely inch by inch. Arriving in the vicinity of the cup, he stops, leans slowly forward from the waist, and peers even more intently at the ground. After perhaps thirty seconds he straightens up and journeys slowly back to the ball. There he takes the putter lightly in both hands, makes two soft, con-

templative practice swings, steps immediately up to the ball, and gently strokes it toward the hole.

The ball rolls up one slope and down another and up another, but appears to be traveling far too slowly ever to reach its target. Six feet from the hole it is hardly moving, but after what seems an eternity it arrives at the right lip, hovers momentarily, then succumbs to the forces of gravity and topples in sideways. The crowd roars. The portly golfer tips his cap, allows the faintest of smiles to flicker across his rosy, rotund features, and proceeds at measured pace toward the next tee.

Between 1947 and 1959 the above episode was as kin to tournament golf in Britain and the United States as tonic is to an Englishman's gin and mustard to an American's hot dog. The perpetrator was, of course, Arthur D'Arcy Locke, universally known as Bobby. A South African, Locke was the first great non-British, non-American golfer. He was also the most bizarre personality and perhaps the most bizarre player technically of all

103

*This slim young man may not be immediately
recognizable to readers who recall Locke in his
heyday, but the swing immediately identifies the
great South African. Modeled originally on Bobby
Jones' action, it is the most idiosyncratic of all the
master golfers'—but also one of the most
repetitive. Among its more unusual features are
the pronounced "inside" takeaway, leading to a
massive "crossing of the line" (pointing the club
right of target) at the top; the huge pivot of the
entire body on the backswing leading to a
high-raised left heel at the top; the
"over-and-around," instead of "under-and-
through," shoulder roll on the
downswing; and the quick roll of the right hand
over the left at impact. Not really the modern
method exemplified, but maybe worth a try if
you'd like to hook everything as Locke did.*

golf's remarkably characterful superstars.

Although he is now but a name to most present-day U.S. tour players, to their predecessors of the immediate postwar years Bobby Locke was a blight of unparalled proportions whose ravagings of purse, pride, and psyche left scars that may never fully heal. Arriving in the United States in the spring of 1947, heralded only by a 12-out-of-16 challenge-match massacre of Sam Snead in South Africa, Locke finished 14th in the Masters and then proceeded to win four of the next five tournaments. When he departed these shores at the end of that summer, he had won seven events, finished second twice, third once, and placed in the top seven on four other occasions. Jimmy Demaret, who played the full 12-month tour, beat him for first place on the 1947 money list by only $3,600.

And it did not stop with that one sortie. Banned from the tour in 1949 for allegedly breaking commitments to play in U.S. events (the truth is that he stayed away because

sponsors would not pay him the appearance money they paid American stars), he was readmitted in response to public demand in 1950. Thereafter he won another six tournaments and—to the home players—a painfully large proportion of the total dollars up for grabs in official prize money, exhibition and challenge matches, and in such perquisites as then existed in pro golf. In seven attempts at the U.S. Open he finished third twice, fourth twice, and fifth once. And all this was just the cream on the cake. During the eight years between the first (1949) and last (1957) of his four British Open victories, only the Australian Peter Thomson rivaled Locke's winning ways outside America.

An interesting facet of professional sports is the fact that the most obviously talented performers are generally the most popular among their adversaries. Jack Nicklaus exemplifies this situation today. Many tour golfers may envy him, but most unreservedly like him, at least partly because they are less upset by losing to him than when beaten by obviously less-gifted players. Perhaps it is simply easier psychically to accept defeat from someone who clearly possesses far greater talents than oneself.

This was the rub with Locke. He did not appear to be in any way more talented than most of the people he beat and in many instances less so. Compounding the irritant was his obvious unathleticism (by Olympian standards at least) and his highly idiosyncratic appearance and competitive demeanor. It was bad enough to be beaten by a fellow who didn't play an orthodox game, but when he also looked and acted like a visitation from another planet, well, that really hurt.

Although a steely competitor who got the greatest relish from beating those who least admired him, Locke was basically a kind and modest man with little if any malice in his heart. Thus it is a near certainty that his bizarre taste in golfing haberdashery, his highly unorthodox shots, his unshakable calm, his ponderous deliberateness, his lack of devotion to the practice tee, his willingness to

105

party, his unself-consciousness (perhaps best expressed after his raiment by his readiness for song) were simply guileless expressions of an unusual temperament rather than calculated competitive ploys. But whatever their source, they served him well in battle, especially in America, where eccentricity has never been as easily accepted as it is in Europe. A top U.S. professional undoubtedly expressed the feelings of the clan when he said of Locke in the early 1950's: "The guy gets to me before we ever hit a shot. I look at that nutty outfit and I'm one down. I listen to that accent and I'm two down trying to figure out what he said. I watch that crazy swing and go three down trying to work out why he doesn't flat whiff it. Then he starts hooking those 50-foot putts into the cup, and I'm done—cooked to a turn."

The bulk of this book is concerned with the technique of the full golf swing, but in Locke's case such analysis would be as unproductive for the improvement-conscious reader as it was for Locke's mind-boggled opponents. In 1972 *Golf Digest* magazine published an article by this writer which described his method of getting from tee to green thus:

"By the time he got to America, Locke had developed and refined to perfection the most individualistic swing of any big winner in history—Hagen with his sway and Palmer with his crashing, flourishing follow-through are models of orthodoxy by comparison. Locke hooked everything. . . . Not drew, *hooked* . . . whipped it around in a high, wide, swinging half-circle. At address, he aimed his entire body somewhere right of first base, with his right foot pulled back a couple of feet behind the left. Going back, he swung the club sharply inside with a huge upper body turn and a lot of flippy wrist action. At the top he had the club pointing into the right field bleachers. Coming down, his shoulders rolled and spun like a wallowing whale. Every shot would start way right, then curl slowly back to centerfield."

We shall not here dwell on the details of

this unique action, but in overall terms it is not without some technical interest. Certainly one very intriguing aspect of Locke's swing is that its basic principles were acquired from a book, making him the only great golfer to have learned the game originally from the printed word rather than from some combination of mimicry, trial and error, or formal coaching. In the article just quoted from he explained:

"When I was thirteen, my dear old dad gave me Bobby Jones' book on golf, and he said to me, 'Son, here is the finest golfer in the world, and I want you to learn how to play from his book. A lot of people are going to try to help you, but just let it go in one ear and out the other. You just model your game on Bobby Jones and you will be a fine player.' So that's what I did when I started, and what I have done all my life."

Another interesting aspect of Locke's technique, rarely if ever mentioned in previous analyses, is its fundamental similarity not only to Jones' method but to Sam Snead's.

Jones swung the club well inside going back, with a very full turn of the entire body and a free cocking of the wrists, pointed it right of target at the top, then looped it back on track with a reciprocal set of actions coming down. Snead does exactly that, only on a smaller and firmer scale. Locke did exactly the same thing only on a much grander and looser scale. Seen from above, the clubhead in all three swings describes a figure eight. Locke's just happens to have been the fattest eight!

By far the most educational aspects of Locke's method for the average golfer, however, are its economy of effort and its repetitiveness. At no time in his career did Locke sacrifice control for distance, and only when absolutely forced to do so by some topographical circumstance would he play a stroke that called for a marked change in his swing pattern.

"I don't feel it is ever necessary to try to knock the ball out of sight," he said many times. "All I try to do is hit the tee shot far enough to get on the green with the second

shot." Even the long, lush U.S. courses and the power-hitting U.S. players did not alter this ultraconservative approach. Consistently outdriven, often approaching with woods and long-irons where others were flying middle- and short-irons into the greens, and continually ribbed about his "weak left hand," he continued to drive with a two-wood—and collect the checks with his right hand!

When it came to changing his swing pattern, he was even more stubborn, as neatly exemplified by the tenth hole on the New Course at Sunningdale, near London, where he won frequently. The hole is a long par-three with tall pine trees closely guarding the entire right side. For the "normal" pro, the shot was a three- or four-iron with a touch of left-to-right fade. Locke would invariably play it with a soft three- or four-wood, hitting the ball up and *over* the trees and hooking it back into the green! (This and similar situations convinced British fans that Locke actually could not fade the ball even if he had been prepared to try. That was not true, as this writer discovered when he tackled Locke on the subject while playing with him in Vermont a few years back. "Maastah, let me show you how it's done," said Locke, who then proceeded to stroke two immaculate fades to a par-four hole—from his normal 45-degrees-right setup!)

These qualities of conservatism and continuity jointly produced the greatest single strength of Locke's tee-to-green game and the one the average golfer most lacks: consistency. By never hitting hard and by always hitting the same "shape" of shot, Locke could "repeat" to a degree that ate deep into the souls of his more spectacular but erratic opponents. He did not hit many great shots, but he also hit very few catastrophic shots. He was invariably "in play." Add to that his patient approach to the game, his phenomenal short game, and his wonderful depth perception (he never paced a hole in his life but almost monotonously stopped the ball pin high), and his record becomes less amazing than it superficially looked to the fans of his day.

Locke was frequently labeled the world's "best bad player," the inference being that Hagen-type scrambling underpinned the majority of his victories. This was untrue and unfair. The purity of strike necessary to fly the ball as consistently from right to left as he did was every bit as great as that achieved by many of his contemporaries in hitting it fifty yards farther. If further supportive evidence is necessary, it is to be found in his command over the *speed* of the ball on landing. A hooked or drawn shot is notoriously a fast-landing hard runner. Locke could float in his high hooks every bit as softly as Nicklaus today can feather down a fade.

That Locke was an individualist of rare proportions was dramatically established by his appearance as well as his playing method. But the eccentricity of both pall beside his unique competitive demeanor, in which lay much of his strength. No one word can describe Locke on the course, but the two that probably come closest are "benign imperturbability." Very early in life he had learned three things: one, that physical relaxation or at least lack of muscular tension is essential to playing good golf shots; two, that the game can be played only one shot at a time; and three, that there will always be an element of luck in golf.

The first recognition, combined with his naturally deliberate temperament, made him the most physically relaxed and unhurried golfer of all the great champions. To quote again from the *Golf Digest* article: "Locke got into endless troubles about his speed of play. He was not like Jack Nicklaus, who careens along the fairways then takes aeons over the shot. Locke had just two speeds for everything—leisurely and slow. Once he actually got to the ball, he played his shot with dispatch. But getting there was the problem. Week in, week out, the writers would record how he took 20 minutes to put his shoes on, 10 minutes to collect his scorecard, five to get a ball from his bag. He had his pace and nothing would shift him from it. Large gaps would open on the course ahead of him; his playing partners would grow red-necked and fiery-eyed; officials would threaten, but Locke remained immovable..Since the war, at least, nothing—but *nothing*—has ever hurried him."

Locke's second recognition, that golf can be played only one shot at a time, aided him tremendously in concentrating and through that in combating pressure. He always played the course, never the man. And he never looked backward or ahead, but simply to the shot at hand. Combined with his third recognition—that the outcome of at least 20 percent of the shots played in golf is largely a matter of luck—this one-shot-at-a-time approach engendered an emotional equanimity and an effortless intensity of concentration rarely if ever matched in tournament golf.

In the final analysis, however, Locke's greatest strength had to be his phenomenal short game. He was a magical pitcher and chipper and almost beyond argument the greatest putter of all time; a man who literally holed out frequently from forty or fifty feet and who thus expected and almost always tried to do so.

Unquestionably his inviolable emotional and physical calmness was a major factor behind Locke's short-game wizardry—psychic and physiological relaxation and the yips are, as Deane Beman might say, mutually exclusive. Another factor was Locke's delicacy of touch: He was born with extremely sensitive fingers. Yet another factor was his excellent memory: He could vividly retain all the breaks and rolls twixt ball and cup in his mind's eye, even at long distances. But the catalyst for all this was his conscious mental approach to the short game, captured in these words from the previously quoted *Golf Digest* article:

"I learned very early in life that, as Bobby Jones said in his book, the real secret of success in golf lies in turning three shots into two. If you miss a third of the greens in every round, but turn three shots into two four times, you save four shots a round. If you do that in every round of a tournament you save 16 shots. Thus, once I had my long game in reasonable shape as a young man, I worked

for many, many hours—many, many days and weeks and months—on my short game. And it paid off very well by taking the pressure off my long game. I always felt confident that I could make pars when I was playing poorly and that, when I was playing well, a few birdies might come my way."

As in seemingly every other department of method and attitude, Locke in putting was highly individualistic, if not downright unorthodox.

Realizing that putting was half the game of golf, he set himself specific targets on the greens, 32 putts representing a fair day's work, 30 putts a good day, and 28 putts a very good day. "But twenty-eight putts was my real target," he says, "and I had a lot of twenty-eight-putt rounds."

His primary objective in actually stroking the ball was to impart topspin to it, by which he meant true end-over-end rotation from the moment of contact, with no skidding, sidespinning, or hopping. The objective here was to take advantage of "the hole's four entrances—the front of the cup if the putt is 'dying'; the back of the cup if the putt is going a little too fast but is on line; and either side of the cup if the putt is the right strength but is marginally off-line." It was because he did not impart sidespin, he averred, that so many of his putts fell in via the "side door" while other players' spun out.

He believed that most putts are missed not because they are mis-hit but because they are misread: hence his incredibly meticulous surveying of greens, especially near the hole where the slower-moving ball is most susceptible to terrain. His first concern was pace, his second break, and he would not putt until he had a clear mental picture of the ball's speed and direction as it ran from him into the hole. Regarding pace, he had a definite rule of thumb for each texture of green. On a fast surface he tried to hit the ball as if the putt were six inches shorter than it really was; on a medium-paced green just to drop it over the front lip; and on slow greens to bounce it lightly off the back of the cup.

Of all his putting rules, the one he most

steadfastly maintained was to stick to what-ever decisions he had made about speed and line. Once he had made up his mind, he never changed it while actually stroking the ball. At the ball he would make two soft practice swings—never more, never less—then immediately stroke the putt. "Second guesses in putting," he said, "are fatal."

To hear them talk about it today, it is apparent that the effectiveness of Locke's actual putting stroke is still as unbelievable to many of his contemporaries as it was when they actually suffered from it. Unorthodox as it may have seemed in some elements, it was certainly a uniquely powerful golfing weapon.

In line with his policy that the fewer the variations in overall technique, the greater the consistency or "repeatability," Locke used the same overlapping grip on the greens that he used in hitting to them, with the exceptions that he held the club even more lightly (primarily with his fingertips) and placed both thumbs straight down the shaft. The position of his hands high on his long puttershaft also never changed, irrespective of the length of putt, primarily because he did not want to vary the "head feel" that was essential to his sense of control during the stroke.

At address Locke used a mini-version of the closed stance he employed for full shots, with the weight comfortably distributed between both feet, the body and neck inclined well forward to place his eyes directly over the ball, and the ball always positioned opposite the left toes. The reason for the closed stance—apart from the fact that he used a closed stance for everything—was to encourage the putterhead to swing to the ball from inside the target line. The reason for positioning the ball opposite the left toes was to facilitate "striking it slightly on the upswing, just after the putterhead has reached the bottom of its arc . . . [which] greatly helps me to impart true topspin to the ball. If the ball were farther back, I might have a tendency to chop down on it and impart backspin or sidespin."

If there was one thing in putting Locke

wanted to avoid at all costs, it was cutting across the ball from outside the target line, thereby imparting sidespin to it. A further insurance against this was his habit of addressing the ball opposite the toe of the putter, then striking it on the center of the clubface. It would seem that few golfers not gifted with Locke's equanimity of nervous system and delicacy of touch would be able to repeat such a maneuver, but he maintained that everyone should try it, in that it counterbalances a natural tendency to swing back outside the line when the ball is addressed opposite the center of the putterface.

So much for the preparation. Now came the part that really got to his adversaries—the actual stroke.

The two cornerstones of Locke's putting method were keeping the clubface square to the ball's starting line throughout the stroke and swinging the blade of the putter forward to the ball from inside that line. He also placed great emphasis on keeping the putterhead low to the ground—"almost brushing the grass"—throughout the stroke, all of these techniques being designed to obviate the hated sidespin and produce the beloved topspin. In 1972 he wrote of these matters:

"[Vitally] important is keeping the blade square to the starting line of the putt, or even closing it a little during the backswing. This is known as 'hooding' the face and is a very important part of my stroke. Walter Hagen proved to me in 1937 that this type of backswing was the only one that would impart true topspin to the ball, and I am very happy that I listened to him and copied his method.

"There is no wristwork in my backswing. Wristwork in putting breeds inconsistency. However, one thing that does result from hooding the face is that my left wrist turns slightly 'under' on the backswing. The longer the stroke, the more the back of my left hand points towards the grass.

"To most observers, it appears that at the completion of my backswing the putterface is slightly closed. It may well be, but to me . . . the feeling is that it is still square to the starting line of the putt. So long as it isn't open to that line, I am not too concerned.

"I have always thought of the ideal putter swing as matching that of a clock's pendulum, slow and very smooth, with the clubhead going through the same distance it goes back. Thus, in returning the putter to the ball, I try to swing it very smoothly at the same pace I swung it back. Again, there is no wrist action. The putter is swung by my hands, wrists and arms as a unit; my left wrist at impact has exactly the same relationship to my left arm that it had at address. This ensures that the putterblade remains square to my target through impact and well into the follow-through."

Although there can be no doubt that this is exactly what Locke actually did, to those who were obliged to observe the stroke at close hand it somehow looked different. Perhaps their impressions were colored by the stunning frequency with which he beat them by toppling the ball into the hole from impossible distances or by the differences between his method and their own perhaps more stylistically "proper" systems. Whatever the reasons, contemporary comments do not always jell with Locke's own description of his stroke. They abound with phrases like "The damn club almost falls out of his hands, he holds it so loose." "The guy closes the clubface through the ball, actually hooks the ball into the cup, and, I ask you, how can anybody putt like that?" "I think he hypnotizes the ball into the hole because he sure doesn't ever seem to hit it hard enough to get there." "Hit it on the upswing? Why, he flat tops it."

To which Locke, with a gentle smile widening his ample jowls, would undoubtedly have replied something like: "Well, Maastah, the truth is that actually I'm a singer. Golf with me is really just a sideline. . . ."

Cary Middlecoff

PLAY AWAY WHEN READY, WHEN READY, WHEN READY, WHEN . . .

For those of us who are made like Dr. Cary Middlecoff, the frustrations inherent in trying to strike a golf ball solidly time after time are especially exasperating. Middlecoff is a perfectionist, which is just about the worst thing you can be if your occupation calls for never missing four-foot putts. Perfectionists make outstanding martinis—and anyone who has been Middlecoff's guest knows how expert he is in that area—but gin and vermouth can be measured far more precisely than can the split second between backswing and downswing or the velocity of a right-to-left wind at a point some 200 yards down the fairway. Golf is a game of variables, literally dozens on each shot, and the player who expects to mesh all these pieces perfectly every time is more likely to end up with a major migraine than a major championship.

Dr. Cary Middlecoff fussed, fretted, and fidgeted his way to 34 PGA tour victories in his first 10 years as a playing professional—more than Gary Player and Lee Trevino won together. He took the Masters once (1955) and the U.S. Open twice (1949 and 1956). Between 1947 and 1956 he won more prize money at golf than anyone else in the world. He achieved his outstanding record, as we shall see, with a temperament and a swing far less suitable than those of many of his contemporaries, and in spite of several physical ailments ranging from color blindness to a shattered spinal disk. In short, logic would seem to have dictated that Dr. Cary Middlecoff should have stayed in Memphis, Tennessee, drilling molars.

We shall here first look at Middlecoff's temperament because it dramatically affected the way he played the game. Next we'll examine the physical limitations under which he played. Finally we'll discuss his swing, pro and con, and try to find the reason why he was so good at a game to which he seems, outwardly at least, to have been singularly unsuited.

Middlecoff comes from a family of dentists and surgeons, a precise world where the slip of a drill or scalpel can cause far graver consequences than a mis-hit two-iron. Though he has not practiced dentistry since leaving the army in 1946 ("I pulled seven thousand teeth before I found out the army had another

CARY MIDDLECOFF

Born: January 6, 1921; Halls, Tennessee

Major victories:
U.S. Open: 1949, 1956
Masters: 1955

dentist"), Middlecoff did absorb his father's intense attention to detail. When he came out on tour in 1947, he sought a similar perfection in his golf game.

"I knew I had a good swing," he says, "and was firmly resolved not to change it. The improvement I hoped for was in making the swing repeat itself more consistently—to reach the point where each swing was my best swing. I thought this was both possible and feasible. It was in pursuit of this ideal that I learned to my disappointment that the game is, indeed, one of constant correction."

To help eliminate the extra pressures that a golfer can put on himself by striving for perfection, Middlecoff pursued the Walter Hagen philosphy that life goes on in spite of three-putt greens. "I was always so highly strung," he says, "that I always tried to accept the most negative outcome I could think of. I figured that no matter how badly I missed the shot, I wasn't going to die and probably wasn't even going to have a heart attack."

While Middlecoff probably did swing more freely whenever he could truly accept that shot results were slightly less than life-or-death matters, and while he realized the rarity of perfect striking, when it came to *preparing* for a shot, he was as much a perfectionist in all his movements as any surgeon. He would approach the ball and study its lie as though it were a rattlesnake waiting to strike. He'd police the surrounding area for any stray leaves, grass clippings, or worm droppings. He'd toss grass into the air to track down the subtlest of breezes, then do it again to make sure. He'd shade the front of his visor salute fashion and squint at the green, then edge over to his bag, tentatively select a club, and salute once again. With the chosen implement in hand, he'd edge into his address position as warily as one steps onto

---

"Clearing the left hip" has long been recognized as a key swing fundamental. Few players ever cleared theirs more dramatically than did Middlecoff.

an icy surface. Then he'd step back, test the breeze, return to the bag, select a new implement, salute, and try again. Once settled over the ball he'd turn his head to and from the target as many as twenty times (yes, it's still there). Finally, if all seemed right with the world, he'd actually swing the club.

On the green he was equally meticulous. "If he spotted a dew drop on a blade of grass in line with his ball and the cup," a reporter once wrote, "he'd wait for the sun to come out and dry it up. . . . Once he deliberated so long that picnickers spread out their lunch under a nearby cypress and finished eating while he made up his mind."

While Middlecoff felt that his slow play was exaggerated by commentators—he did walk swiftly between shots—he admitted to occasional indecision and nervousness. "The most important part of golf," he said, "is getting ready for the shot. . . . It takes a world of self-development and self-control. There is nothing unusual about learning good technique, but conquering the mental side is something else. I ought to know, I've fought a running battle with it for years. . . . My slowness was due to indecision caused by nervousness; didn't know what to do. . . . Anyone who hasn't been nervous or who hasn't choked somewhere down the line is an idiot."

Meticulous, indecisive, nervous—how could a man with such fusspot characteristics withstand the shot-to-shot, day-to-day, week-to-week rigors of professional tournament golf and still maintain such a high standard of excellence?

Well, for one thing it helps to have an understanding wife—a Valerie Hogan, a Winnie Palmer, a Barbara Nicklaus, a Vivienne Player—and in Edith Buck Middlecoff, Cary has one of the best. It also helps to have an outgoing personality, to be able to lose oneself in a convivial atmosphere, and Middlecoff is at heart a friendly, sociable person. It also helps to be outspoken, to blow off steam when the pot begins to boil, and to have enough sense to escape from competition when the nerves

Middlecoff drove the ball farther than most professionals of his day despite his rather short backswing and relatively small degree of shoulder turn. No doubt his tallness gave him some additional leverage, but it was his precise sense of timing that provided most of his length on full shots. By noticeably pausing at the top of his backswing, he gave his legs and hips ample time to lead all else on his forward swing. This lower-body leadership, when coupled with his steady head position, allowed him to build additional leverage early in his downswing, retain it until near impact, and then fully release it into the ball. Golfers with minimal arm and shoulder suppleness similarly should strive for a steady head position and sufficient time between backswing and downswing to allow for their changing of direction.

begin to wear and tear.

"It gets pretty tough sometimes," Middlecoff told reporters in February, 1957, after some six weeks on the winter tour. "All during the winter a collection of minor aggravations build up until a person can't stand it anymore and he lets loose. These things wear on you continually until you can't concentrate. . . . I'm going home; pull down all the blinds, disconnect the phones, rest, and just forget about golf for a while."

At times Middlecoff would pack it in during the middle of a tournament, or he'd pull out before it started. Before the 1954 San Diego Open a newspaper columnist opined, "Middlecoff is one of golf's finest drivers, and few of the pros are better putters. He's always tough—if he doesn't pick up."

During the 1949 U.S. Open at Medinah, outside Chicago, Middlecoff was struggling with wildness through the first round, to the tune of being five over par after 14 holes. On the 15th tee he advised his caddie to pocket the ball if his drive didn't finish in the fairway. It did, however, and Middlecoff birdied the hole, parred in for a 75, shot 69-67-75 in the ensuing rounds, and won his first major championship by a single stroke.

In all fairness it must be noted that Middlecoff's slow play and occasional withdrawals from tournaments were probably due in large part to a rash of physical problems that plagued him throughout his career. The aforementioned color blindness, for instance, made it difficult for him to distinguish between various shades of green. This put him at a time-consuming disadvantage in judging the distance of full shots and in ascertaining

subtleties of length, topography, and grass texture on the green. Also he was extremely allergic to certain grasses and fought a running battle with hay fever. Pills helped, but many a time he approached shots with eyes watering and nose sniffling. As defending champion in the 1956 Masters he shot 67-72 the first two rounds and took the lead by a shot on the third day after going out in 35, despite a severe hay-fever attack. Between nines he rushed into the clubhouse to get the pills he'd left in his jacket, only to find that a friend had borrowed the coat to wear on the course. Red-eyed and suffering, Middlecoff shot 40 on the back side to fall four shots behind. He eventually lost the tournament to Jack Burke, Jr., by two shots after double-bogeying the 71st hole.

Along with color blindness and hay fever,

Middlecoff also had to pace himself slowly on especially hot days to guard against heat prostration. He'd had a mild heat stroke as a youngster of eleven while on a golf course, and it seemed to have left him especially vulnerable to the sun's rays.

But of all his ailments, it was chronic backache that finally did him in. The pain started about 1956. Cortisone shots eased the suffering, but at times Middlecoff had to struggle over the ball at address just to find a comfortable position. By 1963 the pain in his back and right leg had progressed to loss of feeling in his right big toe. When doctors invested his spine with a dye and rocked him back and forth under an X-ray machine, the fluid spilled forth from between two vertebrae in his lower back (lumbar) region. The leakage was due to the fragmentation of the elastic

disk between the vertebrae. One of the splinters had broken through the tirelike covering of the disk and lodged against a spinal nerve, causing both the back pain and the paralysis of the toe. An operation to remove the disk reduced Middlecoff's suffering, but the damage had been done. Cary had won thirty-four PGA tournaments through 1956. Thereafter, from age thirty-six on, he would win only three more times.

No one can say for sure when the disk became deficient. No one can determine for sure whether Middlecoff's particular style of swinging caused the damage or whether from the start some spinal inadequacy caused him to develop the type of swing he did. It can be unequivocally stated, however, that he had one of the most violently hip-sliding, back-bowing forward swings in the history of the game.

Swing theorists have for years advocated the so-called reverse C position during the downswing, formed as the middle of the body from the left hip down to the left knee thrusts forward toward the target and then turns to the left while the head remains back, well behind the ball's original spot. It is a position that provides a massive buildup and release of centrifugal force into the ball.

Middlecoff, normally extremely long and straight off the tee, carried the reverse C position to an extreme. He always advocated and applied a great deal of hip slide and turn on his forward swing, so that his left side jutted out toward the target as he started into the ball. Moreover, after setting up with his head behind the ball, he would slide and turn it even farther to the right, away from the target, during his forward press as he eased his hands and arms toward the target. The result was an extreme inward bowing of the lower back as he lashed through impact and beyond.

No doubt Middlecoff's 6-feet 2-inch stature and relatively short arms had much to do with his swing action. The reverse C position, as opposed to a more straight-up I posi-

tion, had the effect of allowing his hands to swing through the ball close enough to the ground for him to use clubs close to standard in length.

In discussing this matter with this writer a few years back, Middlecoff opined that the taller golfer with short arms was at a major disadvantage because club manufacturers had not found a way to provide them with suitable equipment of proper length. He explained that any shafts that were made long enough to accommodate the extra distance from fingers to ground either became too whippy when attached to a clubhead of normal weight or too heavy if their walls were thickened to provide sufficient stiffness. While he admitted that the newer and lighter shafts helped ease the problem and thus gave taller golfers at least a fighting chance, he felt that the ideal height for golf was still about 5 feet 10 inches.

Thus, if Middlecoff's extreme reverse C position did lead to his spinal damage, it could possibly be construed that his height, in itself, was another physical disadvantage to add to the list.

Another physical drawback of Middlecoff's was the fact that he was rather less physically supple than many of his contemporaries. His shoulder turn was thus necessarily abbreviated—less than 90 degrees—as was the overall length of his backswing. In his case this did not cost distance because, by setting his head and shoulders well back and by leading powerfully with his left side in moving forward, he did achieve a full muscular coiling and stretching. His straight left arm, combined with his height, gave him sufficient leverage in terms of swing width and length. The shorter backswing turn did dictate, however, the most visually dramatic feature of his overall action, the famous "Middlecoff Pause."

Theorists continue to debate whether or not there is an actual pausing at the top of the backswing. Most maintain that something keeps moving at all times—club, hands, knees, or whatever—but if any champion ever did actually come to a dead stop at the top, it had to be Middlecoff. His relatively short backswing turn—along with a tendency to straighten his right leg more than most—forced him to take an abnormally long time to change directions. If he didn't do so with extreme leisure, his hips and legs would never have had enough time to gather themselves for the previously described assault toward the target. Instead, his shoulders, already turned less than most, would take over and shove the club out of proper plane.

"The object of good tempo," Middlecoff wrote in his praised book, *The Golf Swing*, "is to ensure that the downswing is started smoothly with the hips leading and the rest of the power-generating elements following smoothly in their proper sequence. Everything that goes before the transition from backswing to downswing has that objective.

"Here I might cite what I always felt was an advantage in stopping the club at the top of the backswing—as I did so pronouncedly in my best years, but hardly do at all now. I think the pause gave me appreciably more time to alter an incipiently wrong swing—either to correct it or improve it—than the nonpause golfer got. I never urged the adoption of the pause on other players, but I think it helped me."

Apart from the pause and the extreme bowing during his forward swing, Middlecoff's grip, setup, and swing were quite orthodox. He has always been a "fundamentalist" in his approach to the swing, and in the nine years this writer worked with him at *Golf Digest* magazine, where he still serves on the Professional Panel, I cannot recall his ever suggesting any swing technique that departed drastically from a norm accepted by most teachers. His considerable writings on the game stress basics and overall simplicity of movement. I once asked him what one thought predominated during the thousands of swings he made in competition. His answer, in effect, was simply that he tried to strike the ball squarely.

The major influence on Middlecoff's swing during its formative stages was the model supplied by Emmet Spicer, an outstanding Memphis amateur of the early 1930's. "He had a graceful easy style," Cary recalls, "and hit the ball as well as any player I have ever seen since. I did not try to make my swing look like Spicer's, or anybody else's, but I tried to incorporate into my swing what I took to be the fundamental positions and movements that made Spicer's swing produce such powerful and accurate shots. That, I still think, is the approach all aspiring golfers should take."

No discussion of Middlecoff's game would be complete without some mention of his excellent putting. Golf historians still recall the 82-foot eagle putt he dropped on the 13th hole at Augusta National en route to a seven-under-par 65 that helped him to win the 1955 Masters by a then-record seven shots. Less famous, but equally important, was a four-footer he made on the final hole to win the 1956 U.S. Open at Oak Hill Country Club in Rochester, New York. That particular putt, perhaps more than any other, illustrates Middlecoff's ability to eliminate pressure by meticulously blocking out any negative thoughts, no matter how long it took him to do so.

The putt appeared to be straight in, but Middlecoff knew that it wasn't. In a practice round he had putted along the same line, aiming straight at the cup, and found that the ball did take a slight break. Five times he had stroked the ball and each time it had trickled off to the left. Now, with the U.S. Open at stake, Middlecoff found himself forced to allow for a "borrow" that he couldn't see. "I needed five minutes to muster the courage to play the break I knew was there," he recalled later. Finally he allowed for three inches of curve and stroked the ball smoothly into the hole.

Middlecoff used an aluminum-headed, mallet-type putter that was an inch longer than standard and had a relatively upright lie. The extra length and the upright lie allowed him to stand with his eyes over the line, yet carry his hands high. The high hands took much of the wristiness out of his stroke and allowed him to swing almost solely with his arms. An arm stroke, he felt, required a longer swing than did an arm-wrist action and thus allowed him more control over distance, especially on long putts.

As with his full shots, Middlecoff was a perfectionist on the greens in that he tried to hole every putt. He felt the technique used by some—especially on long putts—of trying to make the ball finish within a three-foot circle around the cup produced negativism. "Why not try for perfection?" he asked. "It costs no more." Also, as on full shots, he made it a point in putting to pause slightly between backswing and forward stroke.

These days Middlecoff spends most of his time in Florida, with occasional trips to participate in golf functions. Secure financially, he sleeps late, enjoys a leisurely breakfast, reads the paper, ambles over to the course for a game "with anyone who can play," returns for martinis, dinner, and a quiet evening with Edie. Away from the madding crowd and free of aggravations, he has, in effect, "gone home, pulled down the blinds, and disconnected the phones." It's a life to which Dr. Cary Middlecoff is singularly well suited.

PETER THOMSON

Born: August 23, 1929; Melbourne, Queensland, Australia

Major victories:

British Open: 1954, 1955, 1956, 1958, 1965

KEN BOWDEN

Peter Thomson

"A LIGHT, TENDER, SENSITIVE TOUCH IS WORTH A TON OF BRAWN"

After winning a British Open—or any major championship, come to that—quite a period of time elapses before a golfer can begin to become his own man again. First there is the clamoring of the photographers for "just one more" trophy-clutching, wife-kissing picture. Then there is a moment of seclusion for the checking and signing of the scorecard (a very meticulous process indeed since Roberto de Vincenzo's 1968 Masters). Next there is a television interview, the prize presentation (speeches and more photos), and a trip to the press tent. Then more mass and individual press, radio, and television interviews, and seemingly a million well-wishers and backslappers, and an orgy of autograph signing.

By the time he gets bedazedly through all this, the first self-directed act of the new hero is usually to head for the nearest bar. For Peter Thomson, however, after his fifth British Open victory in 1965, the first move was to walk briskly to a remote corner of the Royal Birkdale press facility, pull out a portable typewriter, and thereon tap out with two fingers and almost no pauses a crisp, fluent,

and highly readable 800-word story for a major Australian newspaper. That done and filed, he then spent fifteen minutes discussing with a group of golf correspondents the merits and demerits—conceptually, structurally, and literately—of a large book over which he had spent many evening hours during the week of the championship. And then, of course, he went for a drink.

Insofar as a couple of his acts can encapsulate a man's character, these capture the essence of Peter Thomson, crown prince of the golf world outside America throughout the 1950's, and arguably the greatest manipulator of the small-size golf ball (1.62 inches) who ever strode a links.

It is a possibility that the name Peter Thomson will not instantly connote Olympian golfing prowess to many present-day American readers, especially any who really do still harbor the outdated impression that the shores of the United States represent the limits of the golfing universe. Until he became a senior, Thomson won only one tournament in this country (the 1956 Texas International Open), placed only once in the

Thomson is the only golfer discussed in this book who has never himself authored a text about how to play golf, despite the fact that as a writer he is probably the best qualified of all the champions. The reason is that he believes that all he has to say about technique—and all that anyone need know—can be said on two sheets of paper of which 90 percent would, incidentally, be concerned with "getting set up right." A point to note about the simple and ultraeconomical swing that has derived from this uniquely simple approach is that it is physically within the capability of almost every golfer, a point that cannot be made for many of the modern champions' actions.

top 10 money winners (1956), and never came closer than fourth to winning a major American championship (again in 1956, in the U.S. Open). Since turning fifty he has returned pretty much full time to become a top star of the flourishing U.S. Senior Tour. However, it is doubtful if all his contemporaries on it rose up and cheered when he re-entered their lives, because Thomson has never gone much out of his way to hide his lack of admiration for certain aspects of American golf (or life), either when here or proffering opinions in other lands.

Be that as it may, the facts of the matter, when one takes a world view (as this book essentially does), are that Peter Thomson was a superstar in his own milieu and, of course, that he had an absolute right to choose what that milieu should be—as do the modern American tour stars who never leave these shores. Another reason present readers might enjoy becoming more familiar with him is that irrespective of his fabulous non-Ameri-

can playing record and marvelously simple technical approach to golf, Thomson is one of the most interesting *people* ever to have graced the game.

Even in lands that he loved, Thomson never won too many most-warm-and-wonderful-human-being votes from his rivals, partly because of his casual self-sufficiency and independence (a common Australian trait), partly because he played so simply and won so easily, but primarily because of his intellect. One cannot fairly claim that he is the most innately intelligent of all the champions, but in breadth of intellectual interest and accomplishment, leading to articulateness and (among those he likes) companionability, he is supreme.

It is often argued that what prevented Thomson from more aggressively attacking the American circuit was simply lack of length from the tee, plus an inability to fly the ball high through the air. It is true that he has never been (and never tried to be) a big hitter and that he much prefers bouncing and rolling the ball onto firm greens to plunging it into puddings. But there was also another factor behind his limited U.S. forays, that being his belief that there is much more to life than acquiring money and momentary glory by winning golf tournaments. Thomson likes to read deeply, go to the theater and to classical concerts, is profoundly interested in the political, economic, and sociological sciences, and enjoys total changes of scene and culture. On the U.S. tour he found limited opportunity either to indulge these interests or discuss them with like minds. There was too much traveling, too much similarity of environment and habitat, and too much preoccupation with golf. In Europe, particularly in Britain, everything—tournaments and libraries and theaters—was easily to hand. Cultures and topographies change dramatically within a few hundred miles, often less. The golf tour was not so rich and much less formularized and therefore competitive-

ly less intense. And because he was a champion and well known, stimulating nongolfing company abounded whenever he removed his spikes.

Beyond his atypical interests and attitudes, Thomson has two other personality traits that have tended to make him admired only by people who know him not at all or very well. The first is his command of the language—as an official of various Australian golfing bodies his ability to think straight and then cryptically articulate his thoughts has often turned totally hostile meetings around to his point of view. With people who bore him, this sharpness of mind can often lead to a caustic turn of phrase or at least to sharply pointed wit. The second trait that has not always won him undying love, especially among his professional brethren, is an unaffected air of assuredness, nicely captured by the distinguished British writer Pat Ward-Thomas in his 1961 book of essays on

The Masters of Golf. Wrote Ward-Thomas: "I never saw a golfer who seemed so assured of his destiny. There is about him an unmistakable air of success. . . . Thomson took success as though it was his due, not as something exceptional but as part of the natural order of things."

Whether or not it was actually part of the natural order of things for him to become a champion golfer, Thomson certainly made the game look supremely easy. Not since Harry Vardon had a champion played with less visible physical or mental strain. To quote another accomplished British writer (and amateur golfer), Donald Steel: "[There is] always something gay, relaxed and vital about [Thomson] as a person, as well as something incredibly soothing and infectious about the simplicity, grace and rhythm of his play. Nobody that I have seen adheres more strictly to the dictum that the best way to play golf is the simplest, and here, to my mind, lies Thomson's secret."

Why—and how—did Thomson play golf so simply? The answer to why lies in his ultralogical approach to the game. The answer to how lies in the ultra-economical, straightforward, and mechanically frill-free swing that developed from that mental approach.

Although eminently equipped to do so, Thomson has never written a book about the mechanics of playing golf, primarily because he believes that all he would have to say would not occupy more than two sheets of paper. Indeed, his entire literary output about method was contained on two pages of the Sunday *Times* of London in 1960, in the form of an interview with Henry Longhurst. But Thomson has been quoted extensively over the years on his mental approach, and there is no better way to capsulize this than through his own words. Here, sometimes paraphrased, are a few of his more illuminative observations:

- "The most important facets of golf are careful planning, calm and clear thinking, and the ordinary logic of common sense. Golf calls for logical observation. Beyond that the big thing is not power but judgment."
- "You have to like and enjoy what you are doing and where you are doing it. It is a good idea to make up your mind to like a course you are about to play, to like the people you are playing with, and to enjoy the weather, hot or cold."
- "Golf is at least 50 percent a mental game, and if you recognize that it is the mind that prompts us physically, then you can almost say that golf is entirely a mental effort."
- "You think best when you are happiest."
- "You can tell when a golfer is thinking freely. He goes along with his head up and a happy attitude."
- "One's best golf is played when the body is relaxed and the nerves are quiet."
- "Your mind can switch from problem to problem and dispatch them promptly when it is working free from the poison of worry."
- "If you think you are striving to your utmost, then you have nothing in reserve for any adversity that might come your way."
- "Success in golf is 50 percent what you do and 50 percent what other people do. So remember that they may not be doing their 50 percent as well as you are doing yours. Stay calm and alert and recognize your opportunities."
- "Be alert to what is going on around you. You have only to be one stroke better than everyone else to be a winner, and if everyone else plays poorly then you can play poorly too and still win."
- "Every tournament has its climax, its winning moment, and if you are not watchful you will miss it and lose your best chance."
- "There is no incentive to be second. Even in stroke-play there are only winners and losers. If I have two bad opening rounds, I will just walk the rest of the way, and try again to win another time."
- "The difference between winning and losing is always a mental one."

And moving toward the area of technique:

- "Anyone who can walk can play golf. It is a walking game. To be a good golfer you must be a good walker; you must condition your legs."
- "Muscular strength is not particularly advantageous in golf. Control of direction pays off better than length. Unbridled power hitting from the tee courts disaster."
- "Plan your round before you tee off. Plan each hole and stick with that plan."
- "Start building confidence on the first hole, and keep building it as you go forward."
- "Walking with a steady, relaxed rhythm, arms swinging freely, will help your game."
- "Think simply about your swing and you will have a simple, uncomplicated swing. Think simply of drawing the club back, gathering your power, and then hitting the ball precisely forward towards the target."
- "A light, tender, sensitive touch is worth a ton of brawn."

After having "got set up right," Thomson essentially does nothing more than swing the club freely back and through as an extension of his left arm. There is no "manipulation" of the club or body in this swing, but, because of his comparatively "strong" grip, Thomson must clear his left side speedily on the forward swing. This makes space for his arms to traverse his body without the left arm being forced to roll or collapse. As these pictures show, he allows his head to rotate toward the target in tandem with the unwinding of his body sooner than do most top golfers.

On the wings of this astutely philosophical approach Thomson has breezed lightly to victory in a modern-record five British Opens—at least one of them, in 1965, against the cream of American golf—and to countless other triumphs in Australia, New Zealand, the Orient, and Europe. He is invariably at his best when playing the small ball in wind and/or on bone-hard fairways and greens. No matter how badly he is outgunned—and he has been frequently outgunned very badly—he continues to drive for safety and position, often with a three- or four-wood (he won at least two British Opens without ever drawing the driver from the bag). The harder the conditions underfoot or the stronger the wind, the more adept he has been at trundling the ball along the ground, often to within one-putt range from vast distances off the greens. Always he has a game plan and always he sticks to it until his instinct or serenely observant eye tells him that here is *the* oppor-

tunity, the climactic moment, of a tournament. Then, when trying to grasp that opportunity and under the greatest pressure, he will dig into his reserves and produce his most telling strokes.

Like Thomson's mental approach to golf, his swing is conservative rather than spectacular. Indeed, the only truly striking things about it are its extreme simplicity of motion and economy of physical effort. From an early age he has regarded the act of striking a golf ball as an essentially simple exercise, adhered to a handful of commonsense fundamentals, and often said that it is not the swing but golfers themselves that make the game so difficult.

Thomson's first and bedrock fundamental is "getting set up right." Indeed, in Europe at least, he may have been the first top player to place really heavy emphasis on that area of form that today has become the foundation of all sound teaching. To Thomson, getting set

up right is not in the least complicated. All that it basically involves is putting oneself as nearly as possible at address in the position one wants to be in at impact. "Think how your body has to be when you strike the ball and work back from there," he told Henry Longhurst, who later wrote:

"There is no reason why any of us, tall or short, fat or thin, should not get set up right. The stance, about which volumes have been written, is a piece of typical Thomsonian simplicity. Lay a club down on the ground, pointing to the hole, and put your toes against it. That is the end of that.

"Now put the ball opposite your left foot with your left arm and the club in a straight line, as they will be, or should be, as you actually hit the ball. Your arm and the club will now be at right angles to the imaginary club on the ground against which you have lined up your toes. If they are not, you have got the ball—*as almost everyone has*—too far

back. . . .

"We now come to the critical point, the make-or-mar of the entire set-up. Your right arm is not long enough. It won't reach. How are you going to get it on the club? . . . Keeping your right shoulder *back* and tilting your left shoulder *up*, you reach under and attach it to the club.

"I tried this experiment on many willing subjects and in every case, regardless of handicap, they at once looked like a golfer. If it feels awkward at first, it only shows how wrong you were before. You can apply a simple test. When you have got 'set up,' keep your body still, lay the club across your chest and see where it is pointing . . . it will be pointing straight at the flag.

"How far away from the ball should you be? . . . Stand relaxed, leaning slightly forward, with your knees slightly bent and your whole body in balance. Extend the left arm and the club in a straight line, not stiff as a ram-rod and you are now measured off."

These are the only "mechanics" with which Thomson has ever concerned himself in print. And from the setup on, his concepts become even more simplistic. Regarding grip pressure, he told Longhurst: "You should start with a light touch, barely enough to lift [the club] off the ground—so that it feels heavy. It is just like using an axe. You lift it with a light grip, just enough to raise it, and it feels heavy. As you bring it down, your grip tightens without you thinking about it and reaches its tightest at the moment of impact. There is another likeness with golf. Using an axe, you do not *hit* with it; you *accelerate* it. That is exactly what you do with a golf club.

Concerning the takeaway, all Thomson had to say was that the club should be *drawn* straight back, with the weight kept squarely on both feet and no body sway. Concerning the backswing, he suggested forgetting all that the books say about turns and pivots and simply letting nature take its course once the club had been *drawn* smoothly back. Con-

cerning impact, his only axiom was that most of the body—and certainly the head—must remain behind the ball as it is struck "precisely and directly forward."

Based on these principles, Thomson's swing at his prime was compact and comparatively short, with a medium-paced tempo, a "quiet" rhythm, and the hit very much disguised by the swing. To the modern stylistic purist, a couple of its elements might have caused some head shaking. For example, Thomson had a comparatively "strong" grip position, with three knuckles of the left hand clearly showing at address and the right hand in, if anything, an even stronger position (turned farther to his right). His setting of the club and left arm in a very straight line, with the ball positioned well forward, forced his right side very much "under" the left at address, which is fine unless it is carried to a point where the entire upper body is turned well right of target into a closed position, which sometimes happened in Thomson's case and caused hooking. One would also notice at times a slight but definite lateral sway of the hips going back, counterbalanced by a pronounced hip slide coming down. His right side also seemed to "release" (turn into the shot) very early on the downswing, and sometimes as a result his head appeared to rotate toward the target a little too fast for safety.

But who has ever swung a golf club flawlessly? Thomson has certainly hit his quota of scruffy shots, but in the final analysis he has had the one quality that is common to all the great champions of golf: repetitiveness, the ability—mentally and physically—to do the same thing over and over again most of the time, whatever the playing conditions and whatever the competitive pressures.

And therein, you had better believe, lies the key to repetitiveness at the prize table as well as on the course.

DICK AULTMAN

Arnold Palmer

A MATTER OF THE MIND

Anyone who has played serious competitive golf realizes that the fine line between success and failure depends more on the mind than it does on the body. This is true because in golf, perhaps more than in any other sport, the player's personal psychology determines how his physical self will perform.

That golf is primarily a question of mind over matter is proved many times daily in dozens of different ways on any weekend at any course in the world. One need only compare the smooth, unhurried flow of the practice swing with the jerky lunge of the actual stroke to realize how even the ball itself can, unbeknown to the player, trigger mental anxieties that doom the shot. How often has the mere thought of shanking caused even expert players to hit shot after shot more than a full inch off clubface center? What golfer hasn't had those occasional days when he just *knew* that a given putt was going to drop and, more frequently, anticipated that only an extremely fortunate combination of skill and luck could possibly cause the ball to finish anywhere near "gimme" range?

Even the very best teachers of golf have come to realize the frustrating fact that no matter how well they do their job, there will always be the occasional pupil whose mind, for some deep, dark psychological reason, simply will not allow him to execute what he has been told, shown, and physically manipulated to do.

In short, golf at its present stage of development is a game in which there is no sure cure for negative thinking short of, perhaps, prolonged psychiatric analysis, deep hypnosis, electroshock treatment, or prefrontal lobotomy.

There may come a distant day when some progressive university offers a course called something like Golf Psychotherapy E3, an advanced study requirement leading to a Doctorate of Mind Control, DMC. If so, hopefully the professor would include at least one lecture analyzing the case history of one Arnold Daniel Palmer, that great American player of the twentieth century.

Between April, 1958, and April, 1964, Arnold Palmer won seven of the 25 major championships held, finished second or third in

ARNOLD PALMER

Born: September 10, 1929; Latrobe, Pennsylvania

Major victories (through 1974):
U.S. Amateur: 1954
U.S. Open: 1960
British Open: 1961, 1962
Masters: 1958, 1960, 1962, 1964

Arnold Palmer swings with far more vigor than most professionals, yet still with a definite sense of rhythm, or "beat." This rhythm allows time between backswing and downswing for his left leg and foot to change direction and lead all else in his forward swing. The fourth and fifth photos show this leg drive as his left knee shifts dramatically forward while his club continues to swing farther back. Palmer maintains firm left-hand control throughout his swing, as shown by the firm left-wrist position at impact. He also retains his head position until well after the ball is away. One of his biggest assets over the years, however, has been the consistency of his takeaway. It has always been smooth, straight back from the ball—at least for a few inches—and "square," with the clubface always aligned at 90 degrees to the path of clubhead movement. Smooth, Straight, and Square are the three S's of the takeaway that breed swing consistency and excellence.

six others, and leaped tall buildings at a single bound, without ever having to dress up like Superman. He could seemingly *will* the ball into the cup from any distance, especially if a major title were at stake and the TV cameras were beaming in. "If I ever needed an eight-foot putt and everything I owned depended on it," Bobby Jones once said, "I would want Arnold Palmer to putt it for me."

In the years since April, 1964, Palmer has won no major championships, seriously challenged in them only about six times, and, recently, found it more and more difficult to survive the 36-hole cutoff.

Perhaps we should admit that when a golfer approaches and passes forty, the odds against his winning prestige tournaments increase rather rapidly. Palmer, however, was only thirty-four when he won his last major title, the 1964 Masters, an age, for example, when Ben Hogan had yet to win eight of his nine majors. What is even more puzzling is the fact that even today, at forty-five, Palmer, as we shall see, seems to be swinging as

well—some say better—than ever before. Over the years it has been said that Palmer's biggest weakness was his golf swing and his great strength his inner ability to generate a great shot—often a putt—whenever it was needed most. In this chapter we shall first discuss Palmer's swing, pro and con, yesterday and today, as well as his personal psychology, in hopes of ascertaining what has happened to him as a total golfer.

A few years ago *Golf Digest* magazine ran an article in which twenty-five touring professionals each selected the fellow pro he felt had the best swing. Not surprisingly, Sam Snead won the most votes. Gene Littler, though inactive at the time of the polling, received several mentions. Tommy Bolt, himself playing only infrequently, finished fifth behind Snead, Nicklaus, Trevino, and Weiskopf. Palmer, then the winner of more PGA tour events than any other player in history except Snead and Hogan, received only one vote—from Trevino.

Probably Palmer would have fared even

worse in a similar poll of the generally less-informed golfing public. We tend to ascribe greatness to those swings that look smooth, graceful, and effortless—Bobby Jones, for sure, Snead, Littler, Bolt, Boros. A Palmer would never make the list. His swing is too fast, too violent, too lacking esthetically. This is unfortunate because, while Arnold's swing will never be regarded as a model worthy of emulation by the masses, a look behind its façade of unruly vigor reveals many admirable qualities.

Palmer's grip, for instance, deserves top marks. Throughout his years as a junior golfer Arnold held the club with his left hand in a so-called strong position: turned well to his right, wrapped across the top of the club-shaft, so that at address he could look down and see the top knuckles on all four fingers, with his left thumb resting on the right side of the shaft.

In 1948 Lew Worsham, former U.S. Open champion and head pro at Oakmont Country Club near Arnold's Pennsylvania home, encouraged Palmer to adopt a more reliable "neutral" grip, one in which the left thumb sat on top of the shaft so that the back of this hand faced down the target line. Some 500,000 practice shots later, Arnold emerged with the excellent grip he uses today, the palms more or less facing each other and aligning with the clubface itself. His hands are firmly melded together and to the shaft itself in a standard overlap grip. He talks about using firm grip pressure instead of the light pressure advocated by many modern teachers, but if he does hold tighter than most, it's simply because he swings faster than most; he needs the extra control. Partly because of his firm hold, Arnold has never been flippy-wristed. He swings with jackhammer firmness.

Palmer made a second major improvement in his technique about 1962 when he began

136

gradually playing the ball farther forward in his stance, more toward his left foot. No doubt this modification forced him to use more leg action in his downswing, which in turn increased the duration his clubhead moved on line and at ball level through impact.

His firm-wristed, "one-piece" takeaway, with the clubhead moving straight back from the ball for at least a few inches, gives Palmer one of the game's wider swing arcs. His straight left arm and full shoulder turn give him a tremendous coiling of back and shoulder muscles without necessitating an overlong backswing.

Palmer's swing tempo is faster than most people could handle successfully. It works for him, however, largely for three reasons: First, though Palmer's overall pace is fast, there remains a definite "beat" to his swing, a specific "one-two" count with sufficient time between the numbers to let him shift gears and change directions from backswing into forward swing. Second, his unusually strong hands and forearms let Palmer retain control of the club while swinging shorter and faster than most. Thus he avoids the sudden increase in grip pressure—the grabbing—that ruins the rhythm of so many weekend swings. Third, Palmer plays well with a fast swing because of his steady head position: While his head does swivel during his swing, in conjunction with the turning of his shoulders, it remains free of any up-down or left-to-right swaying. In short, it serves as a highly effective anchor that helps to keep him in balance despite the fury of his action.

Another commendable feature of Palmer's swing is his outstanding left-hand, left-side control. Readers will note in the photo of Arnold at impact that the back of his left wrist and his left arm are about as firm as they could possibly be. Byron Nelson has described Palmer's impact position as being "absolutely perfect," and this photo would certainly bear out his opinion. There is no indication whatsoever of right-hand takeover, no breakdown at the back of the left wrist, no bending of the left arm, any of which would reduce both distance and accuracy.

Palmer's excellent left-side control stems in part from his emphasis on pulling with the last three fingers of this hand during the early stages of his downswing. This left-hand pulling effort is aided in large part by his legs. They act as leaders in his downswing, making the first move to his left side. Were his extremely powerful shoulders to lead, his right side and right arm would force his left arm and wrist to break down either before, during, or shortly after impact.

Palmer's legwork is unusual and worthy of mention in any discussion of his game. If readers will look closely at the photos in this chapter, they will notice that Arnold's right leg actually stiffens during the middle stages of his backswing. Such stiffening would inhibit most golf swings, making it all but impossible to drive with the legs during the forward stroke. Palmer, however, recovers from this right-leg stiffening before he completes his backswing, by re-flexing the leg once again well before his club has finished moving back and up. Thus, by the time he's ready to move into his downswing, Arnold's legs are both flexed and ready to lead the action. Thereafter he retains this flex throughout his forward swing.

It has been this writer's observation that in recent years Palmer's leg action and footwork on the forward swing have become, if anything, freer. In this respect his swing has improved with age.

Another improvement noted by various Palmer watchers is that his swing plane, which has always been on the flat side because of the distance he stands from the ball, is now more upright, at least in terms of the plane on which he swings his left arm. This arm, which he once swung back and up on the same plane as his shoulders turned, now swings higher—less around and more skyward.

Arnold's more upright arm swing sets his club into a better position at the top of his backswing, by placing it less behind his body and more above his shoulders, not quite so far away from the target line. Therefore, in returning the clubhead back to that line, he is less likely to shove, push, or throw with his

Palmer reaches farther for the ball at address than do most good golfers. This forces him to swing in a relatively flat plane. However, his excellent left arm extension and full shoulder turn do move his hands higher than might be expected at the top of his swing for a full buildup of leverage. He sets his clubshaft in excellent position at this point so that it parallels his target line. His strong left-hand control—no inward cupping at the back of the left wrist—is also evident at this position. At the top, Arnold, though a fast swinger, does give himself sufficient time for his legs to lead his downswing. This leadership helps deliver the clubhead to the ball from inside to along his intended line and also aids in avoiding the hooked shot that frequently results from a flat swing plane.

right shoulder, arm, or hand. With his hands higher and the club set more "above" the line, all he must do is pull it down and forward with his legs, left side, and left arm and hand. The increased left-side control that results helps decrease his chance of hooking or pulling shots to the left.

Thus it would appear that whatever flaw or flaws might be working to undermine Palmer's once-glorious game, they do not originate or manifest themselves in his full swing.

If there was one word that has characterized all aspects of Arnold Palmer's game, it would be "boldness."

"What other people might consider careless and foolish," he once said, "is my normal game. It is my nature to hit a ball hard and usually to go for everything, and therefore it isn't reckless for me to do so."

In the finals of the 1964 World Match-Play tournament in England, Arnold had just won the 33rd hole from Britain's Neil Coles. That put him two holes ahead with just three to play. The 16th hole on the West Course at Wentworth, with its narrow driving area, seems to beg for a three-wood or one-iron from the tee, especially in the case of a long hitter like Palmer when two holes ahead. In previous matches he had, in fact, teed off on this hole with the one-iron. This time, however, he selected the driver, electing to go for all the cookies. Why? "To have taken a one-iron at that stage would have seemed chicken hearted," Palmer told a friend. "Also I just wanted to see if I could drive it straight in that situation."

Palmer finally won the match, 2 and 1. The incident typified his willingness to accept a challenge, even though it was largely one manufactured in his own mind.

In Palmer's heyday the bigger the challenge, the better he seemed to play. He often performed relatively poorly when he had a big lead—witness his loss of seven strokes over the last nine holes against Billy Casper in the 1966 U.S. Open. He played good golf when he was battling more or less level with other contenders. He played outstanding golf

when he was behind—witness his final-round 65 to pick up nine shots and win the 1960 U.S. Open. The need to attack the course when trailing brought out the boldest and the best in Palmer, just as it had in the case of Hagen.

During the four-year period 1960–1963 Palmer went into the final round of 38 tournaments on the PGA tour with a reasonable chance of winning. He finished on top in 29 of those events—over 76 percent. During the next three-year period, however, he challenged in 22 tournaments and won only six—about 26 percent success.

It was during much of this drought that Palmer self-admittedly shed some of his boldness. Instead of attacking with what always seemed to others reckless abandon, he tried, as he said, to "Hogan it." Instead of banging away with the driver and charging the flagstick on approach shots, he became more cautious, more strategic. He began maneuvering his tee shots with a three-wood; he

tried to cut shots into safe parts of the greens. It was not Palmer golf and it didn't work for him. Whereas as a challenger in the 38 events of 1960–1963 he had shot final rounds of 68 or better 17 times—over 44 percent of the time—in the aforementioned 22 tournaments that followed he bettered 69 only three times.

Only after he was able to recover his normal, bold, attacking style did the Palmer charge come forth once again. In 1967 he challenged in 12 tournaments and averaged 69.17 strokes in fourth-round play, a full shot and a half less per round than in the preceding years.

Today Palmer still plays boldly from tee to green, but there it stops. While his full swing remains intact, the same cannot be said for his putting. There was a time when Arnold continually amazed his adversaries, notably Nicklaus and Player, with his ability to clang the ball into the hole off the back of the cup from any distance or angle, but especially from ten feet in. He'd do it on any type of

green, from the slick roller coasters of Augusta to the slow platforms of Las Vegas. And it didn't seem to matter a whit to him if a missed first putt rolled well past the hole—what was a mere five-footer coming back?

Today Palmer is an inconsistent putter. He has the occasional good day or good two or three days, but then his touch seems to disappear. His short putts don't dive into the center of the cup quite so frequently, but rather slide by to one side. The curling sidehillers often fall below the cup, too cautiously stroked, or skin the high side, slightly pushed or pulled.

When a golfer's putts stop dropping, the normal tendency is to try a new technique. The new method may work in practice but not on the course under pressure. Or it may work for a few holes or a few days and then crumble. Then the search must start again.

Experimenting with one's basic putting style is a hazardous enterprise. It can start a vicious cycle. Too much experimentation leads to overconcern about the "mechanics" of the stroke, which inevitably causes a lessened sense of feel, which leads to bad stroking, which causes a loss of confidence, which necessitates yet more experimentation.

The loss of putting confidence also puts extra burden on the rest of one's game, especially those parts that are weakest. Palmer, for instance, has never been outstandingly skillful with the wedges. Gary Player (though admittedly prone to occasional exaggeration) once told him, "Arnold, your wedge and bunker play has lost you at least eighteen tournaments. In fact, I have personally watched you lose twelve of them."

In his prime Palmer could miss a green, make a half-decent wedge shot, and still expect, with reasonable certainty, to save a par with his putter. Today, when putting badly, he must put the same wedge shot even closer in order to approach the putt with a similar expectation of success.

Loss of confidence on the greens is something that has struck down many mighty golfers. Vardon, Hagen, Cotton, even Jones after he had retired are just four who admitted to the disease. Perhaps Palmer, like the venerable Snead, can find a way to regain putting confidence before its absence totally erodes the rest of his game. To do so represents the biggest challenge of his golfing life. To beat that challenge, to make at least one last charge, will be largely an issue of mind over matter.

The astute American writer Herbert Warren Wind once observed that modern golf has indeed been fortunate to have had such a dedicated and selfless gentleman as Arnold Palmer as its No. 1 hero. Certainly no player of similar magnitude in any sport has given more to his public. A vast portion of Palmer's adult life has been spent onstage, willingly giving handshakes, autographs, and kind words to hundreds of thousands of regulars in his "army."

Perhaps that college professor of the future, teaching Golfing Psychotherapy E3, lecturing on the subject of Arnold Daniel Palmer, will conclude that it was too much golf and too few outside interests that drained Palmer of his ability to continue winning. Perhaps he will merely attribute it to the normal attrition of advancing age. Or perhaps he will say that it was simply a matter of Arnold's giving too much of himself to too many who wanted to share in his glory.

Billy Casper

"PLAY SAFE AND PLAY WITHIN YOURSELF"

Billy Casper is the forgotten star of American golf. His career record—including fifty-one U.S. tour victories—speaks for itself, but his personality does not, and in the brash, noisy, thrusting world of professional sports today that can lead only to obscurity. When a quiet man isn't winning big all the time, as Casper often didn't in his later years, then that obscurity can actually become invisibility.

There have been times when Casper was very visible indeed, physically and in the public eye. When he won the U.S. Open in 1959 at Winged Foot, he was, at 212 pounds, one of the plumpest men ever to capture a major championship. Slimming down to 175 pounds in the late 1960's, via a bizarre diet necessitated by some exotic allergies, gained him much newsprint. His defeat of Arnold Palmer in the 1966 U.S. Open, after Palmer had led by seven shots with eight holes to play in the fourth round and then collapsed even more spectacularly on the last nine of an 18-hole playoff, made banner headlines around the world. A then-record $205,168 in prize money in 1968, making Casper the second golfer to win over $1 million on the U.S.

tour, followed by a 1970 Masters victory, caused many to exalt him to the status of the "Big Three" (Palmer, Nicklaus, and Player) by expanding it to the "Big Four." Among the *cognoscenti*, at least, his Vardon Trophy awards for low scoring average in 1960, 1963, 1965, 1966, and 1968 were especially noteworthy. So were the feats of winning at least one tour event every year between 1955 and 1971 and at least $100,000 each year from 1966 until 1971. Even after he began to slump in 1972, the size of his family (nine children, six of them adopted) and his increasingly missionistic allegiance to the Mormon faith made him a subject of periodic interest to sportswriters and of some wonder to their public.

But the hard truth of the matter is that even when at his best, Casper never really received full recognition of his formidable golfing skills. The prime reason, of course, was his outward lack of personal razzmatazz (he is actually one of the most congenial, sincere, and—among friends—amusing people in professional sports). Another reason was his gray strategical approach to the game. Of

BILLY CASPER

Born: June 24, 1931; San Diego, California

Major victories (through 1974):
U.S. Open: 1959, 1966
Masters: 1970

Casper is generally regarded as one of the finest putters in golf history, but—illustrative of the individuality of putting—his technique is totally different from that of many great putters. Unlike, for example, the epitome of "strokers," Bobby Locke, Casper is a "rap" or "tap" putter. Using almost nothing but his wrists to swing the putter, he takes it seemingly straight back with an apparent face-hooding action, then raps or taps the ball crisply with a limited follow-through.

all the American superchampions, Casper has played his golf the most cautiously and conservatively.

"Play safe and play within yourself" is a credo from which he has never himself departed in competition or in his voluminous writings advising others how to master golf. His texts ring with passages like "Golf is a game of thought and management, with a premium on placement, accuracy, judgment and finesse." "Don't be too impatient or greedy. Consider the variables, the margins for error, then go with the percentage shots." "Play every shot so that the next one will be the easiest that you can give yourself." "Play easily, smoothly and unhurriedly. Don't swing too hard or go for shots with little chance of success." "Know your limitations and play within them."

All excellent advice for the everyday golfer, but hardly a clarion call to the masses at a time when Palmer was crashing and grimacing to throbbing triumphs, Nicklaus was driving the ball 300 miles, and Player was gobbling raisins and yogurt and whirling himself off his feet trying to stay up with them.

To any handicap golfer who is ready to put his common sense ahead of his muscles and who has seen Casper play, it should, however, be apparent that he is in many respects a far better model than the three champions who have so regularly overshadowed him. Magnificent as their games are, there is no doubt that either sheer physical strength or special physiological attributes have contributed mightily to each of these golfers' prowess. Casper patently lacks such special assets and is, in fact, physically very much your average country-club *Homo sapiens* (apart, perhaps, from his abstemiousness). What Casper does with a golf club should thus be within the physical capabilities of any passably healthy, reasonably active member of society, and for that reason it is worth looking at his swing in some detail.

Like so many of the methods discussed in this book, the basic character of Casper's swing derives from the way in which he holds the club. Although he states in his writ-

ings that he endeavors to align the palm of the left hand parallel to the clubface—which would face the back of the hand to the target—Casper actually sets his left hand well on top of the shaft in what is generally regarded as a "strong" position. In order for his hands to work as a unit, rather than in opposition to each other, he then must (and does) place the right hand on the club in a comparably "strong" position; in other words, fairly well under the shaft. In other respects his grip is orthodox, with the club pressed firmly against the butt of the left hand by the last three fingers, the shaft running across the roots of the fingers of the right hand, and a normal overlap linking the hands together.

The basic pattern of Casper's grip stems from the fact that he first began to play golf at an age (five) when he was insufficiently strong to hold the club other than with his hands turned well to the right. This generated, as he matured, a pronounced right-to-left pattern of shotmaking. Although at one period of his professional career he did work on a fading technique (as an antidote to violent hooking), his inherent and today consciously preferred shape of shot is a draw. And, indeed, because of his determination never to sacrifice control for distance, it is difficult to conceive that he could consistently have moved the ball far enough by hitting it from left to right to have compiled his illustrious record.

Although they have usually acquired the habit at a much later stage of life than Casper did, many handicap golfers instinctively favor his "strongish" grip pattern and for the same initial reason: It allows undeveloped or untrained hands to grasp the club relatively securely and to swing it with a feeling of authority. So long as they then build a swing around that grip, as Casper has, all is roses and honey, because out of that compatibility will come the right-to-left flight pattern that is so valuable in distance terms to most amateurs. Unfortunately most do not so construct a swing, and therefore we shall shortly use Casper as a model to show then how they could. But before getting into that, let us just

touch on one other basic element of his swing that has grown from his mental approach that also could help many a struggling amateur.

Casper's determination always to play safely and well within himself (never exerting more than 85 percent of his available muscular capability, he says) is reflected in his body action as well as in his maximum-distance-for-minimum-effort grip. A pronounced feature of the modern, power golf swing is an exceptionally full shoulder turn on the backswing—usually well beyond 90 degrees. Casper's shoulders certainly pivot, but rarely more than 90 degrees. He is, in short, much more of an "arms and hands" swinger and less a "shoulder turner" than any of his "Big Three" adversaries. This economy of shoulder motion is, of course, in his case primarily a control factor, and it can offer the same advantage to the physically well-developed but wild-hitting handicap player. To the less physically well-equipped golfer, it could actually represent the best possible way to tackle the game.

Now, having said a moment ago that Casper essentially swings the club with his arms and hands rather than with his shoulders, let us stress that the *real* key to his highly effective use of a "strong" grip lies in his leg action, and quickly resolve any confusion in the reader's mind by once again explaining why good legwork is essential to every strong-gripping golfer (the matter was previously touched on in the Gene Sarazen chapter and will be again in considering Lee Trevino).

To do so, we must clearly understand two incontrovertible facts of golf. The first is that, given comparable swing patterns, the stronger a golfer's grip, the less his club will face to the right of the target as it approaches the ball during the final stages of the downswing (the less "open" or more "closed" it will be, to use the common terminology). The second fact is that a golfer's hands, unless and until they are trained to do otherwise, will instinctively realign themselves square to the target at impact—just as one hand used in a slapping motion instinctively arrives square at its target irrespective of the alignments it has passed through while swinging back and forth.

As photographs clearly show, and the success of their shots clearly proves, the hands of *all* good golfers who grip the club "strongly" have been trained to swing to a greater or lesser degree "sideways on" through impact—in other words, with more or less the *edge*—the butt—rather than the back of the left hand aligned toward the target as the ball is struck. Sarazen's hands did this pronouncedly. Because they have somewhat less "strong" grips than Sarazen, Casper and Trevino do it less so, but still noticeably. If they did not—if these players allowed their hands instinctively to revert to a square-to-target impact position—then the face of the club would be severely closed and every shot they hit would be a catastrophic duck hook.

Delivering the clubface squarely to the ball thus aligned, however, is unfortunately not simply a matter of training the hands (although such training is imperative). Man being built the way he is, for such a motion to become *anatomically* possible, the body *must* get sufficiently *out of the way* of the hands and arms to allow them to swing *past* it without being forcibly realigned. When that doesn't happen—when the body remains "in the way of" the hands and arms in the final part of the downswing—then *anatomically* one of two things is *forced* to happen to the "strong" gripper: His left elbow must bend grotesquely or, and much more commonly, his right hand must roll violently over the left as the club meets the ball. In the first case, of course, the club is severely decelerated, resulting in miserable distance. In the second case, the clubface is severely closed, resulting in horrendous inaccuracy.

How does the good strong-gripping golfer "get himself out of his own way" during the downswing? Very simply, by using his legs to "clear" (turn) his hips toward the target well *ahead* of the arrival in the impact position of his hands, arms, and the club. And among present-day stars few make this move more pronouncedly or more effectively than Billy Casper.

We will better understand the precise mechanics of this critical lower-body motion if

In addition to his strategical approach being the most conservative of the modern American champions, Casper also has the most economical swing. Like Peter Thomson's, his action is basically an arm swing with the club simply going along as an extension of the left arm. Also like Thomson, and because of his comparably "strong" grip, Casper must clear his hips speedily starting the downswing to give his arms room to swing freely past his body. He does so with a pronounced—but smooth and controlled—targetward shift or shuttle of the legs and hips at the start of his downswing.

we examine it in context with the motions that precede it.

Casper's swing is actually one of the most mechanically simple in the modern game. All he does in gathering himself to hit each shot is take the club in his hands as previously described; stand comfortably to the ball in the prescribed manner; and swing the club, straight back at first and then up and around with his arms, without manipulating it by independently twisting his hands and wrists, all the while maintaining a fixed body axis and a steady head. The facts that his shoulders and hips turn, that his left knee bends in toward the ball, that his wrists cock, that his left hand, wrist, and forearm are all in line at the top, etc., are all *results*—not *causes*—of this uncomplicated, stressless swinging of the arms. Here, in short, is a swinging motion about as close as you can get to the simple action of the pendulum.

Once Casper has thus "gathered" himself to strike the ball, he must do two things. Like all other golfers, he must initiate the downswing in a manner that will allow centrifugal force to accelerate the clubhead to its maximum velocity close to the point of impact. And, in his case, because of his strong grip, he must place particular emphasis on making clear passage for his hands to swing freely past his body without the wrists being forced to roll over prematurely or the left elbow to crumble in the impact zone.

Casper achieves both ends through classical lower-body action. First, as his left arm nears its maximum backswing movement, he drives or thrusts or slides or shuttles (choose your own word) his knees *directly* toward the target. This is not the violent or lurching motion that one sees so often at the driving range, but a smooth, controlled, *springy* movement of the legs that is certainly deliberate but is also the natural physical *reflex* response to the coiling of his body during the "gathering" process.

Next comes the master move for the strong gripper, the motion without which Casper probably would have remained in the navy after his period of conscription. In the fraction of a second after his legs have begun

149

their targetward motion, Casper's left hip begins to turn *behind* him—to clear passage for his hands and arms. Once that motion has begun, it continues, smoothly and in concert with his continuing targetward leg thrust, *right up to, through, and well beyond impact.*

At the moment of impact, as the back of his left hand faces 45 degrees right of target, his hips face 45 degrees left of target. He is, in short, entirely "out of his own way"—to such an extent, in fact, that his left hand can continue its sideways motion, without the right hand moving over it, until well after the club reaches horizontal on the through-swing.

And that, if you are blessed (or maybe as you see it, cursed) with a strong grip, is how you too *must* use your body to have any chance of delivering the clubface fast and consistently square to the ball.

Billy Casper has a chameleonlike quality as a golfer that may not always be apparent to the casual fan. The most conservative of the great modern players from tee to green, he becomes one of the boldest the moment he steps onto a putting surface. Underpinning

that often winning switch in character is one of the finest senses of touch and one of the most effective putting strokes in modern golf. Like Palmer in his heyday, Casper in his best years could be an aggressive putter from a long distance because he knew he could always hole out what was left.

It is a strange fact of golf that the two men most generally claimed to have been the greatest putters day in, day out in history, Bobby Locke and Billy Casper, actually used totally dissimilar stroking techniques (although they shared phenomenal ability to "read" greens). Even stranger is the fact that both techniques would have to be regarded as "unorthodox" in a number of mechanical respects. If this proves anything at all, which it probably doesn't, it is the truth of the belief that putting is 99.9 percent inspiration and .1 percent method.

In preparing to stroke the ball, Casper is unexceptional. He uses the most popular of putting grips, the reverse-overlap (forefinger of left hand wrapped across fingers of right hand), with the palms turned slightly upward

and the thumbs down the top of the shaft. He aligns parallel to the starting line of the putt with his feet and body, with the feet about a foot apart (a widish stance for better balance) and the knees "pressed" in toward each other slightly as a means of anchoring himself. He leans comfortably over from the hips with only a slight flex at the knees, his eyes directly over the ball and a "relaxed" (tension-free) feeling in his neck. At this point his one departure from the norm (assuming there is a putting norm) is to rest the back of his left hand against the inside of his left thigh, which, of course, necessitates his standing very close indeed to the ball.

Unlike Locke, who was pronouncedly a "stroke" putter, Casper is categorically a "hit" or "tap" putter. He believes that the function of the left hand is primarily to keep the club in position while the right hand very positively taps or raps the ball. Solid striking of the ball on the "sweet spot" of the putter-face is critical to him, and to facilitate this, he looks very deliberately at the top of the ball throughout the stroke and continues to peer down at the spot the ball occupied for a few seconds after it has departed. Freedom from tension in the neck, he believes, is a great safeguard against moving the head or taking one's eyes off the ball.

Casper's actual stroke derives from his desire to move himself and the putter as little as possible to roll the ball the desired distance. He achieves that goal by virtually eliminating the arms from the stroke, except on longish putts. His stroke on short- and middle-distance putts is actually made simply by breaking the wrists, away from the target going back and toward the target going through, with, in the middle, a distinct and conscious "rapping" of the ball by the right hand, felt, he says, predominantly in its firm-gripping thumb and forefinger.

So "compact" a putting action is in itself

unusual, most golfers (especially the more nervy ones) requiring a more flowing motion in order both to create and gauge the momentum of the strike. Even more unusual, however, is the actual swing path and clubface alignment of Casper's stroke.

Almost from time immemorial, it sometimes seems, golfers have been admonished that they could expect to putt well only if they: (1) kept the putterhead low to the ground throughout the stroke; (2) swung it through the ball traveling along the target line by delivering it from *inside* that line; and (3) kept the clubface square to this swing path throughout the stroke.

Casper does only one of these things. The only way anatomically one can get a putter back purely by hinging the wrists, without any arm swing, is to lift it off the ground pendulum fashion, which is exactly what Casper does. In doing that he also does not swing the club inside the target line, but rather directly along *a backward extension* of the target line, which visually gives the impression that the clubhead is actually moving *outside* the line. Finally, however, he does keep the putterface square to its line of swing during the stroke by hooding the face with a slight "turning under" of the left wrist as it breaks backward, then reverses that motion on the forward stroke so that the putterface is actually *opening* to the target line after the ball has been struck.

Different? It certainly is. Worth trying? Well, as the great British golf teacher John Jacobs is fond of saying, "If you can get the ball in the hole regularly by standing on your head, then keep right on—and don't ever listen to advice from anyone." But if your putting is less than you'd like it to be, maybe Casper's method would hit the spot.

Of one thing you can definitely be sure. Somewhere between his system and Bobby Locke's inside-to-outside stroke there's got to be a way for everyone!

Gary Player

TO BE THE GREATEST, YOU NEED AN EDGE

Some say that you can tell a great deal about a man by the books he reads. In the case of many golfers who play the game for a living, we must look elsewhere for social indicators, their literary standards falling somewhere between the daily sports pages and *TV Guide*.

Gary Player's reading tastes, however, indicate a penchant that goes far beyond box scores and Archie Bunker. Four books in particular have, at various times, strongly influenced his life-style: the Bible, *The Power of Positive Thinking, Imitations of Christ,* and *Yoga and Health.*

These books reflect Player's intensive efforts over many years to improve himself as both a human being and, as a direct result, as a golfer. Gary is a man looking for an edge on life, especially if it puts him one up on those with whom he competes for his daily bread. Chances are that Player would have become a purist even if he had followed his father's footsteps into the gold mines of South Africa, but his avowed goal from the start—to become the greatest golfer in the history of the game—has made his regimen of hard work

and self-denial even more rewarding.

Any discussion of Gary Player the golfer must begin and end with a clear understanding of his unflagging determination—almost compulsion—to become the best. In this chapter we shall thus first look closely at his golf swing and then discuss the nonswing factors that have brought him at least in sight of his ambition.

As is true of so many golfers, the evolution of Player's overall swing is directly related to the evolution of his grip. He started with a "hooker's grip," in which both hands were turned well to his right on the clubshaft. The fact that he is short in stature and thus stands farther from the ball than most further accentuated his tendency to hook badly on occasion.

Shortly after first visiting England as a teenager and noting the comparatively "weak" grip of British star Dai Rees, Player went to the other extreme and adopted a slicer's grip. Instead of showing all four knuckles of his left hand at address, he turned this hand so far to the left that no knuckles were visible. As might be expected, the shape of

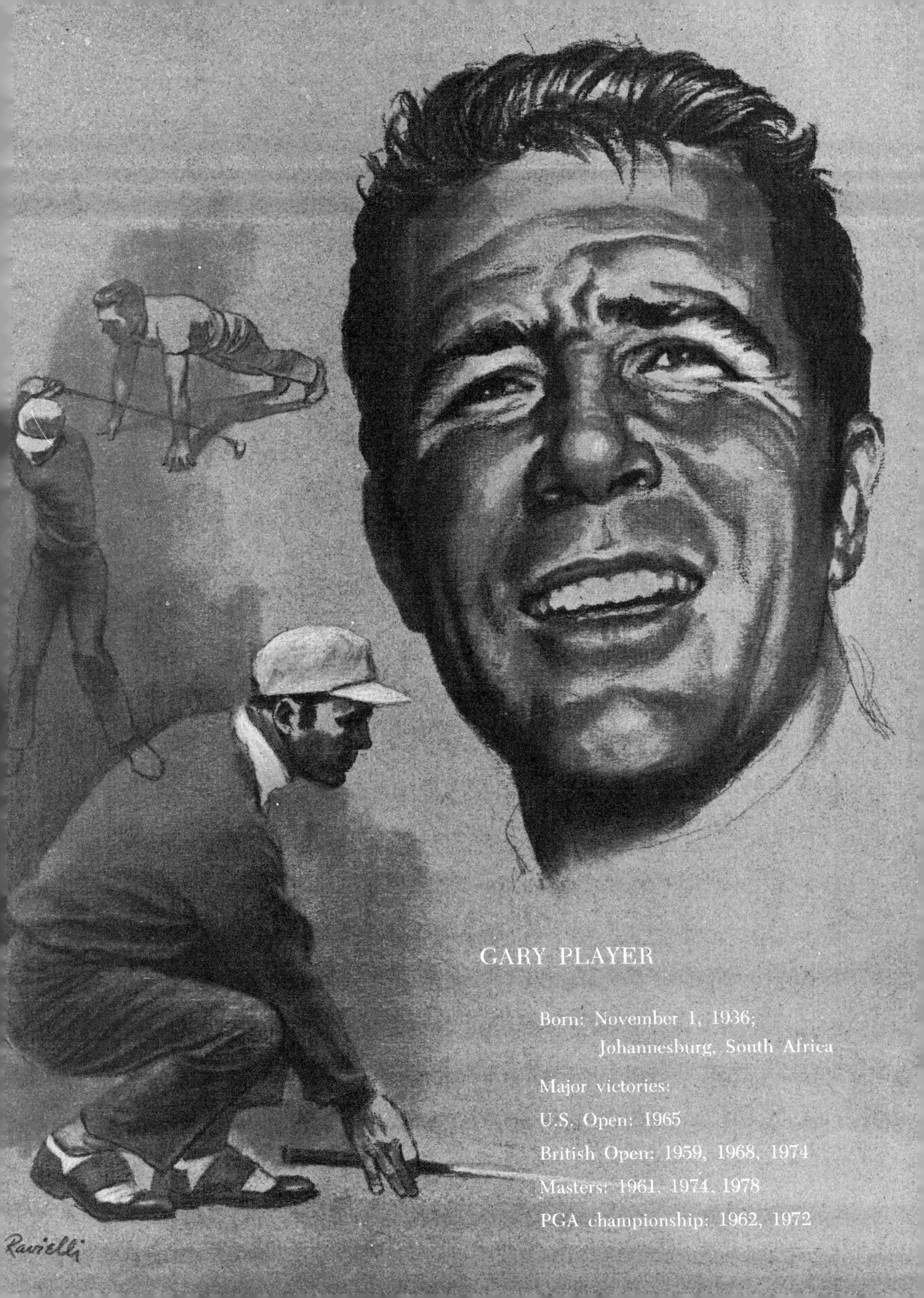

GARY PLAYER

Born: November 1, 1936;
          Johannesburg, South Africa

Major victories:

U.S. Open: 1965

British Open: 1959, 1968, 1974

Masters: 1961, 1974, 1978

PGA championship: 1962, 1972

Gary Player's swing indicates a flexibility and suppleness far beyond that of most humans. Even more remarkable is the fact that he achieves this flexibility despite the obvious arm tension created at address by his extreme reaching for the ball. Note particularly the unusual width of Player's backswing, the full extension of his left arm, and the huge degree of shoulder turn—all accomplished despite a relatively small hip turn and a somewhat flat arm plane. The result is a supertight coiling of muscles and a tremendous buildup of potential energy, which he retains until late in his downswing. The only thing that hurts his normally excellent accuracy is his occasional failure to clear his left hip fully during his downswing. Sliding and blocking with his hips sometimes cause him to push shots to the right of target, but more frequently low hooking results as his hands react to the inside-out clubhead path by closing the clubface.

his shots reversed. In comparing Gary's game with that of his fellow countryman Bobby Locke, the ultimate right-to-left player, one British writer observed in 1956: "When Locke's on the tee the cry is 'fore on the right!' When Player shoots it's 'fore on the left!'"

Player's slice grip eventually forced him to find some compensation that would allow him to draw the ball or at least hit it fairly straight. This compensation was to swing on a very flat plane and bow the back of his left wrist outward slightly at the top of the backswing, thus setting the clubface into a somewhat closed position.

It was Ben Hogan who detected the cause of Gary's flat swing and suggested he again modify his grip slightly by placing his left thumb down the top of the shaft at address instead of down the top-left side. This change made it easier for Player to draw the ball and thus eliminated the need for him to swing so flat going back and to close the clubface by bowing his left wrist.

Today Gary positions his *right* hand a bit farther to the left than most, as an antihook measure, but still sets his left thumb down the top of the shaft as prescribed by Hogan. His swing is still flatter than most, but more upright than it was in the late 1950's. The back of his left hand, wrist, and forearm align straight, not only at the top of his swing but thereon all the way through impact and, on most shots, to the finish. His ability to maintain this straight-line relationship throughout his forward swing, with no inward collapsing at the back of the wrist, attests to his ability to lead with his legs, pull with his left arm and hand, and accelerate both arms freely down and forward as he moves into and through impact. Any right-hand takeover (casting from the top) or slowing down of his arms would force the back of his left wrist to collapse inward. He would then not achieve

the excellent extension beyond impact that he now enjoys. His clubhead would, instead, swing upward and inward too abruptly.

Gary still complains of occasional hooking and seems to come up with a new remedy about once every three months. The hooking occurs when he fails to clear his left hip—turn it to the left—fully during his downswing. Instead of turning his hips, he sometimes slides them too far to the left laterally—"blocks out," as they say—a move that forces his hands and wrists to release a shade too soon and throw the clubface into a closed position during impact.

The need to clear the left hip is particularly important in Player's case because of the way he turns his shoulders on a relatively flat plane during his backswing, largely because his lack of height necessitates his standing a goodly distance from the ball. Then, however, instead of returning the shoulders on a similar plane on his downswing, Gary drops his right shoulder dramatically downward. With this shoulder and his arms thus swing-

ing from so far inside the target line—from "behind himself," if you will—extreme suppleness is required for his left hip to turn freely to the left.

To carry the matter one step further, in this writer's opinion it is Player's head position that dictates the extreme lowering of his right shoulder during his downswing. If the reader will note Gary's head position at address in the accompanying photos, he will see that a line running across his eyes would more or less parallel his target line. A similar observation of Player's head position just prior to impact clearly shows that by that point in the swing, a line across his eyes would extend far to the right of target. If one accepts the premise that what we see tells our subconscious what path we should swing along, it becomes apparent that Player has turned his head into a position from which his eyes are telling him to swing back to the ball along a path from far inside his target line. For normal humans such a swing path would push shots far to the right until an involuntary reaction set

in of throwing the clubface closed to the left. Gary, however, is supple enough to clear his left hip soon enough to swing the clubhead back on line by impact—at least most of the time. When he fails, to avoid pushing to the right, he overreacts with his hands and hooks to the left.

This is not to imply that Player has a bad golf swing, but is merely an explanation of what basically causes his problems on those rare occasions when he gets into big trouble. His swing is otherwise magnificent in most respects, especially as an example of how to generate absolute maximum distance while maintaining outstanding accuracy. Player not only drives the ball farther than most physically bigger professionals but probably—when in peak form—misses fewer greens than anyone since Hogan.

Player's distance stems largely from his unusual suppleness, born of constant physical conditioning. This allows him to make an extremely wide and longish backswing—note especially the full extension of his straight left arm and the unusually full coiling of his shoulders—while resisting with his legs; not that his left heel never leaves the ground. The result is a tremendous buildup of leverage during the backswing that is even further increased—rather than released—early in his downswing.

Gary sets the stage for his left-arm extension—his swing's width—by pushing the clubhead straight back from the ball, along the target line, an extremely long way. He maintains this extension throughout his backswing by turning his chin slightly to his right, a move that makes it easier for his shoulders to coil fully. Meanwhile his legs remain rather immobile, his right knee remains slightly flexed, and his weight remains largely on the instep of his right foot. This lower-body resistance effectively restricts his hip turn and thus further accentuates the stretching of muscles across his back and down his left side resulting from his full shoulder turn.

Player's muscle stretching increases early in his downswing as his left knee shifts to the left while his arms and club are still swinging back and up. Then he actually increases his wrist-cock by slowly pulling with his left hand—instead of throwing with his right—as he starts the forward swinging of his arms. Thereafter his arms continue to accelerate forward freely with no apparent effort either to inhibit or to help the free lowering and squaring of the clubhead through the ball. Again, while his arms freely swing the clubhead forward and gradually turn the clubface to the left after impact, the back of his left wrist remains straight and firm throughout the follow-through.

"I feel I swing as hard as I can," Gary has frequently said. "Some say they don't, but I think all the players on the pro tours hit the ball as hard as they can and still keep it in play.

"I would advise a young boy or girl starting out to do the same," he adds. "It's simple to go from a hard swing to an easy one, but if you've been an easy swinger it's difficult to start hitting the ball hard. More often it goes the other way—an easy swinger develops a lazy stroke as he gets older."

Gary's ability to swing the golf club has been directly affected by his lifelong determination to become the world's greatest golfer. In his particular case the factors spawned by this tremendous drive to excel overshadow even his actual swing technique and thus merit discussion here.

Practice. Player doubts that any golfer in history, except perhaps Ben Hogan, worked harder on his game. Hogan himself was quoted in 1958 as saying that, "I know how hard he [Player] has worked. He's doing what I've been advocating for a long time. That is working hard on fundamentals, and then working the fundamentals into his game."

The late George Blumberg, a close friend of Gary's from South Africa, once recalled seeing him as a teenager practicing bunker shots at the Virginia Park course in Johannesburg. It was six o'clock in the morning. About noon that same day Blumberg happened to pass the same bunker. Gary was still blasting away.

Gary Player is rated best out of sand by many of his fellow professionals. Three things contribute greatly to his success. First, he opens the clubface slightly at address so that it faces right of target and further fans it open as he cocks his wrists early in his backswing. Second, he uses his legs aggressively in his downswing. Third, he attacks the sand with a sharply downward blow. Maintaining the open clubface allows him to swing the club sharply down to the sand without fear of the club's leading edge cutting in too deeply and leaving the shot far short. This sharply descending angle of attack helps assure that the clubhead will not bounce off the sand and into the back of the ball. The strong leg drives produce a long cut of sand. He can plan for it to enter a full six inches behind the ball and thus avoid any chance of picking the shot too cleanly.

"I'd hit shots into the sand," Player recalls, "and then I'd play them to the green. I wouldn't let myself quit until I'd sunk three shots. Sometimes I'd be in there until it got dark."

At other times Player would practice chipping until he'd holed out 10 times. If he wanted to work on hitting the ball low, he'd punch shots under a tree limb until he could do so 10 times in a row. If the 10th shot clipped the branch, he started over.

"A golfer should never quit using a certain club because he believes he cannot use it well," Player once told this writer. "It's best to practice that club until you can master it.

If you ignore your inability, chances are the swing errors that are causing the trouble with that club will creep into the rest of your game."

Gary played his first round of golf at age fourteen (he parred the first three holes) and turned professional at seventeen. Three years later he beat the best British professionals in winning the highly regarded Dunlop Masters tournament in England. His swing in 1956 was too flat, his stance too wide, and his head position downright dangerous—turned toward the target well before impact—but he'd learned enough shots to score 70-64-64-72—270 (plus 68 in the play-off

with host pro Arthur Lees) at Sunningdale. He'd even learned how to play in the rain, having purposely practiced through downpours in South Africa in preparation for conditions in Britain.

Attention to detail. Few top-level golfers in history have been as meticulous about their games as Gary Player. Readers may recall the scene in the 1974 British Open when his ball became lost on the 71st hole. With a six-shot lead and less than two holes to play, the possibility of his blowing the title seemed highly remote. Even if the ball were not discovered, he could all but wedge his way home and still win. But Gary knew, of course, that the

rules allow only five minutes' hunting time. Any searching beyond that limit warrants an additional two-stroke penalty. Thus he borrowed a wristwatch before beginning the search. Nothing would be left to chance.

Such incidents are typical of Player. No top-level golfer, with the notable exception of Jack Nicklaus, is more precise in considering all factors involved in a given shotmaking situation, even if it be a mere two-foot putt. Gary once expounded to this writer on reasons for looking closely at the actual hole before putting. These included:

—Checking the depth of soil above the cup itself (if the cup is set upright so the flagstick doesn't lean, more soil will appear above it on the high side).

—Checking for unusual wearing of grass on one side of the cup (this will be the low side, he says, because more putts will have rolled into it than against the grass on the high side).

—Checking for dead blades of grass on one side of the cup (a good indication that the grain runs cross-cup in that direction because the cutting of the hole necessarily severed the root system of those particular blades).

Only an inquiring mind like Player's, fueled by the desire to gain an edge no matter how slight, would conceive of, absorb, and

apply such detail. He was not out of character, therefore, when early in his career he filmed and studied movies of players like Snead, Hogan, and Cotton. It is not out of character today that he will give at least outward attention to almost any improvement suggestion, whether it comes from a reliable instructor or merely a friendly type in the gallery who happened to have "noticed something when you were hitting those practice balls."

Physical fitness. Player realized as a youth that to become the world's greatest golfer he'd need to get everything he could out of his small body and ever since has been con-

ditioning himself accordingly, running miles daily to build his legs and his endurance, pushing himself up with his fingertips—70 to 80 times a day—to strengthen his hands, arms, and back (later he would minimize upper-body exercise for fear of losing suppleness).

After finishing sixth in the 1960 Masters, he reflected on a comment made by Peter Thomson. The Australian had said that he did not think he (Thomson) could ever win at Augusta because he wasn't long enough to reach the par-five holes in two shots. Player decided he faced the same problem, consulted a body builder on ways to add strength,

added half an inch to the length of his clubs, and otherwise changed his swing to generate the necessary extra yardage. The next year he reached all four par-fives in two and won the tournament.

During the 1960's this writer helped Player with two instructional books. Invariably the taping sessions were held in his motel room starting about 6 A.M., partly because often he was still functioning on South African time, partly because the rest of his day and evening were generally filled with golf and business functions. At various times during these meetings I was encouraged by Gary to:

—Eat lots of fruit (there was always plenty in his room).

—Eat my bacon burned (to avoid digestive problems).

—Avoid showering with soap (bad for the body's natural oils).

—Take wheat-germ pills ("Great for your love life").

—Stand on my head (to improve mental alertness through better circulation).

—Jump rope (to add distance through faster footwork).

While I chose not to follow most of these inspirational suggestions (though I did give

the wheat germ a good chance), I am convinced that such habits have contributed greatly to Player's success as a golfer, not only by directly improving him physically but also by giving him the confidence and psychic well-being that goes with a clear mind and a strong body.

"I really enjoy exercise," he once confided. "Sometimes after a bad day on the course I come home tired and discouraged. But then I do my exercises before going to bed and I feel clean and strong again . . . [or] sometimes I'll deny myself something I really want, like ice cream. This does wonders for me both mentally and physically."

Concentration. "During every major championship I've won," Player has said, "I concentrated so hard that I played rounds without knowing my score. I've often been in a 'don't know who I am' sort of daze—total relaxation with complete control."

Just as Player keeps pushing his body into better service, so too he demands the utmost from his mind, almost to the point of self-hypnosis. He tells of an incident just before the 1965 U.S. Open at Bellerive Country Club near St. Louis, Missouri. He was passing by a board on which the names of former Open winners were lettered in gold. The last entry on the list was "1964—Ken Venturi."

"I'd been past that board before," Player said, "but this time I looked up at it and I saw—I mean I really *saw*—my own name under Venturi's. There it was in gold lettering just like his: '1965—Gary Player.'"

A few days later Player's name was, in fact, lettered in gold on that board.

Another form of mental gymnastics that Player performs is convincing himself that the golf course where he happens to be competing is an outstanding example of architecture and conditioning. At times this appears to be the height of self-deception, but it is merely his way of establishing friendly working conditions for himself. It helps him avoid the trap of self-pity, the attitude of "Who could possibly play good golf on this cow pasture?" that further escalates so many tournament golfers' scores when the going gets tough. It is also an attitude that endears him to tournament sponsors and ensures a friendly gallery from among the membership.

Competitiveness. This is a factor of success in golf that is difficult, if not impossible, to learn. It involves attitudes and behavior patterns that were well established in the individual long before he ever swung a club, and it seems to reach an especially high level in players of small physical stature—Player, Sarazen, Hogan, to name just three.

Some years ago this writer asked a fellow competitor what, in his opinion, was the No. 1 reason for Gary's success. His simple answer is still clear: "Gary is a great success," he said, "because he likes to beat people."

Player is, indeed, one of the most competitive individuals ever to play the game. He has, for instance, added tens of thousands of dollars to his prize winnings over the years simply by never letting down when having a poor tournament or a bad round. He tries his utmost on every shot, whether he be contending for first prize or fiftieth position. It is on these latter occasions, though infrequent, that the effects of his mental and physical preparedness pay the highest dividends.

Though it will never come to pass, the only true way to determine who is indeed the "world's greatest golfer" would be to stage a gigantic tournament in which all leading contenders would play each other, head to head, at least a dozen times in all the various golfing areas of the world. The winner—the man who finished ahead by the most holes—would necessarily have: (1) a well-rounded game that would stand up under all types of course and weather conditions; (2) an intensely competitive spirit; and (3) the physical and mental stamina to sustain Nos. 1 and 2. In this writer's opinion, the winner of such a contest, if held in the mid 1970's, would be Gary Player.

Lee Trevino

FIVE WRONGS ADD UP TO ONE IMMACULATE RIGHT

The golfer, perhaps more than any other sports competitor, is the unknowing *victim,* rather than the *captain,* of his fate. Unlike, say the tennis player, the bowler, or the pool shark, he competes in an arena of varying dimensions over varying terrain. He plays in varying weather on widely varying types of turf. He must choose correctly from a wide selection of tools to strike a ball that rests in a wide variety of lies.

While all these variables add to the challenge—and the charm—of golf, none has as much influence over how a person actually swings the club as does the pattern of his previous shots. Our past shots force a reaction in the way we hold the club, position our bodies, and swing. Our past shots *demand* that we play future shots a certain way.

Usually we are not aware that we are changing our swing to compensate for past blunders. The reaction is subconscious and subtle: The chronic slicer may, for instance, gradually and unknowingly start aligning himself farther and farther to the left of target; the chronic hooker farther and farther to the right. When we *do* react consciously to correct for bad shots, all too often we choose the wrong remedy, either because we don't realize the true cause of the problem or because we actually employ a cure that is vastly different from the one we think we are applying.

It is this writer's contention that the vast majority of golfers fall into one of two classes. There are those who have built swings designed to correct for having a preponderance of shots finish to the right of target, and there are those whose swings have evolved to offset hitting trouble on the left. An experienced player may go through periods when he's trying to cure slicing and other periods when he's trying to cure hooking, but he will always do so within a basic swing framework that was ordained long ago, during its formative stage, as a reaction to a pattern of shots that *finished* either left or right.

It is my further contention that those players who developed a basic pattern designed to keep shots from finishing on the left generally are much more fortunate than those whose swings evolved as a reaction to finishing on the right. (It has often been said that

164

LEE TREVINO

Born: December 1, 1939; Dallas, Texas

Major victories:
U.S. Open: 1968, 1971
British Open: 1971, 1972
PGA championship: 1974, 1984

While several key aspects of Lee Trevino's swing are better shown from a different camera angle (as seen later in this chapter), this face-on view does point up his rather "strong" grip position at address, his early wrist cock, and full left-arm extension during his backswing and, above all, his unusually strong leg action during his forward swing. This leg action helps assure an on-line clubhead path through impact and, along with his firm left-hand control, all but eliminates any chances of his closing the clubface prior to its releasing of the ball. An additional bonus of Trevino's somewhat flat swing plane, excellent leg action, and firm left-hand control is the fact that his clubhead remains at ball level considerably longer than normal through the hitting area.

all great players suffered through the problems of hooking at some time in their early development. Hogan, Snead, Nelson, Palmer, and Player are but five such who come to mind.)

There are good reasons why hooking, rather than slicing, creates reactions that produce better players in the end. For one, the right-hander whose early shots finish right of target faces the challenge of making his shots go more to the left. To accomplish this he invariably relies on his right hand, arm, or shoulder to throw or shove the club in that direction as he strikes the ball. The fact that, being right-handed, he is already right-side oriented makes this tendency feel even more natural. Thus he builds a swing that lacks sufficient left-side control. He becomes a top-heavy shover of the club or a right-handed thrower. In either case, he seldom achieves his full potential either as an accurate striker or as a generator of clubhead speed.

Generally speaking, however, the golfer who builds an antihook swing gradually develops more and more *left-hand* control and more left-arm, left-side downswing pulling action in order to keep the clubface from closing. Usually he becomes more lower-body-oriented; he unconsciously develops good leg action on his forward swing to aid in pulling with his left arm and hand. Thus he automatically develops a proper swing path, one that moves the clubhead from inside to along the target line at impact—more toward right of target instead of outside in and to the left. He thus hits more shots with the clubhead moving on line instead of *cross* line. By learning to pull with his left arm and side, he develops the knack of releasing the maximum force of his swing into the ball instead of at some point earlier in the downswing.

Lee Trevino is a classic example of the antihook golfer, the player who has developed tremendous left-side control to keep the ball from flying and rolling into trouble on

the left—as hooked shots certainly will do on the hardpan fairways of Texas, where Trevino learned his golf. These same antihook measures that keep the ball in play, by ensuring that the hands lead the clubhead through impact, also keep its flight relatively low and boring—ideal for controlling shots in the unusually influential winds of Texas, not to mention Britain, where Trevino has twice won the Open.

In Trevino we see not only classic antihook technique but also indelible proof that several swing compensations—departures from normally accepted techniques—can be made to combine to produce one highly effective whole. Trevino's swing is a mass of balanced compensations, the first of which is the alignment of his body far to the left of target while aiming the clubface directly at the target. This compensation represents an antihook device in that by aligning left, Trevino enhances his ability to lead with his legs on his forward swing, to clear his left hip, and thus

pull rather than throw the clubface through impact. It is this *pulling through* that keeps the clubface square, whereas throwing it through with the right hand would close it to the left, causing violent hooking or pull-hooking.

Because he has aligned himself to the left, when Trevino initially starts the clubhead back from the ball along *the path of his alignment,* he shoves it *outside* his actual target line. Were he to continue swinging back on this outside path, he would be forced merely to lift the club with his hands and arms, wasting much of the power potential of his legs and body. He would also move the club into position for chopping sharply downward along an outside-to-inside clubhead path at impact, from which the normal result would be a weak pull-slice.

To avoid such lifting and chopping, Trevino makes a second compensation, that being to swing the club around his body on a relatively flat plane. In so doing he bows the

back of his left wrist outward and thus sets the clubface into a very "closed" position at the top of his swing. Thereby he has, in effect, all but eliminated the danger of pull-slicing, but instead has now programmed his clubface for a low hook. Trevino compensates for this problem, however, by pulling in his downswing with his legs, left side, left arm, and left hand to such a strong degree that he disallows the clubface from turning to the left of target until well past impact.

If we accept the premise of the stylistic purists that any particular golf technique which depart from orthodox is wrong, then Trevino's swing is a mess. But the fact is that it works supremely well. And the reason it works is that he has developed and "grooved" an action wherein five wrongs add up to one immaculate right by:

—First, setting his hands on the club turned considerably farther to the right than is normal for a player of his caliber—a grip that definitely encourages hooking.

—Second, aligning himself far to the left of where he aims the club.

—Third, taking the clubhead back outside his target line.

—Fourth, closing the clubface by bowing his left wrist and swinging on a relatively flat plane.

—Fifth, dragging the clubhead through impact to an extent that would cause most of us to slice the ball way into right field.

Despite his unorthodox technique, Trevino is regarded by many of his fellow professionals as being the ultimate model of consistency on the present-day tour. His ability to reproduce repeatedly the same shot time after time is the envy of almost all of his adversaries.

"The best golf swing is the one that repeats most often," said George Archer in 1973. "The swing that repeats most often on tour today is Lee Trevino's. I've seen him score badly when he gets to thinking badly, but I've never seen him swing badly. That little old fade just keeps repeating, repeating, repeating. . . ."

"You watch him in slow motion," says Homero Blancas, "and he's the dead same through the hitting area every time."

"Lee Trevino has a very effective swing," adds Jack Nicklaus, "in that it is wonderfully well grooved. Give me an action like Trevino's every time. It may not look pretty, but it sure does work."

How can a swing with so many compensations work so well so repeatedly? Apart from the fact that Trevino has practiced exceptionally hard to groove his action, I think one major reason for his repetitiveness is the fact that his swing does include such *dramatic* compensations. His is a swing of extremes: an extreme openness at address, an extremely outward-moving takeaway, an extreme closing of the clubface, extreme left-side control down and through. It seems to this writer that these actions are so pronounced that they are easily sensed by Trevino as he swings, simply because they are so extreme. He himself has said that he feels his greatest asset is the fact that he always knows at every stage of his swing just where his clubhead is and what it is doing. In short, his unorthodox swing is relatively easy for him to control largely because it is so unorthodox.

To carry this reasoning a step further, it could be argued that Trevino's swing works time after time because the results would be fatal if he varied from his pattern at any point along the way. With such an open position at address, he *must* work the club back to the ball from inside the target line in order to avoid pulling shots to the left; he *must* pull with his legs and his left hand and arm in supreme control to avoid violently pull-hooking the ball.

Some of the effects of Trevino's unique swing are at least as beneficial as those to be obtained from a more orthodox style. The tremendous left-side control that his open address position and closed clubface position at the top demand keeps the clubface looking at the target longer through the impact area than happens with a more orthodox action. This left-side control also forces his clubhead to extend along and down the target line longer than normal before returning to the inside after the ball is well on its way. His relatively flat plane and strong leg action also lengthen the period of time his clubhead moves at ball level—they flatten the bottom

From this camera angle we can see how far Trevino aligns himself to the left of where he aims the clubface, which is more or less on target. During his takeaway he starts the clubhead back on a path that parallels his body alignment but that is well outside his actual target line. From this outside-the-line position Trevino must somehow swing the club far enough inside the line, around himself, so that he can attack the ball from inside to along the target line. In so swinging the club back to the inside, he reaches the top of his backswing with his clubface extremely closed. At this point he is flirting with a low hook, but thereafter he saves the day with his strong leg action and left-hand control as described and shown in the previous series of photos.

of his swing arc for a very solid, forward-hitting delivery of the clubhead to the ball.

Trevino's swing demands extremely strong left-hand control from the start. Without it his right hand would pick the club up as it started back to the outside. Without it he would not set the clubshaft on proper line at the top. Without it he would certainly throw the clubhead back to the target line with his right hand and further close the clubface before impact.

"I try to hold onto the club as long as I can without uncocking my wrists," Trevino says of his downswing. "If I ever release my wrists [too soon] I'll hit a low hook, the way I

170

did when I was a kid. That's because I aim my body to the left. I like to think that I'm backhanding a wall with my left hand as I hit the ball."

Not coincidentally, Trevino has carried the idea of left-hand control even into his putting stroke. "The left hand should be in command on all golf shots," he says, "but especially in putting. I want to get the feeling that the heel [of the putter] is leading the stroke."

Trevino's swing requires not only left-hand dominance but also strong, supple, fast-acting legs and an excellent sense of rhythm. Lee is a great believer in jogging and invariably turns to this form of exercise whenever his swing begins to falter. He also swings to a definite rhythmical beat that gives him ample time between backswing and downswing for his legs to gather themselves to lead his forward stroke.

Trevino is also exceptionally supple for a person of such relatively ample girth. Normally golfers whose upper and lower bodies are closely melded by a generous stomach find it difficult to make a full shoulder turn without their hips following suit. The general result is less muscle stretching—less leverage—than is achieved by the golfer who gains a wide separation in degree of turning between his upper and lower body. Though

Trevino is not your typical "wasp-waisted" Texan, his suppleness does give him a full shoulder turn with minimal hip turning, a blend that results in full coiling and a huge buildup of leverage.

Trevino's suppleness also helps him to retain this pent-up energy until near impact, by allowing him to retain maximum shoulder coiling even after his left leg has started to shift toward the target on the forward swing. The result is even more muscle stretching—and thus leverage—at a point in the swing where less supple players usually reduce stretching by starting to uncoil their shoulders prematurely.

There are, of course, many other assets, beyond suppleness, that have combined to make Trevino a superstar of golf. They include his excellent hand-eye coordination and his willingness to work extremely hard at the game. Hand-eye coordination is partly instinctive, in that the ability to strike an object squarely with an implement in hand undoubtedly has been bred into us since cavemen days. To excel at golf, however, demands the constant polishing and fine tuning of such natural gifts through unrelenting practice, and here Trevino, during his prime, was in the big leagues with Sarazen, Cotton, Hogan and Player.

Lee was a very good golfer when he came out of the marines in late 1960, but he really began to develop the makings of a great golfer only during the early 1960's, when he worked at Hardy Greenwood's driving range in Dallas. He says his normal daily regimen was 18 holes of golf in the morning, then some 1,000 practice shots at the range throughout the rest of the day and evening. Occasionally he would demonstrate his exceptional hand-eye coordination—and his ebullient personality—by playing the par-three course at the range using only a family-size Dr. Pepper bottle for a "club" wrapped with tape to prevent it from shattering. He would throw the ball into the air and swing the bottle at it baseball style. On the greens he used it like a pool cue for putting. Thus equipped, he once played a full nine holes in 29 strokes.

Throughout the years Trevino has not only perfected his antihook technique but also striven hard to hit his shots higher, especially after first seeing Ben Hogan play in 1962. "He worked that ball so pretty from left to right," Trevino later recalled of his fellow Texan. "I was always duck-hooking the thing. That's why I don't hit the ball very high. I'm still hooking, but I'm trying to get away from it. One of these days I'm gonna

get that fade and it's gonna go so high. . . . "

When Trevino won the U.S. Open in 1968 at Oak Hill Country Club in Rochester, New York, he was still basically a low-ball hitter. His victory derived in part from the fact that four days of rain prior to the tournament had softened the greens to the point that they would hold even a low-boring approach shot with dartboard sureness. Such was not the case, however, in 1971, when he won the Open at Merion Golf Club outside Philadelphia. There the traditionally super slick greens were rolled daily to make them even firmer and faster. Trevino's victory at Merion proved that he had learned to hit the high shots when necessary. It also prompted Jack Nicklaus, whom Trevino defeated in the play-off, to suggest to his friend that he should no longer consider Augusta National, site of the Masters tournament, as being unsuited to his game. Augusta National does favor the player who can hit high, long-carrying drives around right-to-left doglegs; but Trevino, applying his excellent hand-eye coordination to maneuver the ball in either direction, certainly would now seem to have the tools to handle this—and any other—

championship site.

Trevino's ability to master and sustain an unorthodox swing stems not only from hard work and a deep insight into golf swing mechanics—it is a little-known fact that he taught the game for seven years before joining the tour full time—but also from his intense competitiveness. Nicklaus and Player are just two who have learned from bitter experience that when the chips are down, Trevino plays head to head with bulldog tenacity. Greatly sustaining this intense competitiveness is his Hagen-like ability to switch his concentration off and on at will during the course of 18 holes. Like Hagen, Trevino jokes with anyone in earshot whenever he feels the need to refresh himself from the pressures of the battle. Then, revitalized, he gets on with the job at hand. His seemingly almost endless stream of chatter is, of course, simply a way of releasing nervous energy. Offstage Trevino can be a very quiet and serious man.

If there is a flaw in Trevino's competitive makeup, in this writer's opinion it rests in his occasional tendency toward impatience. He is at his best mentally when he's in the fight and/or is on his stick. Periodically, however, when he is not in contention and struggling with his game, he seems to lack the dogged determination and patience of, say, Gary Player to really buckle down to competing and giving every shot his best effort. Such instances of faltering internal resources have been rare, however, and, as stated, nonexistent when a major victory is even faintly within his grasp.

Trevino did not start relying on tournament golf for a living until relatively late in life, at the age of twenty-seven. In the seven years that followed he established an amazing record, both in terms of money won and major championship victories. During the late 1970's he seemed to be at a career crossroads with back problems and operations that limited his ability to practice. Would he continue to advance over the next several years and thereby go down in golfing history as an immortal with the likes of Hagen, Jones, Hogan, Snead, Palmer, Player and Nicklaus? Or would he gradually fade away, yet still be remembered with such great players as Cotton, Locke, Middlecoff and Thomson? His victory in the 1984 PGA Championship did much to place him in the former classification.

Whatever his historical position, however, Lee Trevino has already demonstrated to millions of golfers of this era that the golf swing need not be "pretty" to be successful. As he himself has said: "Any golfer can use any type of swing that he can master."

Jack Nicklaus

THE MOST AND THE BEST

In the original edition of this book, the system chosen for its structure, the chronology of the champions' birth dates, made the last subject Jack William Nicklaus. This was most appropriate, in that the Golden Bear was at the time of first publication by far and away golf's most dominating figure.

However, as no one predicted it would more resolutely than Nicklaus, the time had arrived with the preparation of this new edition for others to contend for that position, and, indeed, two of the most prominent of them are the subjects of the following added chapters.

What hasn't changed, though, is Nicklaus' status in the overall history of golf. Dominating he may no longer be, but no one with real knowledge of the game would argue that anyone on the scene today is even beginning to threaten his lifetime record. There never has been a golfer like Jack Nicklaus, and he is unique in so many ways that it is difficult to imagine there ever will be.

The cold record alone is stunning. By the spring of 1986, when he was forty-seven and had been playing professionally for a quarter

of a century, Nicklaus had won, at twenty, six more major championships than anyone else, not to mention the most money by almost a million dollars. He had been winning with sub-par scores in some arena or other since the age of fourteen, and he had won all over the world. As a pro, he had come back from the dead (at least as trumpeted by the press) at least three times, most spectacularly to win the 1986 Masters—his sixth—after half a dozen major-less years. By the end of that twenty-fifth season, out of the 100 majors he had played as a professional he had won 18, finished second in 19, and third in nine, meaning that he had finished in the top three almost half of the times he had teed it up. His overall total of victories in his own country was an amazing 71, and his worldwide total a staggering 89. By then, of course, he had also won every golfing honor and award and citation and professional best and most (except total numbers of PGA tournament wins) in the United States at least once; sometimes, as in the case of year's top money winner, almost to the point of monotony.

JACK NICKLAUS

Born: January 21, 1940, Columbus, Ohio

Major victories:

U.S. Amateur championship: 1959, 1961

U.S. Open: 1962, 1967, 1972 , 1980

British Open: 1966, 1970 , 1978

Masters: 1963, 1965, 1966, 1972, 1975, 1986

PGA championship: 1963, 1967, 1973, 1975, 198

One could go on, but that too would indeed be monotonous. Much more interesting are the flesh-and-blood factors that have made Nicklaus such a unique champion. To begin with, there are his inherent physical and psychological talents for the game.

In the area of physique Nicklaus was gifted with an extraordinarily powerful pair of legs, a strong back, and at least an adequately healthy supportive anatomy—all of which he further developed through an outdoor, sports-mad childhood and adolescence. In the area of the mind he was blessed with better-than-average intelligence that, had his life taken a different turn, could certainly have made him into a corporate titan and that even now is translating itself into creative accomplishment through the vehicle of golf-course designing. In combination, his strong body and sharp mind produced at a very early age a quality that this writer believes to

Since most fans regard Nicklaus as the greatest golfer of all time, so must experts on method regard his swing technique as its ultimate expression so far as it has presently evolved. Extremely powerful legs, an athletic torso, and superb coordination enable Nicklaus to create and control a massive arc primarily through body action. Note especially the tremendous extension of the arms, the ultimate height of the hands, and the "tightness" of the bodily windup going back, and, coming down, the pronounced targetward thrust of the legs, followed by positive hip clearance while keeping the upper body entirely behind the ball.

178

be the true secret of many golf champions: exceptional eye-hand (brain-to-body) coordination.

In the realm of the spirit, Nicklaus was equally if not even better equipped for the game of golf. Almost certainly as a result of his Teutonic heritage, he was possessed from an early age by an amazingly strong desire for perfection, particularly in regard to his own activities. Out of this grew fierce, driving ambition, and out of that grew the determination, dedication, concentration, and competitiveness that, more than any other factors, have made him the superchampion that he is.

Watching the ease and power with which Nicklaus still plays golf today, it is impossible to avoid the impression that his talents come more from heaven than from within himself. His busy nongolfing life and his outwardly minimal dedication to practice reinforce that impression. Actually it is very far from the truth. That he is uniquely gifted is beyond question, but behind the development of those gifts to their present level lies a Herculean and essentially solo effort of body, mind, and spirit. It is true that he was well taught originally by Jack Grout and given great opportunity and mighty encouragement by his late father, Charlie. But they could not supply him with the will or make the effort for him. What Jack Nicklaus is today as a golfer is strictly what he has made himself.

In respect to the bodily effort, his teacher, Jack Grout, puts the record straight in his foreword to Nicklaus' latest book, *Golf My Way*. Writes Grout: "No one ever worked harder at golf than Nicklaus during his teens and early twenties. At the age of 10, in his first year of golf, Jack must have averaged at least 300 practice shots and at least eighteen holes of play daily. In later years he would

179

often hit double that number of practice shots and play thirty-six—even fifty-four—holes of golf a day during the summer. I have seen him practice for hours in rain, violent winds, snow, intense heat—nothing would keep him away from golf. Even a slight case of polio failed to keep him from turning up at Scioto for a golf match."

To which Nicklaus adds in the chapter on his current practice habits: "During my early years in golf I probably practiced as much as anyone in history, but today my temperament is such that I can only practice effectively when I have something specific to prepare for. Just going out and hitting balls for the sake of hitting balls doesn't do anything for me any more."

Because the mind drives the body, the huge physical efforts that Nicklaus has made to master golf were in a sense initially mental and have thereafter been mentally sustained.

In addition, however, he was particularly fortunate or gifted or intelligent in recognizing the need to develop one particular purely mental talent at the same early age that he began to hone his physical game. There have been many fine shotmakers down the years (and there are many today on the pro tour) who have never recognized or accepted the fact that hitting the ball is only one-third of the game of golf. The other two-thirds are course management and self-management. Once a reasonable level of shotmaking skill has been developed, they become the supreme factors in competitive performance.

Nicklaus became a precociously mature course manager while still a teenager, and he offered some clues as to how that happened in a 1974 article in *Sports Illustrated* magazine when he wrote:

"As far back as I can remember I have preferred being outdoors to being indoors, and

natural things to manufactured things. The main reason golf appealed to me so much as a kid was that I could do it by myself, without the dependence on other people that most sports involve. But the appeal of the golf course itself was also a very big factor. A golf course . . . was simply a good place to be; a source of constant pleasure and contentment quite apart from the actual playing of the game.

"From that simple starting point I became more and more intrigued, as my game improved, by the way in which the elements that make up a golf course determine the type and quality of shots a golfer is called upon to play. I became (and remain) fascinated with the effects of grass, trees, water, sand, and the shape and texture of the land itself in determining shot-making values. Seeking to understand each new hole I encountered, I would try to put myself in the mind of the ar-

chitect. I'd try to figure out why he had done, or perhaps been forced to do, particular things in particular ways. Inevitably this intense observation improved my strategical approach to shot-making, which led to better scoring, which encouraged me to develop an ultra-analytical approach as a competitive tool."

Nicklaus also became an outstanding self-manager on the course at an age when even great golfers—Bobby Jones, for one—are still launching clubs in the wake of misstruck shots. Here there can be no denying that Jack's early golfing maturity resulted in large part from his father's comfortable circumstances and great ambitions for his son, by allowing the youngster to play a vast amount of formal competitive golf across the country. As Jack Grout wrote in the book foreword previously quoted from:

"Jack Nicklaus started to play competitive

golf at a very early age, and it did wonders for him. . . . Formal competition puts the game in clear perspective for a youngster, by giving meaning to what he is learning about technique. It causes him to become aware of the need for strategy, as well as fine shotmaking; makes him realize that he will have to think well to win, not just swing well. It breeds maturity by thrusting him into pressurized situations and subjecting him to the emotions of success and failure. It builds self-confidence and self-reliance, and it helps a youngster to overcome nervousness. . . . I believe a lot of Jack's adult successes both on and off the golf course can be traced to the maturity and clear-headedness that grew out of his early competitive experience."

In terms of the spirit, it cannot be denied that Nicklaus was also lucky in his parentage or at least in his ancestry. Perfectionists throughout history have been the great achievers in every area of human endeavor, and it is this writer's view that perfectionists are born, not made. To strive for the ultimate is something that Jack Nicklaus genetically cannot help doing, not only in golf but in every facet of life. It has been this writer's pleasure to work closely with him for almost twenty years on various literary and business projects. He is as determined to attain perfection in these as he is on the golf course. He will not accept a business involvement to which he cannot give 100 percent personal attention and effort. He did not want initially to produce the bestseller *Golf My Way* because he did not think it could be done well enough. It destroys him to have to compromise even the placement of a single bunker in designing a golf course, albeit the entire forces of nature demand and justify compromise. He finds anything less than perfection in himself embarrassing and in others irritating (although he now tolerates it more easily). He has never in his life hit a practice shot without giving it 100 percent effort, simply because he would be disgusted with himself if it were a poor shot. If he gives up golf at what the world would consider a premature age, it will be because he thinks he is not getting any better at it, not drawing closer to perfection, in which case he will annoy and embarrass himself to

the point of not wanting to go on.

One does not, of course, have to look beyond this characteristic to discover the source of Nicklaus' determination to become the world's greatest-ever golfer or for the lifelong dedication he has given to that goal. Nor need one look further to identify the source of his massive competitiveness (well disguised, incidentally, by a strong sense of sportsmanship). What may not be so immediately obvious is the degree to which his perfectionism has contributed to his single biggest golfing asset beyond power and a marvelous putting touch: concentration.

Among the superchampions only Ben Hogan and Gary Player have concentrated as well as Jack Nicklaus, and one has to believe that it was from that same source—perfectionism—that both drew their similar, almost self-hypnotic powers of concentration. Most people will have had at least some personal experience of how this works in their vocational, if not their avocational, activities. When you absolutely *must* do something to the utmost of your ability, as well as you possibly can, then invariably you will concentrate on it with your maximum intensity. Unfortunately for most people this happens only when the imperative word really is "must"; on occasions when it's a matter of perform or starve. In the case of the great achievers, the imperative word has almost always not been "must" but "*want.*" Therein, perhaps, lies the reason there are so few of them.

The total golf game that all these qualities have melded to produce in the mature Nicklaus has been the most formidable in history and will probably remain so for a good number of years, especially with the growth of the Senior Tour and the presence on it of such one-time opponents as Palmer, Player and, about the same time as Jack could join, Trevino.

Nicklaus at his best is the longest *controlled* driver of the ball in the game's history. He is the most powerful consistently *accurate* long-iron player there has ever been. No golfer since the Scots founded the game has been able, when necessary, to hit the ball as *high* with the power clubs, which is the

An infrequently mentioned factor of great golf is clearly evident in this sequence in the consistency of Nicklaus' clubhead plane and arc on both sides of the ball. Frames four, seven, and eleven indicate that the clubhead met the ball while momentarily traveling directly along, rather than across, the target line, which is fundamental to starting the ball on target. All one need do additionally to make the ball fly straight, instead of curving left or right of target, is match the clubface alignment at impact to the direction in which the clubhead is swinging. Jack Nicklaus would seem to have done that better and more frequently than anyone else in history.

key to his ability to hold the firm greens on which major championships are traditionally played. In recent years he has been able to curve the ball left and right and hit it high and low at will. His upright swing and physical strength give him an almost superhuman capability to escape from tall grass. He is an accomplished sand player and has gradually become better at the chip and pitch shots that he was so infrequently called on to play by comparison with less powerful and accurate golfers. He has a superbly delicate, deft, and positive putting stroke that, although it occasionally gets a little out of kilter mechanically, shows no suggestion of the tremors, jerks, yips, or other nervous afflictions that have struck down so many great golfers who were still in their prime from tee to green. His profound knowledge of technique allows him to be his own most effective swing mechanic and to right wrongs with maximum speed and efficiency. And he is marvelously "repetitive" because in all the thousands of rounds he has played and millions of balls he

has hit, he has been doing fundamentally the same things every time.

Those are the shotmaking tools. In the area of course management he is the most observant, analytical, and meticulous golfer in the world today. He identifies, physically measures, understands, and almost photographically memorizes every single element of every hole he plays that can conceivably influence playing strategy. Computing the knowledge thus gained, he makes his decisions about where to position each shot with almost clinical precision and detachment. Having then arrived at the ideal course of action through knowledge and logic, rather than guesswork or emotion, he has the capability, confidence, and courage to attempt the ideal shot. And he almost always *does* attempt the ideal shot, even when swinging below his best. Unwillingness to compromise with what he knows to be strategically ideal has, in this observer's opinion, cost him more than one major championship.

In the area of self-management Nicklaus is probably without peer among superchampions. His life-style is active and healthy without being faddish. He has fought a long battle to contain his business activities to a point where they never more than fleetingly debilitate him mentally or physically. He works hard at ordering his playing schedule and business life in such a way that neither will threaten his happy marriage and close family life. Whatever he chooses or is obliged to do, he does with dispatch and efficiency. He enjoys the perquisites of fame, graciously tolerates most of its penalties, but remains in his own private self an essentially normal and down-to-earth individual. In terms of his playing career his one danger—if that is not too strong a word—is probably the amount of intellectual and physical effort that he increasingly devotes to the designing and building of golf courses, his greatest love af-

ter winning major championships. But he personally sees this as a regenerative, more than a debilitative, agent. "It's a different kind of challenge and effort," he says, "and I need that sort of total change. After a period building courses I'm always eager to get back to playing golf, and vice versa."

The swing with which Nicklaus plays golf is not in its *scale* a swing for all mankind, requiring as it does unique gifts of physique and eye-hand coordination. But in *form* it is the epitome of the modern method and as such a superb model for every golfer. Here are its technical fundamentals as reflected by Nicklaus in his extensive writings over the past fifteen years:

- A grip which *reflexively* delivers the clubface square to the target at impact at high speed without slippage (his small hands and short fingers have caused him from an early age to favor the interlocking system of unitizing the hands).

- A setup in which: (1) the shoulders are *parallel to the starting line* of the shot, which, as he never attempts to hit a dead straight shot, means that they are always aligned slightly left of the direct ball-target line for a fade or slightly right for a draw; (2) the ball is always positioned at the point where the clubhead will reach the bottom of its arc and is momentarily traveling parallel to his shoulder line, a point which for him is opposite the left heel on all normal shots; (3) the left arm and shaft form a straight line from the left shoulder to the clubhead, thus automatically placing the hands as they should be at impact—slightly ahead of the clubface; (4) the weight is distributed evenly between both feet as the knees flex slightly and the body leans comfortably forward from the hips.

- A mental picture of the spine serving as a fixed swing axis, around which the head may swivel but never move laterally and

185

around which the shoulders and hips may freely pivot but not sway.

- A picture of the ideal plane of the swing as being as near to vertical as is consistent with a wide arc and a full upper-body turn.

- A picture of the toe of the club gradually moving farther from the target line than the heel in natural response to the movements of the backswing; then of this process gradually reversing in response to the movements of the downswing, with a fleeting moment of clubface squareness at impact. In other words, an open-to-square-to-closed clubface sequence occurring as a reflex response to the overall swing, rather than from any deliberate manipulation of the club.

- A sense of staying in motion in some part of the body from the moment of stepping up to the shot until the end of the follow-through.

- The slowest, smoothest, and most deliber-

ate "one-piece" movement away from the ball that it is possible to make while actually *swinging* the club rather than "taking" it back.

- A picture of the clubhead moving straight back along *a line parallel to the shoulders at address* (*not* the extension of the direct ball-target line) until it is automatically swung to the inside by the turning of the body.

- Ample extension of the club away from the ball, with the left arm and shaft continuing to form a straight line until the wrists are naturally hinged by the weight and momentum of the wide-arcing clubhead.

- Maximum turning, pivoting, coiling, or winding of the shoulders in response to the momentum of the extended arms and club as they swing backward and upward.

- Free rotation of the hips around the fixed axis of the spine —but only in response to the momentum of the high arm swing and

full shoulder turn, never as an independent action.

- Retention of the weight on the *inside* edge of the right foot as the upper-body coiling pulls the left knee behind the ball, forcing the left foot to roll onto its inside edge.
- The back of the left hand, wrist, and forearm forming a straight line at the completion of the backswing.
- The clubshaft parallel to the *starting line of the shot* (again, note, *not* the actual ball-target line) at the completion of the backswing.
- A feeling of passivity in the hands and wrists throughout the backswing and especially during the initiation of the downswing.
- A replanting of the left foot, a thrusting from the inside edge of the right foot, and a feeling of moving the knees directly toward the target as the first action of the downswing.
- A fast and conscious turning of the hips toward the target, made almost simultaneously with the targetward shuttling of the knees that initiates and motivates the downswing.
- An uncoiling of the left shoulder initially on an *upward* path, and the right shoulder initially on a *downward* path, as a reflexive reaction to the targetward motion of the legs and hips.
- No effort to restrain the swinging of the arms or to inhibit the unhinging of the wrists once the legs have begun to drive targetward and the hips have started to unwind.
- A sensation at impact of driving the ball *directly* forward, deriving from the upper body being almost entirely behind the ball as it is struck.
- No effort to prevent the clubhead from swinging to the inside immediately after impact, but an effort to extend it as fully as possible until the sheer momentum of the clubhead forces the left arm to bend and the right hand to roll over the (always firm-wristed) left hand well into the follow-through.

How did this great golf swing evolve? The answer is from history as first interpreted to Nicklaus by Jack Grout, a man who had actually witnessed it in the making by either observing or playing with every great golfer of the twentieth century with the exception of Harry Vardon.

From Vardon came the foundations on which this swing was built, now long buried but still rock solid. From Hagen, Sarazen, Jones, and others of their era came the basic structure, now also modified but still fundamentally fine engineering. From Nelson, Hogan, Snead, Cotton, Middlecoff, Thomson, and their contemporaries came further refinements, each adding through individual craftsmanship elements that brought the whole nearer to a utopian ideal. From Palmer, Player, Casper, and others of our own day came the penultimate polishing. And then, finally, in Nicklaus, it all came together.

Possibly one day man will devise another and an even better way to strike a golf ball. But here, in Jack Nicklaus, at least for the moment, we continue to see the ultimate expression of the long evolutionary process that is being narrated in these pages.

DICK AULTMAN

Tom Watson

"HUCKLEBERRY DILLINGER," THE CONSUMMATE COMPETITOR

When Thomas Sturges Watson was seven the Huck Finn look was pretty much in place—the rusty hair, the freckles, the sunburned nose. The massive forearms, later compared to cartoon characters Popeye and Alley Oop, had not fully developed, of course. That would require another million or so golf swings.

Also growing, in Tom Watson's guts, was a gigantic competitive force, a gunslinger's dedication to beating the foe. "Huckleberry Dillinger" would be the nickname given by his coaches in high school, where he would excel as a football quarterback and a basketball guard.

It was in the genes. His great grandfather, Isaac Newton Watson, had climaxed his legal career in the late 1930's by busting the notorious Pendergast political machine that had corrupted Kansas City, Missouri, and much of that state. It took I.N. Watson and two retired FBI agents two years to find the deceased Missourians who had continued to vote from the grave for Boss Pendergast, as well as the living whose anti-Pendergast votes were never counted. Some 200 convictions later, the state was clean.

Another great grandfather, Dr. Simeon Bishop Bell, braved the rugged covered wagon trail to Kansas in 1857, survived bloody Civil War guerrilla strife on the Kansas–Missouri border, fought his way to the top in real estate, and eventually gave the University of Kansas land and money to establish its medical school.

Tom's father, Ray, had focused his share of the competitive genes on becoming a successful insurance broker and a scratch golfer at the Kansas City Country Club. There he won several championships and even beat his middle son regularly, at least until about midway through Tom's fourteenth summer.

Seven years prior to that time, however, Ray Watson, better known as "Hook" because of the prevailing shape of his full-swing shots, had taken the family to Colorado on vacation and then to the local course for a round of golf. There the club professional took one look at Tom and objected to someone so young going onto his course.

Hook struck a deal. Pointing down the first fairway, he asked the pro if Tom might be deemed worthy if his tee shot should happen to carry a ditch some 75 yards out.

TOM WATSON

Born: September 4, 1949; Kansas City, Missouri

Major victories:
   U.S. Open: 1982
   British Open: 1975, 1977, 1980, 1982, 1983
   Masters: 1977, 1981

Watson's swing bears resemblance to those of Sam Snead and Jack Nicklaus. At address his left arm and clubshaft form the straightline relationship from the shoulder to the ground that we see in Nicklaus. This helps create the extreme width and height of swing that give both Jack and Tom their unusually fast clubhead speed and resulting length of shots. Watson's excellent coordination of armswing and body turn, both back and through, is most Snead-like, as is the concurrent turning of the chin back and forward.

The pro agreed, and Tom, with one year of golf under his belt, pulled out his sawed-off three-wood. With the family honor on his slight shoulders, he swung the club back and up in the long, high arc that later would become the signature of his technique.

The ball carried the ditch with much to spare. Hook Watson had put his seven-year-old on the spot and the boy had met the challenge.

(Twenty-five years later, shortly after Tom had won his eighth major championship, the 1982 U.S. Open at Pebble Beach, his long-time friend and golfing companion, Frank D. (Sandy) Tatum, a former U.S. Golf Association president, summarized the competitiveness that Hook Watson had kindled in his son: "He is the consummate competitor," Tatum wrote in *California Golfer* magazine.

"There is something akin to the joy of combat that seems to take hold of him as he approaches a competitive round of golf. More than intensity is involved; there is deep-rooted pleasure at the prospect of the challenge. What evolves is total application, total concentration and the focusing of an unusual intelligence on what he is setting out to do. Overlaying all that is the love of and for the game that pervades his whole approach to it.")

The things that Ray Watson did for Tom are what other fathers of would-be golfers might well emulate. He continually encouraged, challenged and played with his son. He established within him a love and respect for the game. This started when Tom was six and nothing has changed 32 years later. When Tom was eleven, Ray did another

smart thing. He turned Tom over to Stan Thirsk, head pro at the club, to oversee the development of his technical skills.

"My father liked to think of himself as a Sam Snead disciple," says Tom, who himself also spent a good deal of time in the early 1970's watching this maestro of rhythm and tempo practice and play. "Dad has a classic swing, a rocking back to the right heel and swinging a bit from in to out. He has good rhythm. He hits it long and high. He never had a great short game, but was always a good putter."

Tom played frequently with Ray and his cronies. "I always looked forward to those Saturday afternoon matches at 1:30," he says. Those $2 Nassaus honed Tom's competitiveness. So did the $1 that Ray gave him whenever he passed a scoring milestone,

breaking 100, 90, 80, and finally 70.

Before Tom was a teenager, the Watson foursome often included Ray, Tom, Thirsk and Bob Willits, another scratch golfer who had won the 1947 Missouri Amateur. Tom played hard, kept his mouth shut, and resisted the temptation to fling clubs after bad shots. Because of his reticence during these matches, Hook's friends nicknamed Tom "Fly" for "Flytrap Finnegan", the mouthy cartoon strip character. When Tom decided to try the PGA tour in 1971, Willits and friends staked him to $18,000 in expense money. He repaid the loan from his 1972 earnings and added dividends in 1973. "Fly is better than General Motors," Willits declared.

Tom began holding his own and then some in the Saturday matches by the time he was

192

thirteen. The next Memorial Day he shot a 67, beat all the older men, and received his first national mention in *Sports Illustrated* magazine. Also that summer, Tom entered the Kansas City Match Play tournament. In the 36-hole finals, he finished the morning round two holes down. During the lunch break, his opponent spotted him in the clubhouse shooting pool. "He's really worried, isn't he?" the opponent observed. Watson won the match, 4 and 2.

A year later Thirsk matched Tom with Arnold Palmer in an 18-hole contest for charity. With the galleries lining the first fairway, there to hang on Arnold's every trouser hitch, fifteen-year-old Tom whaled into a 300-yard drive. "Who's *this*!" Arnold exclaimed. Watson loved it. Competitiveness. Born of playing for $2 Nassaus with the best players his father could find.

And there were other personal virtues established during these formative years. All would be needed for Tom to emerge from the frustrations of the early 1970's and to match, if not surpass, the mighty Nicklaus:

Patience. "My father had a hot temper when he was young," Watson says. "I did too, but Dad let me get it out of my system. I didn't rave too much with him, but I did with my peers. It gets old quick."

Watson needed this quality of patience in the 1975 British Open at Carnoustie. He entered this championship still bereft of a major victory, having lost both the 1974 and 1975 U.S. Opens and the 1975 Masters after being in strong contention. Already he had been branded a "choker" by some of the less astute golf writers, the type that show up at major events in the U.S. as a bonus from the boss for sticking it out through Little League games, bowling, slow-pitch softball, and various water sports.

On the fourth day at Carnoustie, with North Sea winds sweeping across the old Scottish public course, all but drowning out the tootling of commuter trains to and from Dundee, Watson three-putted holes 10, 11 and 12. Patiently he hung on thereafter, birdied 14 and 18, the latter with a 300-yard downwind drive, a 148-yard 9-iron and a 20-foot putt. The next day he beat Australian Jack Newton by one in an 18-hole play-off, again competing patiently, this time in hard, driving rain.

"Anything can happen in golf," he said shortly thereafter. "I'll never get out on the course and give up. If a person gives up once, there is always the chance he'll do it again."

"I don't think Jack (Nicklaus) ever gets down on himself," Watson told the late Jack Murphy of the *San Diego Union* in 1979. "He never gives less than 100 percent of his great talent. That's a wonderful trait. All the great players have it—Hogan, Nelson, Snead, Palmer, Player. You can't explain it—it's a natural phenomenon."

Hard work. Stan Thirsk tells of the times when members at K.C.C.C. would ask, "Who's that cute little kid out there hitting balls? He's been doing it for hours." Many of Watson's fellow pros also expressed awe at the efforts he put into developing his game throughout the 1970s.

"When Tom joined the tour, he had a lot of talent, he was strong, and he had a lot of desire," Steve Melnyk recalled in 1978. "But at that stage he was like an uncut diamond. You didn't know how he'd turn out. What Tom did with his golf swing was not given to him. He's worked very hard to refine it. Now it's one of the best five or six on tour." Watson, himself, is proud of the reputation he's earned as a hard worker, but he's always maintained that it has been a labour of love.

"I've always enjoyed trying to shape my shots," he says "and that's absolutely my father's influence. Whenever he'd see me practicing, he'd always tell me to 'bring it in from left to right,' or 'hit me a high one,' or 'let's see you knock one down,' or 'how about a slight draw?'"

To this day, Tom Watson maintains with professorial certainty, "there's no such thing as a straight shot. That's the essence of golf—shaping your shots." And he bemoans that modern developments in golf equipment—the dimpling of the balls, the lighter-yet-stiffer shafts, the spin-increasing grooving of iron clubs—all have tended to dilute this essence.

"These changes, especially in the balls,

From this view, we again see Watson's Snead–Nicklaus tendencies. The relatively early movement of the torso and legs, unified with the swinging of the arms, is similar to both Jack and Sam. The dramatic raising and lowering of the right elbow is more a Nicklaus trademark. The overall simplicity of Watson's swing, with the backswing and downswing planes being all but identical and the clubhead path being well from the inside, is again akin to Snead's form, which Tom's father tried to establish in his own game and Tom, himself, often studied first-hand.

are why the scores are so much lower," he says. "Mishit shots don't curve the ball into trouble so much anymore.

"We all complained about the narrow fairways at the British Open last year (Turnberry, 1986). And I was the most outspoken of all. But maybe that's not right. Maybe we should have 15 to 17-yard-wide fairways now that the balls go so straight."

Watson's intensive work habits at the Kansas City Country Club also extended to the short shots. As a boy he'd frequently seek out a particular short-game situation that he felt would be almost, but not quite, impossible to solve. An example might be from a downhill lie in deep rough to a close-in flagstick on a downhill green. He would practice such a shot until he felt he had developed the technique and the touch to pull it off a vast majority of the time.

Watson entered the 1982 U.S. Open at Pebble Beach with the pall of never having won this event clouding his otherwise brilliant career, much as the same want has been the single blight on Sam Snead's. Tom went into the final round at Pebble tied for the lead, moved ahead early, but fell back as Nicklaus scored five straight birdies in the opening holes.

Then Watson made sensational putts on 10, 11 and 14. A 60-footer on 16, with 10 feet of break, missed by inches. He came to the 210-yard, par-three 17th tied with Jack, who had already finished and was watching Tom's play via a TV monitor behind the 18th green. It looked like Jack's tournament after Tom hooked his 2-iron tee shot into deep rough left of the green, some 10 feet from the putting surface. Nicklaus knew the flagstick position allowed only 10 more feet of down-

Photographs by Stephen Szurlej.
Permission *Golf Digest* © Golf Digest/Tennis Inc.

hill, triple-cut putting surface for stopping the ball. Watson's playing partner, Bill Rogers, later swore that no human could possibly even toss the ball onto the green by hand and stop it anywhere near the hole. Impossible.

Almost. Watson approached the ball and noticed it was on a downhill lie, but set well up in the shin-high grass. "I can handle this," he said to his caddie, Bruce Edwards.

"Get it close," Edwards replied.

"I'm gonna make it," Watson stated.

The shot would be a cut-lob with the sand wedge. Tom opened the blade, made a couple of practice swings, and set up for the shot. Then he adjusted his aim and alignment more to the right, to allow for some 18 inches of right-to-left curve on the green. He made a soft-handed, out-to-in swing. The ball floated upward about two feet, landed gently just on the green, took the break, and ran down into the cup.

Watson leaped into the air, ran onto the green and then wheeled towards Edwards, just enough to intimate, "I told you so!" He said at the time that the shot meant more than any other he'd ever made. It surely must remain as such in terms of his overall record. However, it was not, by Watson's standards, the 1,000-to-1 shot that so many thought it to be.

"I've practiced that lob shot from deep rough for hours, days, months, years," he said. "It's a shot you have to know to do well in the Open." In fact, he'd practiced it just that week, on a downslope behind the second green at Pebble. Hard work.

Perfectionism. Those who have known Watson well, such as Gary Vanier, his roommate in the Alpha Sigma Phi fraternity at

Stanford University and a golf squad teammate, often mention his striving for perfection.

"He was always making little changes, trying to be perfect," Vanier, 1982 California Amateur champion, has said. "He would hit balls on the range for hours while the rest of us were on the course playing."

The drive for perfection, along with the emphasis on hard work, is a staple of society in Middle America. The area is a fertile spawning ground for over-achieving corporate executives, but migraine headaches and ulcers abound. Watson is part of this culture, but he also learned long ago that the search for perfection in golf is on a par with the Holy Grail and the Fountain of Youth. It might lead to a supremely struck, 40-yard wedge shot in Japan in 1976, or an outstanding 1-iron into a 40-mile-per-hour wind at Muirfield Village in 1979, but the real value of the search is simply that it makes the mishit shots a bit less disastrous.

Once Tom really started to believe this fact, in the mid 1970's, he finally began to let go of a self-defeating attitude. Once he realized that his game need not be in perfect order for him to win, he began to do just that with much greater frequency.

. *Self-sufficiency.* Serious golfers need a healthy dose of this characteristic. A trust in oneself, even a somewhat inflated sense of well-being, is vital cushioning against the everyday psychological trauma of tournament golf. Thus it is that most touring pros continually blame their failures on outside factors; the course, the weather, bad luck, an ache here, an overly hectic schedule there— anything but a lack of ability.

Unlike the norm, but in common with men like Palmer and Nicklaus, Watson has always been extremely realistic in assessing the strengths and weaknesses of his game. However, his strong self-sufficiency may well, at times, have prolonged and deepened the slumps in his career. His attitude, oft-expressed in print, has frequently been, "I've been playing badly. I'm not sure why. One day it's this and one day it's that. But I know if I keep working and searching something will click and it will all come back

together. I know it's there; I've just got to find it."

A classic example occurred at the 1987 U.S. Open at Olympic. On the Wednesday, Watson greeted a writer friend with "I'm fine personally, but I'm not playing worth a damn." On Sunday evening, he lost the Championship by a single stroke.

A danger in diagnosing oneself at golf is that what you think you are doing or not doing may be far removed, even diametrically opposed, to what is really happening. Home movies and video have made self-diagnosing less risky, but the need for help from a good teacher is also vital for shortcutting the improvement program and avoiding trips down counterproductive paths.

When Watson has sought outside help, his primary sources have been Stan Thirsk at Kansas City C.C., and the legendary Byron Nelson, usually at Preston Trail in Dallas. Thirsk, a former touring pro, became Watson's primary teacher in 1961 when Tom was eleven, and remains as such.

"At that age you don't have to throw a lot of information at a kid," Thirsk has said. "Tom's dad has an excellent swing, long and upright. Tom simply imitated Ray Watson's swing."

One thing Thirsk did for Tom was make his swing still more upright. "He thought I needed to hit the ball higher," Watson explains. "And he was right." He also taught Watson how the swing and its various parts should feel. This was particularly important, because Tom does tend to dwell on swing positions, a focus that, though important, can detract from rhythm and pace and cause a decrease in naturalness.

Nelson's help has been both technical and attitudinal. "He's helped a great deal in slowing me down," Watson says. "He was a fast player, as I was, so he's told me things he's actually experienced. He's worked on the rhythm of my waggle, improving my footwork, trying to make me take everything a bit slower, to be less fidgety."

Nelson also taught Watson about competing successfully, a valid topic from a man who won 18 tour events, 11 in a row, in 1945. Most importantly, Byron was able to

197

convince Watson that less-than-perfect ball-striking did not necessarily ordain poor scoring. He made the young man realize that his overall game was sound enough to win major championships.

And Nelson's advice often happened to be extremely well timed. Before the final round of the aforementioned 1975 British Open, with the wind blowing and rain threatening. Byron told Tom, "No matter what happens out there today, even if you make three bad shots in a row, don't let the weather discourage you. Everybody else will be making bogies, too. Just play the best you can."

Nelson also talked to Tom by telephone the night preceding the final round of the 1977 Masters. He told him he had watched him play on television that day and thought he was driving the ball well and that his tempo was OK. This seemingly slight conversation was significant, because Tom had just lost two tournaments in a row after leading by three shots. Again, the reporters were asking how he felt about his nerves. Patiently, he had tried to explain the difference between choking and merely swinging badly, as he felt had been the case.

Watson started that final round at Augusta National tied for the lead with Ben Crenshaw and with Nicklaus three shots back. After an out-nine 32, with birdies on holes 5 through 8, his lead over Nicklaus was four. It was back to two after he bogied and Jack birdied the 10th hole. It was only one after Jack made an 18-foot birdie putt on the treacherous par-three 12th.

Watson stood in mid-fairway at the par-five, dogleg-left 13th and watched Nicklaus, on the green ahead, raise his arm after sinking another birdie, this to tie the race. Tom thought Jack was challenging him with the gesture, although later Jack explained he'd merely been acknowledging gallery applause. With competitive juices flowing even harder as well as Nelson's words of confidence in mind, Watson then made his own birdie after reaching the green in two.

Thereafter, he three-putted 14 to again lose the lead, but fought back with a birdie on 15 and another great one on 17, with a downhill 16-foot putt that broke some four feet from right to left. That won the tournament. It also put the choke label to rest once and for all.

It is difficult to pick out for discussion any particular aspects of Watson's overall game and swing technique that have dominated his thinking over the years. It is difficult because at one time or other he's given full attention to virtually every aspect. "Tom will never be satisfied with his swing," Nelson once said. "Even if he got to the point where he was hitting every shot just right, he would still find something he wanted to change."

Among his strengths and weaknesses, length off the tee has never been a problem. Width has. "Losing the ball to the right—the pushed shot—is something I've always had trouble with," Tom says. "That's probably the key fault in my swing. It's basically a posture fault. I'm too straight up at impact, more so than I was at address." (Watson has frequently said that he feels the setup should pretty much reflect where the player would like to be during impact.)

He also lists tempo as an ongoing challenge. "I still get a little too quick," he says. "Pressure seems to exacerbate that problem." And he mentions setting up too open at address, aligned too far left with his right arm and side too high, as a negative tendency that keeps returning like an unwelcome relative. "Setting up too open restricts my hip turn going back," he observes. "I don't get the club set deep enough behind me, and, to draw the ball, that's where you need to be."

Though drawing and fading shots at will has been Tom's forté since Hook Watson set the tone for his practice sessions, his upright swing plane did make left-to-right shots the more comfortable shape. In 1976 and 1977 he made conscious efforts to flatten his swing a little. This made his basic shots fly lower and less left to right. Further flattening—and now we are talking about minute altering—allowed him to fly the ball still lower on a more boring or penetrating trajectory. He finds this shape particularly useful in the wind, especially on British Open links (he has, of course, won five British Opens).

Watson's preoccupation with shaping

shots resulted not only from his father's influence, but also from the nature of the Kansas City C.C. itself. (Usually the course where a person plays most of his or her golf during the formative years has a decided influence on the type of game that evolves.) As young Tom, Hook and the gang played it, the Kansas City course measured about 6,700 yards. It is tight, twisting, well-treed, and most of the greens are rather small. In short, it is a layout that rewards making the ball curve, as well as fly high over trees and low beneath their limbs.

Often courses with narrow fairways breed restricted swings that shorten a player's distance potential. In Watson's case, however, it would seem safe to assume that the ever-present model of his father's long, high, flowing swing negated such restricting, as did the sheer need for Tom to drive far in order to compete with the adults. To this day, he still plays the par-fours and par-fives at K.C.C.C. with a driver off the tee, but admits he'd cut back to more-lofted clubs if he were competing there in a tournament.

Small greens tend to generate good short games, which Tom has always had in spades. For a time in the late 1970's, his ability to save shots with his excellent short approaching and deadly putting led to a new phrase on tour. A "Watson par" was what you made from out of the boonies. Watson feels that the small greens and the resulting short-game prowess also helped strengthen his game in another way. It is quite probable that no other American golfer has ever competed so well in bad weather. A typical example occurred at the ever-awesome Muirfield Village, in 1979, when wind and cold combined for a 13-degree chill factor. Watson shot 69 that day. The average score for the field was 79.5, and a couple of players were in the 90's.

No doubt Tom's patience and competitiveness contribute to his hanging in so well in bad weather. No doubt all the hours he's practiced and played in oft-inclement Kansas City have also helped. But, as he points out, to play well in wind, rain and cold, you also need a good short game, as one develops on tight courses with small greens.

Before closing this chapter dealing with influences on Tom Watson's outstanding career, it would be an atrocious neglect not to mention the two people with whom he has spent the most time. They are his wife, Linda, and his caddie, Bruce Edwards.

Linda Rubin Watson, his childhood sweetheart and mother of Meg and Michael, twice refused to marry Tom for fear that life as a touring pro's wife would not work out. Looking back, it is impossible to imagine anyone handling the role better than she has.

Edwards has been Watson's "Watson," his caddie and close friend, for fourteen years, helping on a face-to-face basis for some six or seven hours a day, reading greens, measuring distances, giving moral support during the trying times. The impact he has had on Tom's success is, like Linda's, incalculable.

Watson, by what he has accomplished, deserves to be remembered as one of the truly great players along with the likes of Nelson, Hogan, Nicklaus and Jones. There are those who would wish that, as leader of the pack for several years, he had shown more charisma—a flashier dress code, more Trevino-like one-liners—but such was not his way, at least not while on the job.

To these critics, Watson has always answered in the vein suggested by Stan Thirsk. "You don't make your reputation by dressing flashy or talking a good game," Tom has said. "You make it by playing well and winning."

And that is exactly how any Kansas City gunslinger would have gone about it.

Seve Ballesteros

THE DASHING LATIN GENIUS

The best golf shot Jack Nicklaus ever witnessed was played on the 578-yard par-five 18th hole of The Champion course at the PGA National Golf Club in Palm Beach Gardens, Florida, on Sunday, October 16, 1983.

The shot, executed under the most intense competitive pressure, was cut with a three-wood from a severely-uphill, feet-below-ball sidehill lie in a sand bunker, over a man-high front lip only a few paces ahead, to the fringe of the green 245 yards distant. Nicklaus's exact description of it that day was the "finest shot I've ever seen." When the shot came up in a discussion a few weeks later, Jack volunteered not only that he probably could not himself have brought it off once in ten tries, but that he doubted if anyone else could either, except for the man who had done so that hot and muggy Sunday afternoon.

The player of that incredible shot was Severiano Ballesteros. When asked later whether it was the greatest of his life, he pondered a moment, then in a tone of simple factuality untinged by the slightest air of braggadocio, said "No." And this was, of course, indubitably the correct answer. Seve Ballesteros had by then hit so many awesome, unbelievable, impossible shots since his stunning arrival on the world golf scene in the summer of 1976 that there truly was just no way he could validly anoint one over another.

Since then the count has continued to climb, to a point where Ballesteros' status as the game's all-time champion stroke innovator and manufacturer is now virtually beyond dispute. Not even those of his adversaries who feel less than warmly about other aspects of the man would deny that, in this regard, he is touched with genius. In a tournament locker-room one day Lee Trevino capsulized it this way: "Seve Ballesteros can do things with a golf club that no one even *thought* about before, let alone tried." Overhearing him, Tom Watson added: "Not even Ben Hogan." It is difficult to imagine a weightier accolade.

Of all the champions examined in this book, Ballesteros presents the most enigmas, especially in the complexity and capriciousness of his hairtrigger psyche. But there is no mystery about the origins of his peer-

200

SEVE BALLESTEROS

Born: April 9, 1957; Pedrena, Spain

Major victories:
    Masters: 1980, 1983
    British Open: 1979, 1984 , 1988

SEVE BALLESTEROS

The enormous centrifugal force that generates the speed of clubhead that drives a golf ball Ballesteros-type distances is impossible without a complete hinging and unhinging of the "lever" formed by the left arm and club shaft. No doubt an awareness of this at some stage of his career, conscious or unconscious, led to Seve's major backswing idiosyncrasy, a comparatively early cocking (or hinging) of the wrists. But, whereas for many golfers this would lead to a lifting of the club with insufficient arm extension and upper body coiling, his width of arc and degree of coiling at the top is absolutely flawless. As the rest of the sequence indicates, this is the backswing of an athlete: storing up and unleasing massive power, but keeping it totally under control all the way.

less shotmaking abilities, any more than there should be about what fuels his desperate compulsion to excel and his seemingly neverending wars with authority and establishment.

Ballesteros is the classic throw-back to the days before professional tournament golf got middle-classed and collegized and mechanized and blandified, to the time when "disadvantaged" kids taught themselves to play behind caddie shacks by mimicry and trial and error in between hauling the bags of their "betters" for pittances, plus, hopefully, a generous tip. In the major golfing nations the social egalitarianizing that followed World War II had pretty much eviscerated this system by the time Seve discovered golf, but in the highly and rigidly stratified class structure of Spain, the tardiest of Western European nations to embrace democracy, it was approaching its zenith. Just as boxing and basketball offered passage out of the ghetto to so many American blacks, consciously or otherwise golf became for Ballesteros, the fourth son of a farmer who lived above his animals, the best—indeed, perhaps the only—escape route from a lifetime of second-class citizenship.

A couple of generations previously, an even less "advantaged" Texan kid by the name of William Ben Hogan had perceived then labored savagely to grasp a similar opportunity; and there was a representative, too, from the intervening generation, and from much the same geographic and social environs as his famous predecessor: Lee Buck Trevino. Different as they are from Seve and from each other in so many ways, the fascinating similarity between this trio is

Photographs by Stephen Szurlej.
Permission *Golf Digest* © Golf Digest/Tennis Inc.

their commanding superiority as shot-makers—and particularly, in the case of the two younger men, the inventiveness and dexterity that came from originally having to learn the game and play every shot with a single and often highly inappropriate club.

In his new instructional book, *Natural Golf*, Seve admits to a fiery youthful envy of the college-golf-scholarshipped, always-professionally-coached, parentally-subsidized brand of champion typified in his mind by Jack Nicklaus, but then quickly adds that, if he had enjoyed the same advantages, he probably wouldn't be half the player he is today.

In other words, teaching yourself the game may be the toughest way to learn it, but it can also make you in the end a better golfer than you ever could become by any other means.

Seve's early social, financial and golfing circumstances have been well documented since his emergence as a superstar, but every aspect of his game is so deeply rooted in his formative experiences and environment that any useful analysis of it demands at least a snapshot look at them.

Severiano Ballesteros was born two days after Douglas Ford surprised pretty much everyone but himself by winning the 1957 Masters, to Baldemero and Carmen Ballesteros Sota, in their home in Pedrena, a small farming and fishing village situated across a pretty bay from Santander, a city of about 140,000 people some hundred miles west of France on Spain's green and fertile but often chilly and weather-battered northern coast. Not far to the south of Pedrena and Santander the Cantabrian Mountains form a kind of barrier to the rest of the country, and the

montaneses, as the people of the region are known, are said to possess certain distinctive characteristics, among them courage, resourcefulness, and thriftyness sometimes to the point of meanness. They are also reputed to be by nature suspicious of just about everything and everyone, highly superstitious, radiant and broodingly grim by turns, and even more matriarchially inclined in their family lives than the rest of the country.

The Ballesteros family lived in a century-old stone farmhouse built by Seve's maternal grandparents, immediately overlooking the Real Club de Golf de Pedrena, probably the best and certainly the most exclusive club in northern Spain. The stables for the animals formed most of the ground floor, with the family living quarters above. Writers who have visited the home describe it as having supplied the essentials but very little more, which also seems to sum up the family finances from farming, at least until the sons were able to contribute. Most of the visitors have remarked on the smallness and simplicity, almost approaching starkness, of Seve's bedroom, and invariably on the fact that it was windowless.

Seve is the baby of the four surviving Ballesteros offspring, having been preceded by a boy who died of wasp stings at the age of two, then by Baldomero Jr., Manuel, and Vicente. The brothers are respectively ten, seven, and five years older than Seve. Manuel played the European tour for a while, his achievements perhaps being more than a little limited towards the end by his intense devotion to shepherding Seve. Now, like Baldomero and Vicente, Manuel is a well-employed and highly regarded club professional in Spain. All three have taken time out to caddie for their brother in major championships in recent years, and the relationships between the four are very close.

The initial Ballesteros connection to golf came through Seve's mother, the former Carmen Sota Ocejo, whose brother, Ramon, after discovering the game as a caddie at Pedrena, became in the late 1960's Spain's best player pre-Seve, with five national Open victories across Europe and six Masters appearances in the U.S. Ramon Sota is now the professional at Pedrena. For whatever reasons, he appears to have been disinclined to give his nephew much help with his game during his early years, and one senses a certain coolness in their relationship, at least on the younger man's side.

Seve's father, Baldomero, Sr., only became an occasional golfer of sorts a few years before he died of cancer at age sixty-seven in the spring of 1986, chiefly so he could spend more time with his sons. But he was an accomplished distance runner and oarsman in his prime, and a commanding figure from whom his youngest offspring obviously inherited his superb physique (Seve is 6 feet tall and weighs a well-proportioned and muscular 190 pounds). Ballesteros Sr.'s legacy in terms of mental toughness is perhaps best measured by the fact that, knowing he might receive a long prison sentence or worse, he shot himself through the left hand rather than fight for the Republicans when shanghied into their army in Spain's Civil War.

Friends of the family say that, as is often the case with the youngest in a large family, there has always been an intense closeness between Seve and his parents (his brothers goodnaturedly talk about how much they spoiled him), and people in golf around the world saw clearly how devastated he was by his father's illness and death. Still unmarried at the time of writing, Seve continues to live with his mother in a fine but unpretentious house he built in 1980, about a drive and long-iron from their old home (which, inevitably, Señora Ballesteros avers she much prefers).

Seve's first direct contact with golf came when he was seven and someone gave him an old three-iron head. He cleaned it up, made shafts for it out of sticks cut from shrubbery (which broke almost daily), and, because golf balls were too expensive for his brothers to part with theirs, used in their place stones gathered from the nearby beach. The "holes" to hit them on he scraped from farmland and seashore. Invariably alone, and often so preoccupied he failed to hear his mother calling him home to meals,

One of the most common – and destructive – faults of middle- and high-handicappers is "losing the angles" at some point in the swing, generally during its backward segment and usually by raising or dipping the upper body, often as a result of poor or improper leg action. Along with its many other lessons, this sequence provides a superb example of the antidote. All of the angles Ballesteros establishes in his magnificent set-up to the ball – the forward inclination of the torso from the hips, the "geometry" from the waist down – remain constant deep into his follow-through. As with all great players, this constancy of bodily attitude throughout the swing is a major key to Seve's constancy of arc and thus his purity of strike time and time again.

he would beat his pebbles to and fro, to and fro, on his improvised courses, hour upon hour, day after day.

At age eight the uncommonly handsome but often intensely *severo* (serious) little boy began to caddie at Pedrena, at which time he acquired his first real golf club from Manuel, without which, the brother remembers, he immediately "could not exist—he was like a man with no legs". It was a complete three-iron, but desperately cumbersome in shaft length and heavy in head weight for his size and strength. Nevertheless, almost at once Seve could hit a real golf ball with it from the farmhouse forecourt over a stand of pine trees onto the second green of the golf course 150 yards away. By often painful and invariably frustrating trial and error, he would also come to be capable of playing just about every type of golf shot in the book with this lone club, including lovely delicate little high floaters from deep sand bunkers.

The shot from the yard to the golf course was risky beyond the trauma of losing a precious ball, in that, with very rare exceptions, caddies were permitted on Real Club de Golf de Pedrena only to carry the bags of members and their guests (for the then equivalent of about 40 cents a round). Nevertheless, as his skills developed and his passion for the game became unconstrainable, the youngster would sneak onto the course whenever he thought he had the slightest chance of getting away with completing even one hole of real golf. Mostly he played his illicit games at night, listening his way around, or raced through the dew and the mist to beat the sunrise, battling par when alone and betting his fellow caddies with more pesetas than he could afford to

lose whenever their nerve and his uncle permitted him to satisfy an ever-growing hunger for human competition.

His favorite hole was the second, a par-three of 198 yards, partly because it was so near to his home, but even more because it allowed him to measure his ball-striking progress by how close to the green he could come with the three-iron. It infuriated him that his brothers could get home with irons, while, even as his technique improved and his muscles grew, he for so long had to borrow woods to have any chance. "My ambition to reach that green with an iron," he once recalled, "was every bit as intense as my ambition later to win a major championship."

Before his tenth birthday, he had completed the Pedrena course with a couple of clubs in under one hour and one hundred strokes, and shortly after it he scored 51 in a nine-hole caddie tournament after starting with a 10 and ending in tears of frustration. By the age of twelve, whenever he could get all the way around the 6,315-yard course, he expected to complete it at or in very little over par. A couple of years after that he got his first pair of real golf shoes, an over-large pair discarded by a member, and in them quickly beat Manuel for the first time.

By then, golf had become virtually Severiano Ballesteros' whole life, consuming him to the point of constant truancy from school, self-imposed abstinence from alcohol, tobacco and girls, and endless fantasies about winning every golf championship in the world by at least 20 strokes. Two more years of this and any possibility of a prominent amateur career disappeared with his acceptance of the gift of a fine new set of

matched clubs—his first—and a bag from an American serviceman friend of his brother Vicente. Six months after that, on January 1, 1974, Seve became the youngest accredited tournament professional in the history of Spanish golf—and conceivably European golf as a whole—when the Royal Spanish Golf Federation issued him with a player's card. He was sixteen years eight months and twenty-one days old.

In that first year as a professional his highest finish in seven European and four South African tournaments was second place in the Italian Open. In 1975 he competed fourteen times in European tour events and once in Japan, with a third place in the Lancome Trophy in Paris his best performance. In July of 1976 he made world headlines by tieing for second with Jack Nicklaus behind Johnny Miller at Royal Birkdale in the British Open, after driving the ball wondrous distances but frequently into places no one had ever been before. He was then nineteen and a quarter years old. By the time he reached thirty, in the spring of 1987, his victory total exceeded fifty in more than a dozen countries on five continents, including two Masters and two British Opens. By that time he was also generally regarded as, day in and day out, the finest golfer in the world.

It often seems to the befuddled weekender that there are far more elements of golf technique about which professionals disagree than there are points of consensus, and this book certainly doesn't do much to negate that notion. One exception, however, is the setup, at least if one employs the broad definition of it as everything that happens from the moment a player selects a club to the instant he begins to swing it. Although celebrated players and teachers differ on some of the details, they are pretty much of a mind that the process of getting ready to strike a golf ball is by far the most critical part of the enterprise. Jack Nicklaus, for instance, has frequently gone on record to say that, in his opinion, the relative importance of the setup and the swinging action are 80–20 in favor of the former. Sam Snead's down-home way of putting it is that, "If he don't aim it right, the best swing God ever gave a man won't git him where he wants to go."

Another exception to the seemingly infinite and ever more arcane inconsistencies that dizzy all deep delvers into golf technique is tempo, or rhythm, or timing, or whatever you might choose to call the quality of the pace, or flow, or "togetherness," of the motions inherent in hitting a golf ball. Nobody is able to explain or describe this quality very well, but there is *total* consensus—Hosannahs!—that, whatever "it" is, it is fundamental to golfing excellence. Indeed, some even regard "it" as the game's absolute holy grail.

It is my view that, of all Ballesteros' many remarkable physical assets, his setup and his tempo/rhythm/timing are by far and away the ones most responsible for his prodigious competitive record. From around late 1979/early 1980, when he stopped trying to drive every par-four and began to make the constraining adjustments to his full swing necessary to play a more percentages-oriented (i.e., brainier) brand of golf, it seems to me that he has arranged himself at the ball as well as if not better than anyone who ever played the game. I believe the same to be true of the quality of his swinging motion. Further, I believe that any golfer of reasonable health and strength who could emulate Ballesteros' setup in all its particularities, then move the club to and fro with, say, about 75 percent of Seve's freedom and fluidity, would have one heck of a job averaging much over par.

What is most impressive about Seve's setup is the repetition and economy and gracefulness of movement with which the whole thing eases—almost oozes—so confidently into place; always smooth as silk and consistent as clockwork whatever the upcoming shot, routine or out of the ordinary, from drive to tap-in putt. As with the Ballesteros tempo/rhythm/timing, the best way to appreciate the excellence of this procedure—and perhaps to absorb a little of all of these qualities into one's own game—is to observe the man in action as often and for as long as possible, perhaps trying at first more to sense or "feel" what happens than to chart the mechanics involved.

If that's not possible, then knowing those mechanics will certainly do no harm, because they are impeccable. Let's look first at those of the setup:

- It should go without saying that everything flows from a truly superb grip, as mechanically fine and functional and orthodox as it is possible to see, either in this book or on any golf course in the world today. As to firmness of hold, the writer and famous Ballesteros analyst, Peter Dobereiner, after having Seve grip his forefinger golf-style, reported: "The pressure would not have squeezed the toothpaste from the tube."

- Seve's stance may seem to be on the wide side to some, but he is broad-shouldered and the distance between his heels with the driver precisely equals his shoulder span. Like other top modern players, he has found that such distancing provides the best compromise between the somewhat conflicting needs to strenuously coil the upper body on the backswing for torque or leverage, then vigorously lead the downswing from the ground up, while at all times retaining perfect balance and stability.

- At one time, Seve set a little more weight on his left foot than his right at address, which sometimes sent him into a slight but often fatal reverse pivot (curing this in practice before the 1984 British Open at St. Andrews played a big part in his winning there). These days, the distribution tends to equality, or even a slight favoring of the right side, which encourages and facilitates a complete weight shift and upper-body coiling in that direction. (The foregoing applies, of course, only to what might be called "routine" shots. A big factor in Seve's ability to invent and manufacture off-beat strokes is the skillful apportioning of little-to-large amounts of weight one way or another to promote a particular swing effect.)

- Both feet are angled outward, the right barely to serve as a brake on torque-

diminishing excessive backswing hip turn; the left a little more to facilitate sprightly leg and hip action into and during the throughswing.

- The amount of flex is identical at each knee: sufficient to promote "centeredness" of the torso as it coils and uncoils; insufficient to restrict the "spring" in the swing; but, above all, unexaggerated and therefore comfortable.

- The feet, knees, hips and shoulders are all precisely parallel to the ball's intended initial starting path (which, in the case of the accompanying photographs, as Seve was attempting a dead straight shot, means an imaginary direct ball-to-target line). If you want a superior example of a "square" set-up, here is one.

- It is almost impossible to strike a golf ball solidly in its rear unless the "radius" of the swing formed by the left arm and clubshaft is completely restored at impact. Like Jack Nicklaus, Seve pre-programs or rehearses this critical piece of geometry by setting his left arm and the shaft in a straight line at address. Also like Nicklaus—who believes this to be a "must" of fine golf—Seve lets his arms hang very easily from his shoulders, as exemplified by their almost vertical alignment.

- Cary Middlecoff once described Ballesteros as "free as a bird at address, particularly in his distance from the ball." Major contributors to both the distancing and the great sense of freedom for arm-swinging it connotes are his postural body angles. Seve arranges his spine, neck and head virtually in a straight line, then gets down to the ball by inclining forward from his hips, then counterbalances his weight by sticking his butt out (which is partly responsible for his degree of knee flex). Proponents of present-day pro-tour swing ideals in particular would say that the end product is about as close to postural perfection as anyone has yet come. Perhaps even more important for the struggling weekender to note, however, is that, having established fine angles at address, Seve maintains or "stays in them" beautifully throughout his entire swing. That seems to be one of the things poor players most commonly don't do, perhaps because the need to is somewhat neglected in both the teaching end of the game and its technical literature.

- Finally, regarding the setup, note that a line descending vertically from Seve's left ear would intersect with his clubhead, which means he positions his head where he wants it to be at impact—well behind the ball. There are essentially two reasons why such a relationship is vitally important. The first is to enable the clubhead to be swung into the ball on a path both low to the ground and from inside the target line (forward head positioning and/or movement causes the out-to-in, steeply-descending, oblique, weak contact of the inveterate slicer). The second reason is to facilitate the uncoiling motions of the knees and hips swinging down and through that is essential in order to deliver to the ball all of the centrifugal force generated in the clubhead, by making space for the arms to swing freely past the body. (Such motion is inhibited proportionately to the amount the head and upper body move targetwards along with the clubhead, which is a principal reason why so many high-handicappers hit the ball so short.)

Moving now from Seve's pre-motion qualities to his second great physical asset, the tempo/rhythm/timing of the swing they so beautifully prepare him for, we immediately run into the chief bugaboo of all sports instructional texts. While the texture of a star athlete's motions may become "sense"-able and thereby partially or wholly mimicable via direct observation, to convey it with words and still pictures in a manner that makes it applicable by a third party is virtually impossible. Therefore, beyond one final exhortation to watch the man in the flesh at any and every opportunity, just a couple of thoughts on this aspect of Seve's game.

Like almost all of golf's greats, irrespective of mechanical preferences or idiosyncrasies, Seve's motion from the milli-second of its initiation to that of its completion is smooth, oily, fluid, *flowing*: no jerks, snatches, hesitations, sudden changes of pace, or other denominations of hitch and glitch. Second, its progression has a distinct and unvarying kind of gather-and-go beat: O–n–e, *t–w–o*. O–n–e, *t–w–o*. O–n–e (up and back), *t–w–o* (down—*whomph!*—and through). Third, although he undoubtedly knows that the scientists say that the laws of centrifugal force are such that the speed of the clubhead peaks some distance before impact, and that there is nothing any human can do to prevent that, like most exceptionally powerful but rhythmical golfers Seve thinks about, tries for, and senses acceleration of the clubhead not only to but through and then well on past the ball. Fourth, he believes that rhythmic movement is the single most important factor in the golf swing, and that relaxation—or, more precisely, absence of excessive muscle tension—is the key to achieving it.

Is the sum of these qualities sufficient to account for the magical quality of the Ballesteros swing motion? My belief is that they are all contributors, but that in the final analysis the most critical ingredient is simply innate talent.

It seems to me that, over the century and a bit in which formal tournament play has spotlighted such things, a handful of people just happen to have been supremely gifted in this dimension of the game, and, because it is so critical, have all become superb—and superbly "natural-looking"—players. In every case, if this is true, they have inevitably started much nearer to the top of the mountain by having this component already in place as they set out as youngsters to learn and refine mechanics; and in my view it is this quality that people have alluded to, knowingly or otherwise, when they have used words like "genius" to describe their talents.

Harry Vardon was perhaps the first of these golfers, and Sam Snead was the last. Seve Ballesteros, to me, is the latest.

Compelled by some kind of inner gods or demons to attain ever greater golfing heights, intelligent enough to have analysed and absorbed golfing cause and effect as well as anyone who ever played, and strong enough to work stupendously at golf physically, Seve Ballesteros has constructed out of his masterly setup and around his peerless rhythm an exceptionally fine set of full-swing mechanics. Let's look at the major components, keeping in mind, first, that, although he often speaks of the swing as being a two-handed, two-sided endeavor, Ballesteros believes he controls his principally with his right hand and side; and, secondly, that when he stands at ease his right hand hangs two inches lower than his left:

- Seve's sense of his initial swing movements, according to most of his writings, is that of the classical shoulders/hips/knees/hands-all-starting-back-together, one-piece action so favored and so well exemplified by Jack Nicklaus. However, photographs both still and moving tell a different story, i.e., that the first Ballesteros move is a distinct rotation of the hands away from the target, the one-piece process then flowing quickly along just as Seve says it does. Black and white evidence of this is to be seen in the first photos after address in both the face-on and down-the-line sequences printed here: the back of the left hand was looking at the target at address, but, long before the amount of Seve's upper-body coiling could solely have realigned it thus, it is now looking directly at the ball. Tom Weiskopf made almost the identical initiating move in recent times, as before him during certain periods of his career did Ben Hogan (at which times he talked about "pronation"). Many other good players have done the same thing to a greater or lesser degree down the years, and have claimed multiple benefits from it. Perhaps principal among them are that the move obviates any hook- or block-producing shutting down or closing of the clubface during the critical early part of the swing; helps to ensure that the back of the left hand and the wrist and forearm remain in line, or "square," as the action progresses; and promotes setting of the hands very supportively well beneath the club's shaft at the top of the backswing, which is generally regarded as the ideal positioning from which to vigorously release the clubhead into the ball.

- Although there is almost certainly no conscious effort to cock the wrists early, the fact that in the second down-the-line photo the clubhead has risen to a point above Seve's knees, while his hands have raised only fractionally higher than their address position, is an indication that the setting begins virtually concurrently with the clubhead leaving the ball. The cocking then gradually increases throughout the remainder of the backswing, involuntarily in response to the momentum of the clubhead, to an admirably full set at the top. Conceivably, without the early start, this process of "hinging the lever" would be neither so smooth nor so complete, which would eat heavily into Seve's power by reducing his capacity to generate clubhead speed by unhinging it. Also, the early initiation of the setting is a further aid to reaching the top with the hands well underneath the shaft.

- Simultaneously with the actions described above, Seve's chin cocks to the right, à la Snead and Nicklaus, to facilitate full upper-body coiling. Then, as with many big-turning, high-arm-swinging long hitters, his head moves progressively farther away from the target until, at the completion of the backswing, it is some four to six inches back of its address position. And, of course, that's where it remains until the ball is on its way.

- What's the proper "plane" of the golf swing? John Jacobs, the eminent British teaching professional, has always stressed—sometimes as a voice in the wilderness—that there are in fact *two* planes in the finest swings, and that they don't and never should match. The easiest way to strike a powerful and accurate golf shot, Jacobs insists and religiously instructs, is with, going back, the shoulders turning on a shallow or flat or close to horizontal plane, while the arms swing upward on a steeper or more upright or closer to vertical plane—each component then more or less reversing its plane on the way down and through. If you would like to be convinced of this, lay a straight-edge along Seve's shoulder line at the top of his backswing, then through the center of his left arm, and compare the two angles: then repeat the process, but with his right arm instead of his left, at the completion of his follow-through. Another interesting exercise is to lay the straight edge along the center of Seve's left arm at the top of the backswing, then slide it down until it meets the ball. You'll find that it connects dead center, which indicates two things. The first is that Seve's arm-swing path or plane is perfect for his build and setup posture. The second is that he has perfectly retained at the completion of the backswing the postural angles he established at address. Finally, note how at the top of the Ballesteros backswing the left forearm, left wrist, back of left hand and clubface are all in the same alignment. "Square" just doesn't come any prettier than this.

- At one stage of his career, when he was younger and not as wise and wily, Seve in swinging the driver would sometimes turn his shoulders through 130 degrees or more. The ball would then quite often travel well over 300 yards. However, he would frequently never find it, or, if he did, have to conjure up some special piece of magic just to get it back on short grass. These days, a reduction to somewhere between 90 and 100 degrees of shoulder coil, along with a less forced extension of the arms—"my serene swing," he calls it—provides much greater control over the direction of shots, while still permitting drives only an insignificant few paces behind those of the game's top cannons. The freedom and the scale of the Ballesteros upper-body coil is thrillingly evident in both photo sequences: he still coils as fully as he can without losing any of his right knee flex, or pushing his weight to the outside of his right foot. What anyone seeking to emulate this textbook backswing coiling should carefully note, however, is how the behavior of all the body parts below the waist are strictly *reactions*

to the swinging arms and the winding torso. Seve's legs and hips really don't do much of anything until his hands are at about hip height, at which time they are simply pulled into their final top-of-the-backswing positions by the actions taking place above. The result is an immensely powerful build up or torque or leverage, the release of which eventually translates into both very high clubhead speed and precise squaring of the clubface to the ball at impact.

Every time a great or good golfer heads to the first tee, he takes with him one or more "swing keys" that he hopes and believes will keep everything meshing smoothly for at least the duration of that particular round. These are self-determined, short, technical, reminder-type admonitions—"Initiate with left hip," "Complete the backswing," "Keep head back," that type of thing—selected from among scores of such thoughts for their degree and tenure of workability over the years. Sometimes they take the form of mind-pictures rather than phrases, such as Nicklaus' envisioning of a razor-blade-embedded wall so located that it will shred his hands if they fail to follow the desired path as the backswing is initiated. Usually these thoughts or images for the day are finalized on the practice tee during the warm-up session, emerging from or being locked into place largely by the feel of the action as it is tuned for battle. The majority of players prefer to limit such keys to one or two at a time, both to "keep it simple" and to save most of their mental faculties for the analytical and strategical decisions so vital to good scoring, but Nicklaus has admitted to playing critical major championship rounds with as many as five of them in mind. As in the game of golf all good moves seem eventually to become exaggerated, even among the best, most top players have a store of around a dozen such thoughts, which they rotate or interchange as mood, feel or score suggests.

Over the years I've been privileged to learn many of the swing keys of a lot of the game's top performers. While each is interesting on its own, the most intriguing thing about them is that collectively they relate almost entirely to things that occur prior to and including the completion of the backswing. And, of course, just a moment's reflection about the sheer speed of the remainder of the golfing action provides the reason why. The human neuro-muscular system simply won't work fast enough for the down-and-through-swing ever to be consciously controlled. Once you get to the top—or perhaps progressively sooner the less skilled the player—that's it for the intellect: whatever's on your mind, your body by now functions entirely by reflex or instinct, or some combination of the two.

The truth of this has been proven scientifically, but it is perhaps even more convincingly evidenced by every fine player's intense and never-ending preoccupation with even the subtlest details of the geometry of the setup and the backswing. What they would seem to be thereby demonstrating is that the quality of the striking part of the action, because it can only be reflexive, is totally dependent on how well it is prepared for.

Because he prepares so superbly for it, Seve Ballesteros' striking part of the action is, it seems to me, about as good as there ever has been. And, although none of us can achieve the moves that comprise it other than as effects, knowing what they are can sharpen our focus on the setup and backswing factors that cause them:

- As we've seen throughout this book, all good golfers swing down from the ground up, or with the following progression of targetwards pulling motion, at least up to the point of impact: feet, knees, hips, belly, chest, arms, hands, club shaft, clubhead. Remember, though, that the sequence occurs not by conscious direction, but as a *reaction* to the almost involuntary release of the torque created by the coil-spring-like winding of the upper half of the body against the resilient resistance of the lower half. A player who tried to copy Seve's downswing motions without having built plenty of torque into his backswing would simply throw all of himself too far

forward too quickly and weakly to strike the ball effectively.

- As the downswing progresses, and particularly during the release of the clubhead by the hands and wrists, Seve's head moves slightly down and incrementally farther away from the target. By this point in his career such head motion has become purely a reflexive response to the powerful driving of his knees and unwinding of his hips, but, like all fine golfers, preventing his head from sliding forward with the club—as nature always urges it to do until it is trained otherwise—was something Seve had to work especially hard on in originally constructing his game. So, if you feel you absolutely have to have a downswing key, make it: "Head moves back as club goes forward."

- Notice in the accompanying photographs how the initiation of the foward motion from the ground up pulls Seve's arms and club into a slightly lower or flatter plane than they swung back on. That's common to all great modern golfers, and is the supreme, slice-killing, distance-improving medicine for all the rest of us.

- Notice in the seventh down-the-line photo how beautifully Seve swings "under" rather than "around" himself. Positional indicators of that enviable pattern include: shoulders still partially coiled as still-fully-cocked hands descend below waist level; right elbow relaxed and almost on right hip; knees almost parallel; right heel only just beginning to leave ground. There are a lot of golfers playing professional tours around the world who would happily give a year or two's winnings to be able to swing through such marvellous positions even half as repetitively as this man does.

- Finally, take a moment to admire and reflect on that wonderfully free, full, relaxed and perfectly balanced finish: weight almost entirely on the outside of the left foot; torso facing the target; eyes tracking the ball over the upper right arm; shoulders and arms replicating their top-of-backswing positions; folding left elbow and well-cupped left wrist indicating a complete, perfectly-timed and thrillingly powerful release of the clubhead into the ball.

Truly, this is a one-in-a-million golf swing, and a golf swing for the ages.

The phenomenal Ballesteros three-wood bunker shot described at the beginning of this chapter was played the final afternoon of the 1983 Ryder Cup match. Seve was first out that day for the Europeans, and the shot enabled him to tie his single with Fuzzy Zoeller, giving each player half a point. However, the Spaniard had had the American three down at one stage, and, with the series tied at the start of the day, Ballesteros was distraught that, as spearheader, he had not provided his teammates with the inspiration of a clear victory. Then, when the U.S. finally prevailed by just a single point in one of the great cliff-hangers of all time, he was even more upset about his supposed lack of leadership qualities.

Ballesteros does not easily forgive himself for any golfing lapse, but surely the enormity of his overall impact upon European golf must one day quench the fires of such occasional hiccups, even in his ultra-perfectionist soul. Two years later the Europeans won the Ryder Cup easily in England, with a team consisting of seven Britons, four Spaniards, and one German, including the reigning Masters and British Open champions in Bernhard Langer and Sandy Lyle. Two years after that, they won it for the first time in America with a comparable mix of nationalities on the twelve-man squad.

From the long-ago days of the Great Triumvirate of Harry Vardon, J.H. Taylor and James Braid to the age of Seve, such achievements by European golfers, with rare exceptions like Henry Cotton and Tony Jacklin, were barely more than patriotic pipe-dreams. At the time of writing, just a dozen years after the Spaniard's dashing Royal Birkdale debut, the best of the Europeans have become consistently the equal and increasingly the superior of any golfers in the world; more and more are grinding and clawing their way to the summit each season; and the aura of hang-dog inferiority that cost the old-worlders so dearly for so long against the colonials, Yankee and otherwise, is but a shadowy memory.

The jury may remain out for some while yet on exactly where Seve Ballesteros is ultimately to rank among the all-time greats of golf, but, if there were prizes for inspiring others, he surely would have already won first place.

BIBLIOGRAPHY

The following are the documentary sources from which this book was researched. The authors are particularly grateful to *Golf Digest* magazine, its librarian, Francine Delphia, and to Janet Seagle, of the United States Golf Association, for their help in locating and making available many of the references.

HARRY VARDON

Vardon, Harry. *The Complete Golfer.* London: Methuen, 1905.

———. *The Gist of Golf.* New York: George H. Doran, 1922.

———. *How to Play Golf.* London: Methuen, 1912.

———. *My Golfing Life.* London: Hutchinson, 1933.

——— et al. *Success at Golf.* Boston: Little, Brown, 1914.

WALTER HAGEN

Hagen, Walter. *The Walter Hagen Story.* New York: Simon & Schuster, 1956.

Martin, H. B. *Fifty Years of American Golf.* New York: Argosy, 1966.

Rice, Grantland. *The Tumult and the Shouting.* New York: A. S. Barnes, 1962.

GENE SARAZEN

Sarazen, Gene. *Better Golf After 50.* New York: Harper & Row, 1967.

———. *Gene Sarazen's Common Sense Golf Tips.* Chicago: Thomas E. Wilson Co., 1924.

——— et al. *The Golf Clinic.* Chicago: Ziff-Davis, 1949.

——— with Herbert Warren Wind. *Thirty Years of Championship Golf.* Englewood Cliffs, N.J.: Prentice-Hall, 1950.

BOBBY JONES

Jones, Bobby. *Bobby Jones on Golf.* New York: Metropolitan Fiction Co., 1930.

———. *Bobby Jones on the Basic Golf Swing.* New York: Doubleday, 1969.

Jones, Robert T., Jr. *Golf Is My Game.* New York: Doubleday, 1960.

——— and O. B. Keeler. *Down the Fairway.* New York: Minton Balch & Co., 1927.

Keeler, O. B. *The Bobby Jones Story.* Atlanta: Tupper & Love, 1953.

HENRY COTTON

Cotton, Henry. *Henry Cotton Says.* London: Country Life, 1962.

———. *My Golfing Album.* London: Country Life, 1959.

———. *Study the Golf Game with Henry Cotton.* London: Country Life, 1948.

———. *This Game of Golf.* New York: Charles Scribner's Sons, 1948.

BYRON NELSON

Nelson, Byron. *Winning Golf.* New York: A. S. Barnes, 1946.

SAM SNEAD

Snead, Sam. *The Driver Book*. Norwalk, Conn.: Golf Digest, 1964.

———. *How to Play Golf*. Garden City: Garden City Books, 1946.

———. *Natural Golf*. New York: A. S. Barnes, 1953.

———. *Sam Snead on Golf*. New York: Simon & Schuster, 1961.

———. *How to Hit a Golf Ball from Any Sort of Lie*, ed. Mark Cox. New York: Blue Ribbon Books, 1950.

——— *et al. The Golf Clinic*. Chicago: Ziff-Davis, 1949.

——— with Al Stump. *The Education of a Golfer*. New York: Simon & Schuster, 1962.

BEN HOGAN

Hogan, Ben. *Power Golf*. New York: A. S. Barnes, 1948.

——— with Herbert Warren Wind. *Modern Fundamentals of Golf*. New York: A. S. Barnes, 1957.

BOBBY LOCKE

Locke, Bobby. *Bobby Locke on Golf*. London: Country Life, 1953.

CARY MIDDLECOFF

Middlecoff, Cary. *Advanced Golf*. Englewood Cliffs, N.J.: Prentice-Hall, 1957.

———. *The Golf Swing*. Englewood Cliffs, N.J.: Prentice-Hall, 1974.

———. *Master Guide to Golf*. Englewood Cliffs, N.J.: Prentice-Hall, 1960.

PETER THOMSON

Nagle, Kel, Peter Thomson, *et al. The Secrets of Australia's Golfing Success*. London: Nicholas Kaye, 1961.

ARNOLD PALMER

McCormack, Mark H. *Arnie*. New York: Simon & Schuster, 1967.

Palmer, Arnold. *Arnold Palmer's Golf Book*. New York: Ronald Press, 1961.

———. *My Game and Yours*. New York: Simon & Schuster, 1965.

BILLY CASPER

Casper, Billy. *Chipping and Putting*. New York: Ronald Press, 1961.

———. *Golf Shotmaking with Billy Casper*. New York: Doubleday, 1966.

———. *My Million-Dollar Golf Shots*. New York: Grosset & Dunlap, 1970.

———. *295 Golf Lessons with Billy Casper*. Northfield, Ill.: Digest Books, 1973.

GARY PLAYER

Player, Gary. *Gary Player's Golf Secrets*. Englewood Cliffs, N.J.: Prentice-Hall, 1962.

———. *124 Golf Lessons*. Chicago: Golfers Digest Association, 1968.

———. *Positive Golf*. New York: McGraw-Hill, 1967.

———. *395 Golf Lessons*. Northfield, Ill.: Digest Books, 1972.

JACK NICKLAUS

Nicklaus, Jack. *My 55 Ways to Lower Your Golf Score*. New York: Simon & Schuster, 1969.

———. *Take a Tip from Me*. New York: Simon & Schuster, 1968.

——— with Ken Bowden. *Golf My Way*. New York: Simon & Schuster, 1974.

——— with Herbert Warren Wind. *The Greatest Game of All*. New York: Simon & Schuster, 1969.

TOM WATSON

Seitz, Nick. *Super-Stars of Golf*. Norwalk, Conn.: Golf Digest, 1978.

Watson, Thomas S. (with Nick Seitz). *Getting Up and Down*. New York: Random House, 1983.

SEVERIANO BALLESTEROS

Ballesteros, Severiano and Doust, Dudley. *Seve: The Young Champion*. London: Hodder & Stoughton, 1982.

OTHER BOOKS

Camerer, Dave. *Golf with the Masters*. New York: A. S. Barnes, 1955.

Flaherty, Tom. *The Masters.* New York: Holt, Rinehart and Winston, 1961.

———. *The U.S. Open.* New York: E. P. Dutton, 1966.

Flick, Jim, with Dick Aultman. *Square-to-Square Golf in Pictures.* Norwalk, Conn.: Golf Digest, 1974.

Jacobs, John, with Ken Bowden. *John Jacobs Analyses Golf's Superstars.* London: Stanley Paul, 1974.

McDonnel, Michael. *Golf: The Great Ones.* New York: Drake Publishers, 1973.

Michael, Tom. *Golf's Winning Stroke: Putting.* Norwalk, Conn.: Golf Digest, 1967.

Price, Charles, ed. *The American Golfer.* New York: Random House, 1964.

———, ed. *Golf Magazine's Pro Pointers & Stroke Savers.* New York: Harper & Row, 1959.

———. *The World of Golf.* New York: Random House, 1962.

Scott, Tom, and Geoffrey Cousins. *The Golf Immortals.* New York: Hart Publishing Co., 1969.

Steel, Donald, ed. *Golfers' Bedside Book.* London: B.T. Batsford, 1971.

Toski, Bob. *Bob Toski's Executive Golf Diary.* Memphis, Tenn.: Sports Marketing, 1973.

Ward-Thomas, Pat. *Masters of Golf.* London: William Heinemann, 1961.

Wind, Herbert Warren. *The Complete Golfer.* New York: Simon & Schuster, 1954.

———. *The Story of American Golf.* New York: Simon & Schuster, 1956.

PERIODICALS (defunct)

The American Golfer, 1909–1932
Golf, 1909, 1910, 1938, 1939, 1941
Golf Illustrated (U.S.), 1921–1935
Golfers Magazine, 1922–1931
The Metropolitan Golfer, 1924-1929
National Golf Review, 1937–1939
The Official Golf Record, 1906, 1907
*Professional Golfer of America,** 1933–1949
Spalding's Golf Guide, 1928–1931
Sports Illustrated, combining *The American Golfer,* 1936–1938

PERIODICALS (current)

Golf Digest
Golf Illustrated (U.K.)
Golf Magazine
Golf Monthly (U.K.)
Golf World (U.K.)
Golf World (U.S.)

*Now *Professional Golfer.*